THE ROAD TO
ZAGORA

The author on the road to Zagora

THE ROAD TO
ZAGORA
RICHARD COLLINS

SEREN

Seren is the book imprint of
Poetry Wales Press Ltd, Nolton Street, Bridgend, Wales
www.serenbooks.com
facebook.com/SerenBooks
Twitter: @SerenBooks

ISBN 978-1-78172-259-6
Mobi: 978-178172-296-1
Epub: 978-178172-297-8

A CIP record for this title is available from
the British Library

The publisher works with the financial assistance
of the Welsh Books Council

Cover Artwork by Flic Eden

Printed by The CPI Group (UK) Ltd, Croydon

CONTENTS

Author's note

My partner, Flic, and I have travelled a great deal in recent years. I was diagnosed with a progressive, incurable disease in 2006 and it seemed like a good idea to see some of the world while it was still possible. We went to India and Nepal three times, travelled in Peru and Ecuador, visited the Middle-East and also spent some time in Turkey and Morocco.

This book tells the story of our travels and of the great misfortune and great good fortune that sent us on our way. It also includes some backstory – tales of times and events that have shaped my life and the life we have lived together.

Flic carried sketchbooks on our travels and wrote, drew and painted along the way. Her immediate response to our surroundings and experiences created a vivid record. Looking though the books has been a great pleasure and I have drawn on her account unreservedly.

The Road to Zagora is dedicated to Flic, my favourite and best travelling companion, with a very big thank you for all that you have given and all that we have shared.

Photographs and some of Flic's watercolours can be found in the blogs:

http://richflicjordan.blogspot.co.uk/
http://flicrichperu.blogspot.co.uk/
http://richardandflic.blogspot.co.uk/

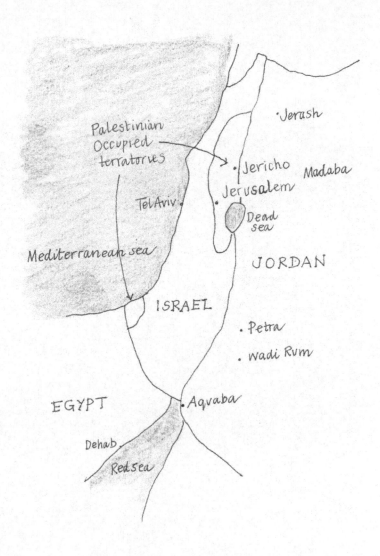

Palestinian Occupied territories

• Jerash

• Jericho   Madaba

Jerusalem

TelAviv •

Dead sea

Mediterranean sea

JORDAN

ISRAEL

• Petra

• wadi Rum

EGYPT   • Aqvaba

Dehab

Red Sea

1

The Most Weird Place

The wind has come round to the north-west and we have changed our plans. We will now take the train to Morfa Mawddach, a little station on the salt marshes at the head of an estuary, and cycle home from there. We will wait for an hour here, at Dyfi Junction, a station at the head of a different estuary, and look up at the surrounding hills, and out across the marshes towards the sea, and talk about long gone times and faraway places. It is the right thing to do.

I am with Bill, who I have known for nearly thirty years; he's a dear friend and has come to help me while my partner, Flic, is away. Nowadays I am ill enough to sometimes need help with the simplest of tasks, buttering a slice of toast, let's say. And well enough to be looking forward to a day of cycling up and down the steep Welsh hills; at least if the wind is behind me. I see this might need some explanation; more on this later. Right now it's eight o'clock on a late August morning; summer seems to be coming to an end and a new season has begun. The air is cooler and clearer, the sun less bright, and the very first hint of autumn colour, very early this year, shows on the leaves of some trees and bushes and on the bracken and long grass.

Dyfi Junction station has been revamped with shiny new shelters and seats, new tarmac and paving slabs, and a row of unnecessarily tall lamp-posts on an unfeasibly long platform. A public address system beeps from time to time and an automated voice speaks its name: *Systemtech Public Announcements*. It doesn't say anything more than that as there are no trains due for a while. And as there is no car access to the station, just a mile long rough track, there are only two

13

passengers for it to address, Bill and myself. The whole thing is incongruous set here in the vast space of the marshes. It could be the railway station at the end of the universe.

We walk to the end of the platform where the railway crosses a body of water a little larger than a ditch. It is the Llyfnant, a small stream that comes down out of the hills and runs across the marshes to join the Dyfi Estuary. We are maybe eight miles from the sea but the tide has come right up here in the night and now flows out quietly between the reeds. Two cormorants fly past. There are some gulls out over the water. And we can hear a stone-chat somewhere nearby but we can't see it. Perhaps it is the unpeopled quiet of this place that makes me think of its opposite, the station at Varanasi in India, where I spent part of a night waiting for a train a few years ago. I tell Bill about it and his opportunity to commune with nature, light, space, and silence is interrupted for a while. I hope he doesn't mind too much.

Flic and I were in Varanasi some years ago. It's a huge, dirty city beside the foul, polluted, pure and sacred River Ganges. A place of pilgrimage that every Hindu should visit once in a lifetime, a place to be cremated and have your ashes cast upon the water, and a particularly good place to die, as you may escape the cycle of death and rebirth and instead reach Nirvana, the Hindu equivalent of heaven. It is also, and people forget to tell you this, a very beautiful place, with the temples and *ghats* strung out along the bank of the wide river. But after a few days the intensity of experience, the heat, holiness and hassle of the place, were enough for us and we decided to move on. The travel agent who sold us our railway tickets told us that he had special connections that would allow him to find seats for us even though the train was officially full. These seats came, as you can guess, at a special price. The travel agency doubled as an internet café and the proprietor also told us that he was a Brahmin and that his people were the first intermediaries between God and man. *We had*, he was pleased to tell us, *connectivity*.

The Indian railway system handles twenty million passengers per day. Unbelievable but true. There were several hundred of them (500 or so I wrote in my diary) in the foyers and on the platforms when we arrived at Varanasi station at ten in the evening. Hundreds of people were stretched out asleep on the ground. They looked poor, perhaps destitute. But no, I noticed that one man was propped up in such a way that he could watch a film on his iPhone. The trains in India travel vast distances over periods of several days and can be very much delayed. It is not unusual to hear an announcement in Hindi and English something like: *India Railways regret to inform passengers that the Punjab Express to New Delhi is running approximately eight hours late*. And so people have to wait and while they wait they stretch out on the ground and sleep.

We found our platform and waited a mere four or five hours for our train. It was a memorable experience. It seemed a good idea to sit comfortably with our backs against the wall and watch our fellow travellers. But nobody did this, they all sat or lay in the middle of the platform. When we saw rats making their way along the bottom of the wall we knew why. And we weren't that surprised to discover later that the railway carriages each had their own population of mice that travelled the length and breadth of the country.

The station was busy with people coming and going and with others trying to make a living by selling chai, or fruit, or cheap plastic toys (why toys?) to those passing through. We saw a whole tribe of village folk come in from the countryside carrying sacks of vegetables to sell at the market. They wore similar red and yellow turbans on their heads and nothing at all on their feet, they were that poor.

Flic took out her sketchbook and started drawing as she does at such times. A very poorly dressed young woman came and sat close by to watch. She smiled and her face lit up like that of a child. Then she moved away and we saw that she was crying. I bought chai for us and a cup for the young woman and we decided that we would give her some money before we left. She was certainly destitute and possibly mentally disabled. Then our train arrived and in the rush we forgot all about her. But I thought about her later. So many people with places to come from and places to go. And maybe a few like this woman, poor enough to spend her days and nights on the station platform, checking out the litter bins in the hope of finding something to eat. Stuck on Varanasi station platform because there was nowhere else for her to be.

Bill and I don't have that long to wait for our train; we are soon riding in comfort and watching the hills pass by on one side and the sea on the other. Then we have a good day of cycling through wild and beautiful landscapes with the help of a following wind, tea and cake in Dolgellau and Machynlleth, and the way-marks along the *Lon Las Cymru*. And I get some extra help and encouragement from Bill when I struggle to get my arms and legs to do as they're told.

Back at home in the evening I find myself thinking again about some of the places Flic and I have visited in recent years and the way that this country looks so different when you return from abroad. Perhaps this is something I could write about. I find one of Flic's India journals and read the words on the last page. We had been away in India and Nepal for three and a half months finally returning from tropical Kerala on the last day of January to a home that just wasn't the same. She wrote:

Now back in Wales these things strike me. It is cold and colourless. There are no leaves, no noises accept the wind blowing, nor anything like the warm bustle of India or the heat of the tropics. It is the most weird place we've been.

A is for Aqaba (Jordan)

Travelling enriches your life and changes your understanding of quite a few things. Home is a different place on your return. You are a different person, having travelled. I have had some preconceptions of other people and places quietly overturned. I spend a lot of my time at home now because of my poor health and have the opportunity to reflect on these things. Or I do something daft like make an A to Z of place names, each from a different country, and write a little anecdote about each one. I once spent a couple of rainy days doing this, starting with Aqaba in Jordan:

Forget Lawrence of Arabia arriving in Aqaba on camelback at the head of a Bedouin army: we crossed the desert by bus, in comfort, with wi-fi and air-con and reclining seats.

Aqaba is a port but also a seaside resort, a holiday destination for Jordanians. We were at the beach on a Friday, the Muslim holy day, and found that it wasn't wall-to-wall joylessness as Sunday is in some parts of Christendom (we once saw a children's playground in the west of Scotland with a sign *Closed on Sundays*). People may have been to the mosque in the morning but now they were having fun. Women were dressed conservatively, some in long black robes, but it didn't stop them from going into the sea, snorkelling or messing about on inflatable plastic ducks.

We had already had our preconceptions of Islamic society challenged in the first Jordanian town we visited. The shoe shop proudly displayed in their window a number of pairs of hi-heeled thigh-high leather boots in a choice of colours, red or black. Did the women we passed on the street wear these under their long robes? In what other context, we wondered, would they be worn? I really can't imagine.

The people of Jordan are renowned for their hospitality, friendliness and sense of humour.

2

An Elephant, Passing By...

The best part of a year passes by and Bill comes to visit again. My health has deteriorated now but we try a more adventurous day out. We are at Dyfi Junction station earlier, this time for a seven o'clock train. And it is a little earlier in the year too; no hints of autumn this time. We walk to the end of the platform and look towards the local osprey's nest. One of the birds is flying towards us but veers away when it recognises our human shapes. It climbs and circles, then folds up its wings and dives, stoops I should say, to attack a random crow that may be a threat to its young. Then the train comes in and we are off to Penrhyndeudraeth, from where we cycle to the foot of Snowdon, climb one of its sibling peaks, Y Lliwedd, and return home by bike and train. Quite a day out.

A couple of weeks later my partner, Flic, and I are on the bus home from Aberystwyth. I am feeling rough and we have a conversation something like this:

'Is it that thing where you feel like you're lying naked on a cobblestone street in the rain and an elephant, passing by, stops to rest and lies on top of you?' she asks.

'No, of course not.' I reply. 'That's how it feels at night. Or not exactly how it feels but a measure of the discomfort. That's how uncomfortable it feels in the middle of the night.'

'So what is it now?' she asks. 'Is it like you're just recovering from flu and have recently been run over by a bus?'

'No, that's what it's like in the evenings, or not exactly like that but comparable, you know what I mean.'

'What is it then? You don't look too bad.'

'It's indescribable. You know how I am with words but this is indescribable. Only it's a bit like... you know those science fiction films where the guy's body is being taken over by an alien? Or when an insect has a parasite eating it live from the inside? It's not like that but it's... you know, my body feels unbearably weird and my speech and my movement and my facial expression are all fading away. And... and I never get used to it. It still makes me feel panicky.'

With the lack of a mountain to climb my body has packed up and we are abandoning a trip to our local seaside town. We talk about the hidden symptoms of my illness, the indescribable half of it, by means of ludicrous analogies. They are, of course, exaggerations, but not so much as you'd think. And today I've been unable to walk far at all and when we get home I have to do some thinking.

I have Parkinson's disease, a neurological condition, in which the brain's messages to the body are somewhat interrupted. The symptoms vary from hour to hour, day to day, and over longer periods. So two weeks ago I cycled 30 miles and climbed a mountain with Bill but today I can't walk a few hundred yards along the prom. Why is that? I have to think this through.

There are, I know now, psychological triggers. The excitement of a new challenge or the stimulation of a friend coming to stay will have a beneficial effect; suddenly I can do more. And exercise, hard exercise like that of climbing what we in Wales call a mountain (anywhere else in the world it would be a hill), always makes my body work better. At the end of such a day I am much more functional than at the end of a day at home. More than that, I realise, is the determination to go on.

Y Lliwedd was tough. Cycling there I was hunched forward and to one side, as if about to tumble sideways off the bike at any minute. It took all my concentration to make my feet stay on the pedals. And when on the mountain we tried a steep short cut to the summit and my legs refused to work. I collapsed onto the slope and Bill had to help me to my feet. This happened a few times. Cycling home he fed me sesame seed snacks and encouragement when it seemed like I couldn't go any further. Aberystwyth prom, on the other hand, is not a challenge and to carry on when you can hardly walk seems daft not to mention embarrassing.

There you are, I have explained a little why a man who sometimes cannot butter a slice of toast can climb a mountain. And why a man who cannot work can, with some help, have adventures in faraway places. That is what the disease has done for me; it has taken me to India and Nepal, Peru and Ecuador, Turkey, Morocco, and the Middle East. When we knew that I faced a future of severe disability Flic and I panicked. And in a spirit of *now or never*, we travelled. We saw a volcano erupting in Ecuador, were guests of honour at a Hindu ceremony in India, came across fresh snow leopard tracks in the Himalayas, snorkelled in the Red Sea, and much, much more.

We did it for the experience of being in beautiful and strange places not knowing that it would enrich our lives and change our understanding of the world in the long term. That's a bonus. It makes me want to write about our travels and about the things we have learned. And there's a temptation to look at the longer journey that I have made, that we all make, you know the one I mean. You'll have to excuse me if I find myself wondering, just for a moment or two, about some of the deeper meanings behind such an adventure.

B is for Bethlehem (Wales)

It was quite early on in that longer journey to which I have referred, and I was maybe twenty-two years old, when I visited Bethlehem, in south Wales. I was working on a small organic dairy farm close by.

I had read a lot of Thomas Hardy as a teenager and loved the rural settings and country life of the stories as much as anything else. I was brought up in leafy suburbia and had romantic notions of the countryside. I loved the beauty of the natural world and wanted to be immersed in it by working out of doors. It might not match up to my dreams but I thought I would give it a try. I had an opportunity through an organisation called WWOOF, Working Weekends on Organic Farms, to volunteer on a small dairy farm near Fairfach. I loved it.

The new owner of the farm, a woman with a Ph D in soil science keen to put into practice her organic theories and ideals, had brought her cows with her down from Scotland. They were Ayrshires, brown and white and very handsome. I was soon able to tell them apart by their markings and got to know the individual characters of some.

There was Ticky, a sleek intelligent animal who always tried to sneak her way into the hay barn on the way to the milking parlour and once managed to break off a car wing mirror in the process. There were Celandine and Buttercup, similar looking cows who had markings the colour of a new conker when it is first squished out of its case and who were great friends and grazed side by side. And there was a big daft cow called Meg who was way down on their butting order, the cow's hierarchy, and was bullied by most of the others. When she had a calf which she would get to see at milking time she got so excited that she pushed her way through the herd, bravely fending off her persecutors. If I thought about it for a while I could probably remember some of the others.

There is, as you know, another Bethlehem in another part of the world, the Middle East. Towards the end of our travels we visited Israel, Palestine and neighbouring countries. We spent some time in the city of Jerusalem and visited nearby Bethlehem. I have enjoyed the interest and beauty of many places on five continents and I'm going to enjoying sharing some of that with you in the following pages. But it was in the Middle East that we were most engaged with political issues and it was there that we had our preconceptions most thoroughly challenged. I don't know why we went to those countries but it feels right that we made that journey after the others, as if we were building up to it. And so you too will have to wait a while before we pass through Israeli checkpoints and visit the town made famous by Jesus and Banksy. You'll have to make do with Bethlehem in Wales and a herd of Ayrshire cows.

3

The Limp, the Alien
and the Aurora

I was diagnosed with Parkinson's disease in the summer of 2006. I had been walking with a limp, cycling with a limp and even driving with a limp (my right foot refused to lift up when I changed gear and I revved up like a boy racer – brrrrrrrrrum!). Sometimes my right arm hung loosely by my side when I walked. When it got worse I had to spend two weeks in Morriston hospital, Swansea, waiting for a brain scan. They found nothing that shouldn't be there (no blood clots, no cancer) and decided that it must be Parkinson's. I returned home and found my symptoms getting worse. My body refused to work when asked, did things I didn't require of it, and seemed to be occupied by an alien. When I closed my eyes at night great waves of coloured light drifted up behind my eyelids. I had always wanted to see the aurora borealis but not like this. I felt too ill to do anything and spent whole days lounging around lying on the sofa.

Then one bright sunny morning in January 2007 Flic decided to walk up the hill behind our village in west Wales. I was too ill to go with her but it was too lovely a morning to miss so I tried anyway. We got to the old spoil heap and a view of the Dyfi estuary and the sea and the Lleyn Peninsula in the distance. Wonderful. I waited while Flic went on to the top of the hill. She came back soon, told me how beautiful it was up there and insisted that I come up too. When I got to the top my Parkinson's symptoms pretty much went away. The exercise, the beauty of the morning, the relief at being out in the world again, maybe all these things together worked a cure. We walked for an hour or so and I came home a happy man. That walk was the start of something big for us.

A few weeks later we walked up Cadair Idris. I felt I could get as far as the lake half way up. It was easy and we continued to the summit. We saw the seaside town of Barmouth in the distance and decided to walk there, some eight miles away, arriving after dark. I cannot express how special a day that was for me.

Flic and I love the outdoors and we continued walking in the hills. We spent six days in the Swiss Alps in the summer. In November we arrived in Kathmandu, ready to walk the Annapurna circuit. It was to be a one off, an unrepeatable trip of a lifetime. We had travelled together many years ago, before we had children. Now Kit had left home and was at art college. Peter, at seventeen years old and with friends in the village, could manage without us for a month. We were ready for a long walk.

A few years ago I was walking along a stretch of the Pembrokeshire Coast Path, with Flic and her sister, Anna. I had been limping for a while but not so badly as to spoil my day. It was a different way of walking not, as it can sometimes be, a difficult struggle. Anna said something like: *It's strange that you like walking so much when you find it difficult.* The truth was, and is, that most other things are more difficult for me; walking is one of the few things I can do. More than that, the repetitive motion often makes my body function better while more complicated tasks cause me to become more dysfunctional. And I've always liked walking.

Flic and I have covered a lot of ground on foot in the years since my illness became apparent and our shared pleasure in the outdoors has brought us closer together. And so it causes me great sadness to realise that it's becoming much more difficult for me and that increasingly I choose to stay at home rather than attempt and fail to enjoy a long walk. But I shouldn't make myself too miserable yet. There are three things I can think about to come to terms with this.

The first is to remember the time when I injured my foot by treading on broken glass when I was wandering around Greece as a young man. I limped along painfully and slowly, there was no possibility of hurrying, and I began to take note of much more in my surroundings. *The slower you go, the more you see* I thought and I still think it now. Secondly there's this: I can still walk quite well, quite often, if only for short distances. Finally I have to celebrate what has been possible for me. Flic and I had a wonderful time walking a hundred and fifty miles around Annapurna. We can't do it now but we did it when we could and it was marvellous, as were the travels that followed. And here's the strange thing: if Mr Parkinson hadn't come knocking on my door we quite probably would have stayed at home.

C is for Copacabana (Bolivia)

The shores of Lake Titicaca are wild and unspoilt and beautiful, for the most part. But not at Copacabana in Bolivia. It's a rundown tourist resort with untreated sewage spilling into the lake, street dogs hungry for titbits and affection, and more pedalo boats per head of population than anywhere else in the world.

Our Lady of Copacabana is the patron saint of boy racers, who come to the town in large numbers on her feast day to have their cars blessed. Then they get drunk and drive around for a while. Gringos are advised to stay away until the festivities are over. But when we were there we did watch a street marriage celebration with music and dancing. I thought something was wrong with the beer – people kept pouring some of it onto the ground. I later discovered it was in honour of Pachamama, the Inca Earth goddess who is in the fertility business. The Spanish imposed Catholicism all over South America but Pachamama is still alive and well and living in Copacabana.

4

Around Annapurna

Of course an essence of Nepal. Ever present at the end of the slightest alley that reminds Nepal a loyally paradise of gallant shade the 'Nature'.
From the website of Hotel Nature.

From our hotel window I can see banana trees, lemon trees, ducks, vines, pot plants, crows, washing, solar panels, brick walls, and flags. The roofs have a tower on them for water tanks – with a spiral staircase you can climb. Hear – dogs, cars beeping, voices, motorbikes, brakes squealing.
From Flic's journal, November 2007.

I don't know the hour but it is early morning, sometime between first light and sunrise. I am up on the flat rooftop of Hotel Nature, looking out across the city through a haze of pollution and humidity. Kathmandu stretches, in some directions, as far the eye can see; only to the west I can make out hills touched with the green of something like woodland or farmland, and to the north, between drifting clouds, glimpses of snow covered mountains.

Low-rise square buildings of brick and concrete surround me, all of them with black plastic water tanks on their roofs, some with pot plants and even small trees, some with washing hanging out, a few with early rising people. A man nearby clears his throat and cleans his teeth. A woman below me is preparing vegetables. Further away a small boy waits until his mother has gone, jumps up onto the parapet and balances along high above the street. There is the sound of a small handheld bell and I look down and across at a man chanting a prayer. There is the smoke of burning juniper leaves and then the bell again.

I can see no old buildings, just these newly decrepit, multi-occupied blocks, a few vacant lots awaiting development and some half-built concrete shells of buildings-to-be. Further away are few scattered little tree-covered hillocks, like tiny islands above the streets. And a bigger hill with trees and what might be a temple, I can make out two white towers and a golden dome.

I don't know it yet but this is to be only the first of a great number of early morning rooftop views, in a dozen countries on four continents, that I will experience during the next few years. Views over cities and mountains and farmland and desert and the sea. I wake up early in a new place, excited by life, looking out and around, maybe wondering what's ahead. It's the best time of the day.

Walking the Annapurna Circuit is, for the most part, easier than walking in Wales. The old trade routes that are now popular with trekkers run through settled countryside and there are villages every few miles along the way. In every one of them you can buy food and drink and find a cheap place to stay the night. There are no way markers but friendly locals will put you back on the path if you get lost. The only problem is the altitude. The route takes you up the valley of the Marsyangdi River and down the valley of the Khali Kandaki. You just have to cross from one to the other by way of the Thorong La, a 17,000 ft pass, where cold and altitude sickness will kill you if you are unlucky enough to get benighted. I really didn't know what effect altitude would have on my illness so we employed both a guide and a porter. On the Thorong La I was pleased we had.

Our guide was called Ram Rai, an easy going but reserved man who spoke some English. Our porter was a sweet young guy called Take. We met them in Kathmandu and set off by bus for the beginning of the trail at Besi Shah. Ram sat across the aisle, a little separate from us but there if needed. That was to be his way over the next three weeks, polite, unobtrusive but with an uncanny habit of being around at the right time. The bus passed field after field of a handsome green cereal crop that I hadn't seen before and didn't recognise. I asked Ram what it was and he showed no surprise at my ignorance. *It is rice*, he said with a smile.

Ram always smiled, always seemed at ease. He had the broad face and narrow eyes of the Rai people (hence his surname, Ram *Rai*, in the Nepali manner) and that contributed to his seeming contentment. Nepalis are lovely people, kind and friendly to foreigners. On the trail they greet you with a smile and the word *namaste*, which translates as *I salute the God within you*. I never, ever heard a Nepali say *namaste* to another Nepali. I guess it's archaic and sounds something like *good morrow kind sir*. No wonder that they keep on smiling.

We set off from Besi Shah early in the morning and walked down a flat, grassy trail along which jeeps or buses would sometimes pass. The buses had very high clearance and could travel over rough ground. After a short distance the path became too rough and narrow for them and we were in a world completely free of wheeled vehicles. Everything had to be carried on the back of a Nepali porter or a donkey. We passed by fields of millet and rice, terraced into the hillside. Lentils were growing on the banks of the terraces. Sweetcorn had been harvested and was stored on the cob hanging in special racks on under the eaves of houses. There were sheep, goats, chickens and water buffalo along the way. Any questions I had about the agriculture there would be answered by Ram who was from a farming background. And when we passed a patch of semi-tropical woodland he showed us the movement in the trees where there were monkeys.

This is what I remember. But Flic carried her sketchbook journal and now I have it in front of me. She wrote and sketched as we went along, not often reflecting on our experiences, just recording the day to day details. It makes for a vivid account, a very special record of a very special journey. Here are some of her observations:

There are cattle trees which are holy and have stones around them to rest on. Giant mango trees with strange noises coming from them – frogs? crickets? Burbling from birds. It's quite humid and cloudy. We stop for tea after a couple of hours and watch passersby – porters carrying huge loads with a strap around their foreheads. There are mule trains carrying stuff up to Manang and returning empty apart from rubbish. All the while the Marsyangdi roars along beside us.

We stopped for lunch at a simple guesthouse close to the bank of the Marsyangdi River in a place called Ngadi. Ram asked if we should stay the night there and we agreed. We pottered about among the boulders on the river bank and then Flic walked up to the village with some local children. That was our first day. I would like to impress you with our courage and fortitude on the hard trail, challenges met, unforeseeable problems overcome. It wasn't like that. At the beginning it was, as we said at the time, a walk in the park.

In the evening some villagers organised a dance for the trekkers. They persuaded us to join in and laughed at us good naturedly and got some money out of us to help with the building of a new school. A girl in her early teens talked to the trekkers in reasonable English. As Flic recorded she was pretty and very aware of it. She sold me a woven good luck charm which has been attached to my rucksack ever since. She seemed worried that she was charging too much at something like 35 pence in our money. As the light faded the locals walked back up to the village. We watched fireflies glowing in the bushes around us and, looking up and along the valley, got our first view of a snow-capped mountain reflecting the sunset

It now occurs to me that we met and talked to women in Nepal as you would at home, no surprises there; but it was in great contrast to our later experiences in India, where ordinary women don't generally talk to foreigners or indeed to any men outside the family. We noticed that men and women share heavy physical work in Nepal and we often saw men looking after young children too. It looked like there was a fair amount of gender equality – who knows?

Our second day's walking was a little harder, not much, and we began to have the animal encounters that are so much a part of rural life in poorer countries. We saw water buffaloes crossing the river. One was swept off its feet and carried downstream a little. When it managed to get out of the water it found itself on the wrong side and had to go back in and struggle across to catch up with the rest of the herd. When we stopped for lunch two kids (the four legged kind) jumped up onto the table and had to be shooed away. Flic noted: It is a festival time and today is the dog's festival so the dogs, a few, have been decorated with garlands and tinsel and one has red paint on its head.

Both the Marsyangdi and the Kali Kandaki valleys have been important trade routes for a long time and, as the paths are not too steep and the altitude not too great, there are many mule trains, as we came to call them although they are made up of donkeys. The foremost animals wear quite grand woven headdresses. We were warned to stand on the uphill side of the path as they passed because you can get knocked off. We met a woman who had been pushed off the path by a well-laden donkey and fallen a few metres – enough to make her nervous when they came by.

We stopped early again and checked into village guesthouse. We made love enthusiastically in the late afternoon. Then we became aware that we hadn't drawn the curtains properly and that a young girl was watching us from the next door rooftop. It left us with an uncomfortable feeling as if we had done something wrong. I had vague worries, I can't say exactly what they were, perhaps I imagined we would be confronted by an angry parent. I was relieved when we left the village the next morning.

The next day we walked through a higher, steeper landscape and reached the village of Tal. For the first time we were in a Buddhist rather than Hindu world. There were prayer flags and prayer wheels, rough stone monuments known as chortens and stupas, mani walls with Buddhist mantras carved into the rocks. There was something very powerful and moving about the marks the religion made on the land. It may be only super-stition (I'm sorry but that's what I think it is) but somehow the expression of belief and connection between the physical and spiritual universe moved me. I think it was just the beauty of it all. And the feeling that these beliefs grew out of the mountains themselves.

There was no electricity in Tal. We ate our supper by candle light and went to bed at eight to escape the cold. Outside the stars shone very bright in the gap between the steep sides of the valley. Flic wrote of humming birds sipping nectar from deep yellow flowers and of walking through villages that seem to be from the Middle Ages, dark and wooden, full of different smells and sounds and mules goats dogs chickens donkeys sheep and children. Women wearing beautiful coloured clothes and being so graceful. They walk the same paths as us but with sandals and bare feet and flip-flops and carry great loads. And a sentence that might give you an idea of the richness and intensity of our experience: now it is Saturday and Friday seems so long ago that I can hardly remember it.

The next day we walked through a changing landscape: steeper and rockier and with pine trees and strange high altitude palm trees in place of the rice fields. We were stopped by Maoist insurgents at a formal checkpoint which consisted of two men sitting at a table by the side of the path. They were polite and unarmed and asked for a *donation* for which we were given a written receipt.

It was the third day of the festival and the turn of cows to be decorated. We took a photo of one wearing a garland of marigolds. In the evening first a group of boys and then girls came to sing in the yard. Ram kept time on a drum while the children danced. Then they carried on around the village with call and response songs and dancing.

We travelled gradually from semi-tropical farmland to pine forests to high altitude yak pastures and eventually, on the Thorong La, to snow and ice. Walking through these steadily changing physical and cultural landscapes felt worthwhile and meaningful.

One morning we were walking through a landscape that I thought must be like that of Arizona. The valley had opened out and at times we experienced an eerie silence that came from being away from the noise of the river for the first time in quite a while. Instead of farmland there was a scattering of stunted pine trees through which we could see a massive sheer rock face with a crack running down its length and patches of snow clinging to the top edge. We met three children walking some distance to school. One of them, a girl of eight or nine years, was practicing her English spelling out loud: S T R A I G H T, straight. She said it over and over again as she walked down the winding trail under the crooked mountains towards the meandering river.

At Pisang we took the high route to Manang through a dry mountain landscape of austere beauty. It was November, with very clear light and blue skies and now, after a week and a half of walking, we were surrounded by very high mountains, sharp peaks jutting out above the ice and snow. We stopped at the small village of Ngarwal where there were maybe forty flat-roofed houses built of rough stone and timber, most of them flying a single prayer flag on a tall pole. We sat on the roof of our very cheap, very simple guesthouse watching the light fade. At sunset the temperature dropped fast and Flic had to stop writing her journal. The ink had frozen in her pen.

We were tourists, on a well-known tourist trail, with all the advantages and disadvantages of that. Accommodation was cheap and plentiful (as little as 70p per night for a double room, if you must know) and there was always rice and lentils (*dhal baht*) and sometimes chocolate cake. OK, there was no hot water and no heating so we didn't take our clothes off for days at a time. And the nights were very long and dark. Doors and windows didn't fit so the temperature indoors dropped close to freezing. But sometimes we were treated to a brazier of smouldering charcoal under the dining table. Everybody would tuck the heavy table cloth around their legs and we would be warm from the waist down at least.

We met and got to know some of our fellow trekkers, people from all over the world and with a wide range of ages. We met a tough retired German woman who had trained as an engineer and had worked at CERN, home of the hadron collider, near Geneva. She was trekking in the Himalayas while waiting for a heart bypass operation. She had been very ill in the Everest region and had been carried down in a basket on the back of a Sherpa. Now, having recovered, she was trying the Annapurna circuit. We met a couple of guys with mountain bikes: a young, clean-shaven Dutch man and a younger Nepali who was his country's junior champion. Not only did they carry the bikes much more of the way than the bikes carried them, they also had a porter carrying their personal gear. He would arrive at their accommodation, on foot, well ahead of them. We met a young Swiss woman who upset the locals by wearing tiny shorts and a Scotsman who amused the locals by wearing a kilt. We spoke to a young Korean woman travelling alone through the countries that shared her religion – Buddhism. And we met, of course, quite a few more.

After twelve days of walking we arrived at Manang, a small town at 11,500 feet. On the way into town there was a wall maybe thirty yards long in which there were niches containing prayer wheels, actually brass cylinders, marked with Tibetan script. An old woman was making her way along the wall, keeping it on her right as is the custom, setting every wheel in motion to send prayers up to heaven. Another tiny old lady came past with a huge bundle of firewood on her back. And at the entrance to the town was a metal sign bearing two images: a young man galloping on horseback and another man on foot leading his horse by the reins. The first image was struck through with a red line signifying prohibition. It seems that boy racers are a problem even in a society without cars.

We spent a few days in Manang acclimatising to the altitude so that we might cross the Thorong La safely. We stayed in a tiny, primitive guesthouse with notched tree-trunks for stair-cases and stupendous views across the valley to the Annapurnas. The people were friendly and kind and pious. Two older men of the family spent the entire day on the roof chanting and praying and reading from religious texts. Across the road a brown cow kept trying to enter through the door into a hotel.

After leaving Manang we walked for three days through a steep and empty steep landscape of high pastures. We caught sight of a herd of *thar*, a sort of wild goat, and we saw yaks for the first time. I had some scary intimations of altitude sickness but I didn't tell anyone; I wanted to carry on. At one lodge Flic insisted on going out exploring alone on the mountain-side as night fell and temperatures sunk down way below freezing. I was worried that something like a twisted ankle would be enough, at that altitude and in that cold, to result in tragedy. I was relieved when she came back.

Then we arrived at a place called High Camp. Now we were high above and far away from inhabitable land. This was just a squalid overnight stop before crossing the Thorong La. Just before nightfall a fellow trekker showed me the route that we were to take the next morning. It was an icy path cut into a steep snow slope that ended, I think you could safely say, in oblivion. You could see the path higher up winding back and forth across scree slopes and snow fields. I went indoors and told Flic that I couldn't do it.

Remember that I had Parkinson's disease, was unsteady on my feet, and had a very reasonable fear of falling. Added to that was the fact that we had to start at four in the morning, in the dark and cold, to make it across the pass safely. Flic was quietly furious that we should have gone so far and then have to turn back. Ram said something like *don't worry – I will take you*. He was completely understanding, kind and confident. I trusted him.

It was scary but not as bad as I anticipated. Ram held my hand crossing one or two dodgy slopes early on and then I was OK. But it was a tough climb up to 17,000 and something feet. There is, at that altitude, not enough oxygen in the air. You have to take a few steps, rest and breathe, then take a few more. As it got light and we got higher I felt that I would faint before reaching the top of the pass. Take, dropped our stuff off at the top and then came back and walked beside me looking very concerned, ready to catch me if I fell. Of course, we made it. The top of the pass was bleak and unspectacular but there was a café serving hot drinks (yes, it's true). We both felt quite ill and soon went down the other side.

As we descended views opened up over a vast arid mountain landscape of great beauty. We walked down and down until we reached the town of Muktinath, a holy place and pilgrimage destination for both Hindus and Buddhists. It felt, I must say, pretty damn good to get there. The town is famous for its shrine, built around a cleft in the rock where there is a little jet of natural gas, the eternal flame of Muktinath. I will always remember the town for something else. Early the next morning

I washed some clothes by hand and put them out to dry. Not a single drip fell from them to the ground and I really couldn't understand why. I touched a t-shirt with my hand and understood: my clothes had frozen, stiff as boards, the moment I hung them up.

Before leaving Muktinath we visited the temple compound with its temples and shrines, the hundred and eight water spouts under which the devout would bathe, and the eternal flame, which was the size of a pilot light on an old style gas cooker. Outside of the compound was the sacred helicopter pad, used by rich Indian pilgrims who need to fit their moment of spiritual enlightenment into a busy schedule.

From Muktinath we carried on down to the valley of the Kali Kandaki river and followed its course for a few days. Then we cut up into the hills again before reaching a road and taking a beaten up old taxi to the lakeside town of Pokhara. This return section of the Annapurna trek was busier, with a small airstrip at Jomsum adding to the numbers of visitors. Sometimes we followed jeep-tracks rather than footpaths and sometimes we would actually see a jeep or a tractor. There wasn't the feeling of being so remote from the twenty-first century. But it was still beautiful and interesting; we were still a long way from home in a very foreign landscape and a very foreign culture.

Near a village called Jarkhot we saw a man ploughing with oxen, probably dzos, crosses between domestic cattle and yaks. He was far away in the valley below us but we could hear him singing as he worked. People seemed happy and they worked without machinery in an unspoilt land of great beauty. On our trek we saw lots of farming activity. We saw rice being harvested with sickles and spread out to dry in beautiful patterns. We saw it being threshed by being beaten with sticks and winnowed by being tossed into the air from woven baskets. We met teenage girls walking down the track, laughing and joking, carrying baskets of manure on their backs. We were aware that farming was a sociable activity, with whole families taking their meals together out of doors, in the sunshine.

It sounds, and it seemed, an idyllic lifestyle that the people led there. We can't know what it feels like to lead that life. It includes high illiteracy, short life expectancy, limited choices, and there are preventable (to us) illnesses. Most houses were without chimneys and the smoke from cooking fires fills the rooms and just leaks out between the roof tiles. This leads to eye problems and chest complaints. Perhaps much of the beauty that a visitor sees is merely commonplace to those who spend their whole lives there. It is, to us, picturesque poverty, but it is poverty all the same. Or is it? The local farmers where we live in Wales don't sing at the tops of their voices as they drive their multi-thousand pound tractors alone, through a relatively unpeopled landscape. So who is poor? That's a big question.

And how should we feel taking time out from our affluent lives to walk alongside people who have none of the wealth and opportunities that we have? All I can say is that our being there contributed directly to the local economy. We bought food and paid for accommodation so the people we dealt with, and their communities, benefited. And it was trade not aid, they sold us goods and services with, as it were, their heads held high. We saw a trekker trying to barter with a woman who had carried apples high into the mountains to sell them at a better price. *Five rupees*, she said (or something, I can't remember now) and the trekker, trying to be clever by bartering, asked, *but how much for two?* She looked at him as if he was stupid. *Ten rupees*, she said, and laughed in his face as if to say *can't you count?*

And the issue of hiring someone to carry your luggage; isn't it a bit like having a servant? I don't know. In a world without cars portering is normal job, not one of high status but perhaps no different from being a taxi driver in our world. And a porter earns a livelihood and feeds his family.

In the valley of the Kali Kandaki we looked for fossils and found a yak's horn. We saw the Dhaulagiri Icefall high above us. We saw the wind blowing fiercely down one side of the valley and fiercely up the other side at the same time; that is to say that we saw the trees being blown about by the two winds. At Poon Hill we watched the sunrise over the Himalayas accompanied by some, I don't know, fifty or so other tourists and listened to their conversations about mobile phone networks and first cars. And then, too soon, we were at the end of the trail. In front of us was a road with buses and lorries and taxis passing by. Another world.

We had walked for twenty-one days through a landscape of both man-made and natural beauty and our only regret was that we had gone too fast – we should have taken longer. Then we spent a couple of days in Pokhara and a few days in Kathmandu.

It was in Kathmandu that on our last day we visited a Hindu temple complex by the side of a dirty river. There were sadhus dressed in saffron robes and monkeys coming down out of the nearby trees. There was strange music and chanting. We saw corpses being cremated on huge pyres and their ashes being swept into the river. A group of boys played football on the river bank while others waded into the water and searched around with their hands for... for what? We didn't know. We spent two hours there just looking, only taking in the extraordinary sights. We felt that we could have been there a much longer time. It was, we believed, the end of a trip of a lifetime, a never to be repeated, wonderful experience. But we were fascinated by what we saw on that last day. We wanted more.

D is for Damp 2000 (Germany)

A little way further down that longer trail that I mentioned (I was something like 26 years old) I got to visit a place called Damp 2000 on the Baltic Coast of Schleswig-Holstein, Germany. It consisted of a number of 1960s style apartment blocks and a yachting marina stuck in some dreary flat farmland by a grey sea. It must be one of the least beautiful places I have ever visited. I remember looking around with incredulity and asking who could have been responsible for the hideous architecture. One of the people I was with muttered the name *Hitler* and there was a ripple of awkward laughter.

I was helping out with a holiday for disabled old ladies from the East End of London. One of the other volunteers was a middle-aged woman who told me that all her family were professional criminals. Her husband had once been a driver for the Kray Brothers. As it happens I was a driver on this trip, driving a sort of ambulance minibus. And I was asked by a dodgy friend in London to bring back a large amount of cannabis and make us both some money. *Who would search an ambulance full of argumentative old ladies?* he said. I decided against it.

I had gone along at the request of a friend, a young woman for whom I had, let's say, *warm feelings*. She had a hard time running the trip and was rightly quite focused and not romantically inclined while we were away and was very cool towards me. Then, back in London, she and I were invited to supper by two of our fellow volunteers. Janet (there you are, I've said her name) and I found ourselves to be the only straight people present among what turned out to be a gathering of ardent lesbian feminists, eighties style and complete with dungarees, short hair and dangly ear-rings. I'm enough of an ineffectual wimp of a guy to be acceptable in such company and I had a good time. Hard drinks and soft drugs came our way in large amounts and we got wrecked. And so it was that there came a point in the evening when Janet and I fell backwards off our chairs onto the floor and into a passionate embrace. After a short while we made it to our feet, staggered through the door and headed off to her bed.

We spent some time together over the next few months; most of it sober and often with our clothes on. It was fun.

5

The Sex Bus

Memory is the story we tell ourselves to make sense of the past.

I heard a psychologist say something like that on the radio many years ago and the words stayed with me. There are so many ways to tell a story and sometimes mere chronology has its limits. Memory doesn't work like that, it drifts backwards and forwards in time, sometimes sticking with a theme rather than a time or a place. Sometimes I like to remember bus journeys.

I am now convinced that the best way to travel abroad is by public transport. On a bus, for example, you can look out of the window and watch the world go by as you would in a private car or taxi. But you get much more than just that; the world, in the shape of your fellow passengers, gets on and off the bus, meets old friends, gossips, laughs, argues, eats and drinks, buys and sells, and gets on with life in all its extraordinary foreignness. The world squeezes up close. Sometimes it sits on your lap.

Our worst and best bus journey started in Tansen, in the central uplands of Nepal. We were on our way from the hot lowlands of northern India to Pokhara, a lakeside town close to the Himalayas. There had been no rain in the Tansen area for months but that morning it was raining heavily as we walked down to the bus station. So far so good; they needed it badly. There was a bus ready to leave and we asked a young man if it was going to Pokhara. He answered *yes* as Nepalis do (out of politeness) when they don't understand what you're saying. We got on and travelled along winding roads between the hills, down and down and down – almost as if we were going back the way we had come the day before yesterday. We asked a fellow passenger, *is the bus going to Pokhara?* He smiled and answered *yes* as Nepalis do when they don't understand you but wish to be polite.

Altitude is the big thing in Nepal. It is possible to travel continuously downhill by bus for many hours – something you can't imagine here in Wales where the landscape is so flat that you need hardly raise your head to see the top of the highest 'mountain'. We travelled, yes, that's right, continuously downhill for two hours, maybe more, until we came to a town we recognised close to the Indian border. Then we got off and waited, in the rain, for a bus going the other way. We were at a road junction and there were shops around about with signs written in English. My guess is that this gave them some sort of status. Nobody in the shops or outside of them could speak a word of English and besides that a substantial proportion of the population is illiterate there. But the signs look foreign and that suggests quality.

A digression here in the form of a Peruvian joke. The English tell jokes about the Irish, the Russians about Poles, Swedes about Norwegians (or is it the other way around?) and so forth. Peruvians tell jokes about themselves:

> *Father to son: what do you want to be when you grow up my boy?*
> *Son: A foreigner.*

Maybe the Nepalis have that same excessive modesty and admiration for foreign cultures; I don't know. And I can't remember now how it was that we were convinced to get on a more than full bus going back towards the hills and, we hoped, Pokhara. But we did. The nice young men in charge of the bus squeezed us on with promises that they would get us seats and we would get to our destination. Both these things turned out to be true.

I remember that with all the luggage and people on the bus I could only find floorspace for one foot. I stood, one legged, for many miles, perfectly safe, wedged in tight by the other passengers and with no chance of falling over. And when some people got off we were given seats straight away. Perhaps it had something to do with the 500 rupees each that we had been charged for the journey. The ticket vendor liked to show the other passengers these 500 rupee notes, smile and nod in our direction enthusiastically. I guess we had been charged at the top end of that sliding scale used in some countries in place of the rather dull system we have at home in which goods or services have a fixed price.

The journey took seven hours. A nightmare on wheels that we somehow came to enjoy. The rain stopped and the sun came out and shone on the extraordinary landscapes that we passed through. The hills were very steep and were sometimes covered in forest. Or they were moderately steep, terraced and farmed for crops like rice and millet. There were pale blue snow-melt rivers in the bottoms of the valleys and as the day went on we began to get glimpses of the Annapurna range of mountains, reaching very high up into that part of the sky normally occupied only by clouds.

As well as the driver there were the two handsome young men running the bus, one to sell tickets and the other to hassle people and their luggage on and off. It worked like this: we would overtake the bus of another company, a competitor, and then arrive ahead of it at some town or village. The young guys would be hanging out of the door or on the metal ladders that led up to the roof shouting *Pokhara, Pokhara, Pokhara*. We would just about stop and any new passengers would be grabbed and pulled onto the bus as we accelerated away before we could be overtaken by another bus.

The guys were having a great time shouting out encouragement and abuse to other road users and climbing up and down the outside of the bus. They both wore bandanas, like pirates. And the nautical feeling was enhanced by the swaying of the bus as it went round endless hairpin bends. Quite few people (not us) were throwing up into plastic bags which they threw out of the window. We got a puncture and the guys changed the wheel at the side of the road. And so it went on. The mountains grew closer and looked increasingly fantastical as the sun went down. We reached Pokhara in the early evening having spent maybe nine hours on busses. Perhaps it sounds like a nightmare. It felt like an adventure.

In India we once travelled on a luxury express bus with numbered seats. The bus left the terminal with each seat occupied by just one person and the aisles free of passengers. It felt comfortable and spacious. A few hundred yards later we stopped to let some village people on. They stood in the aisle or perched on the edge of seats. Half a mile up the road we stopped for some more. We carried on like this for seven hours, very few people getting off, more and more getting on. A woman sitting on the edge of my seat was soon sitting on the edge of my lap. A man was wedged so close against me that I thought we might as well go the whole way and get married. When we arrived (at Jodhpur was it?) the bus took an age to empty of its passengers. Were people getting on again through a back door and passing us two or three times? We wondered how a day spent sitting down could leave us so exhausted.

A cow falls from the sky and kills a young woman on a boat. A glacier advances on New York at 200 miles per hour. A plane turns into a robot and lands on a pyramid. An ant pours a magic potion into the ear of a small boy. A bus travels along the edge of the desert for ten hours. Richard and Flic try not to watch fifth rate Hollywood movies dubbed in Spanish. They arrive in Pacasmayo, en route to Ecuador.

On our later journeys I wrote a blog and this was my blog post after a bus journey in Peru where the buses show endless videos to keep passengers entertained. The videos are often violent and always loud. If you have seen a film called *Precious*, about family life in a poor part of Harlem, New York, and heard the amount of swearing in it, you might understand why, at the end of a day passing through the quiet wild beauty of upland Peru, a passenger was heard to say *let's getting our mother-fucking asses off the mother-fucking bus*. That passenger was me.

Another day, another bus, another blog post, this one from Jordan:

Taxi into Amman and hardly any traffic, shops shut and shuttered. Of course, it's Friday, the day off, the day when people get religion. We get on the bus to Petra and instead of music from the speakers there's wall-to-wall chanting – verses from the Koran, I think, going on for an hour. But nobody seems to listen; people chat, young guys are listening to music on their mobile phones. And in front of me a heavily headscarfed and long coated woman gets her laptop out and checks out her hotmail, facebook and youtube. The chanting stops but is soon replaced by what sounds like a sermon, rather joyless and hectoring in tone to our ears. We hope the guy is preaching the Islamic code of generosity towards all foreigners. Then the bus stops by a mosque and a few of the more pious travellers get out for a while. The laptop woman turns to us and explains in English – 'they are praying, it is a good thing.' We arrive at Petra after 3 hours and find ourselves waiting outside a cheap hotel for the man to come to the door and let us in. We can see what he's doing through the window. He comes out and welcomes us when he's finished saying his prayers.

I could write a piece about the place of livestock on public transport in the developing world. I would probably call it *The*

Bus that Crowed. I could write about bicycle rickshaws, about the world record for number of people riding in a *tuk tuk*, about rides in milk-trucks and pick-ups. I could speak of the *boda-boda*, a bicycle taxi in Africa that takes a passenger on the back rack. And more. But I think the point has been made. Public transport is one of the best ways for a traveller to get close to the life of another people in another country. As close as you could ever want to be.

Here, in Wales, my favourite bus used to be called the X32. We have taken it many times in recent years for a day out on our nearest mountain, Cadair Idris. Once or twice when we were on a bus in Peru and the on-board entertainment was too much to cope with I longed for home and the X32 bound quietly northwards for Dolgellau. And there's something else. You would be travelling home on, let's say, a wet Monday evening in November. You are passing through Machynlleth or Aberystwyth in the rain and dark. Just for a moment you catch sight of the bus number, brightly lit and reflected in the window of a shop or office. You weren't thinking about it before but you are now; X32 in reverse spells SEX. That's why some people referred to it by its local nick-name, the sex bus.

E is for Entebbe (Uganda)

I arrived at Entebbe airport in Uganda and was met by Joseph Sekiku and his old friend Macarius. I was on the way to Joseph's village in NW Tanzania as a representative of a link between his community and ours in Wales. I had been on a night flight, it was now early in the morning and Macarius took us to his home for breakfast. He was a long-serving police officer and as such he was given accommodation with the job. It turned out to be a two room metal hut in a compound of other huts with children and goats running around.

Breakfast consisted of sweetened sliced white bread, perhaps a special treat they had bought for me – I don't know. Macarius' partner, Sharon, had the difficult job of serving the menfolk their food (our food, I should say) while keeping her head below our eye-level. As far as I could make out that was the appropriate etiquette. She also kept a sort of glazed expression on her face that I saw Joseph's wife adopt later; maybe it was a type of politeness used in formal situations. It all looked wrong to me and I felt uncomfortable. Then she and the other women in the room stood around while we ate. They took no interest in the conversation and I assumed they spoke no English.

When I returned three weeks later Sharon greeted me as a friend, in good African English. She asked me why I hadn't got a suntan. It's a different culture there. It would take quite a while to understand it.

6

Ballsy

It was in the spring of 2008, a few months after our once in a lifetime trip to Nepal, that Flic and I met Bill's friend Glynis. I saw her running from her car carrying a pair of crutches and then walking slowly and awkwardly with them as she approached the hostel we were staying in. I understood straight away; *that must be the woman who has Parkinson's disease*, I thought. It was good to meet her, someone a few years down the road from me, experiencing the illness as it progressed further. Or was it?

She wanted to be my friend, to talk to me about her struggle with the disease. She got out her laptop and showed me photographs and poems. She described waking in the night with her hand formed into a rigid claw shape that she couldn't release. She talked of being stuck in the park and a friend coming to get her with a wheelchair. I must say I felt a great warmth and sympathy towards her. Then in the evening she began her dyskinesias, involuntary writhing movements of her whole body, something brought on by the drugs she was taking. She didn't have much to eat at supper time because she couldn't get the food to her mouth. She struggled to keep her face turned towards us to maintain eye contact as she spoke. Both Flic and I found this disturbing. It was my future.

Glynis wanted to keep in touch but I never replied to her emails. I just couldn't. It was selfish and cowardly of me but I had to cope with Parkinson's the best way I could: by denial, by not looking ahead. But Flic and I had a renewed sense of urgency now. We should make the most of the time we had while my health remained.

On the last day of that first trip we visited a Hindu temple complex in Kathmandu. It was the strangest and most exotic experience of our lives, of a culture so different from our own. So when we decided to go back to the Himalayas and walk this time in the Everest Region we thought we would go on to India. We would be away for three and a half months.

We flew to Delhi in October 2008 and made our way overland to Kathmandu. My younger son, Peter, is in India as I write this. His first email home started with text-speak: OMG IDFBI. Oh my God, I don't fucking believe it. Yes, that's how India hits you. It's mad, it's strange, it's ugly and sometimes beautiful. It's an assault on the senses. In India you are intensely alive. Just being there, looking around you, is an experience.

We had just twenty-four hours in Delhi before catching an overnight train that would take us to Gorakhpur near to the Nepalese border. Our plan was to stay at least a month in Nepal before returning to India and spending time in Rajasthan (in the north) and then Kerala (in the south). I look at Flic's journal now and read:

This morning in Delhi. I want to go to the Modern Art Gallery near India Gate. We eat breakfast then walk out and a cycle rickshaw man stops and we jump in. He takes us not far to his friend who has a taxi who takes us to India Gate a huge archway to commemorate the people who died in the first world war we think. There are rows of red flowers and strips of water and grass, fascinating birds, people of all sorts. Some men bathing in the canals, some Muslims, snake charmers, grass cutters, soldiers, families. It is New Delhi designed by Lutyens in the 1920s. Thank goodness that he did and the roads are really wide. You risk injury or death crossing them they are so full of traffic but if they were narrower it would be much worse. Animals mingle with the motorised vehicles – horses, bullocks, donkeys, dogs. Although it's 95 degrees it isn't too hot. The museum has some good paintings and sculptures in the garden. We got a tuk tuk to a famous garden and saw a Gandhi memorial and watched everyone take off their shoes to show respect. The Indians we have talked to are very polite and thoughtful though the price of rides varies a lot.

Proximity. That's the word that springs to mind when I think of India and Indians. There are little three wheeler taxis (tuk tuks, or auto-rickshaws) which have a seat for the driver in the front and a seat for three passengers behind him. There are times in India when a tuk tuk pulls up with a family of four or five sitting in the back and the driver invites you to get in because there is plenty of room. There is no room. So the two of you, with rucksacks, get in somehow. There are lots of arms and lots of legs in the tuk tuk. You know that some of them belong to you. There are torsos and there are hands and feet and luggage and some of it belongs to you too but you lose track for a while. It's only when you need to get out that you decide which body parts and which items of luggage are yours and need to be untangled and removed.

The infrastructure of New Delhi, the streets and buildings, were put in place by the British and are appropriately grand and spacious. But even here the road traffic operates in a way that goes beyond proximity; it challenges the physical laws of the universe as we know it. There is a stream of traffic, perhaps three or four lanes of cars, buses, lorries, taxis and so forth, tightly packed, moving fast, approaching a roundabout carrying the same density of vehicles. There are no spaces between the vehicles on the roundabout into which any of the approaching traffic might fit. It comes on in a constant unremitting stream and, *without slowing down*, merges with the roundabout traffic. Two into one don't go. But this is India and two into one do go and they do it (note the tone of incredulity indicated by italics) *without slowing down*. But I think I can explain.

All over the sub-continent lorries have the words *horn*

please painted on the back. This is to remind you to sound your horn when overtaking because they may suddenly change lanes without looking in their mirror. Why don't they look in their mirror? Because in India you look ahead all the time; you can't take your eyes off the road in front of you because a child or an old lady with a herd of goats, or a cow with painted horns, or a small motorbike carrying a family of four, or a lorry with a hand-painted portrait of the god *Shiva* (to make it accident proof) on each side or... or any number of improbable vehicles, people or animals are about to pull out in front of you (without looking). You do not look behind and your reactions are very, very fast.

The other thing is proximity; did I mention proximity? I finally understood when in south India I saw a man standing up on a boat about to go under a bridge. He ducked at the very last available moment, his head inches from the concrete. And I understood that we non-Indians carry around with us an envelope of extra space into which we cannot imagine other people or objects intruding. The Indian universe is envelope-free and you can bump right up against anyone or anything. And people take up less space. In a country with a population of more than one billion this might be considered a good thing.

We stayed one night in Delhi, pottered about a little, paid a lucky young cycle-rickshaw driver about a month's wages for an hour's pedalling, and in the afternoon got ourselves to the station. I am always appropriately nervous before long journeys; I have a preoccupation with issues such as getting on the right train, not losing my luggage and so forth. Flic is relaxed and carefree. The more carefree she gets the more nervous I get. I was uncomfortable, it has to be said, when she got out her sketchbook and started drawing the people on what may or may not have been the right platform for our train. And when it arrived it was the longest train I have ever seen. We were the only foreigners among a multitude of Indians. Somehow we found our carriage and settled in.

We are on the 2nd class AC sleeper. While the light lasts it is like watching a silent film, factories, fields, brick kilns and other trains and people some dusty some bright, some cutting rice and some sleeping.

Now it is dark outside. In our carriage there are lights and curtains but further down it is dark and the carriages are more crowded and there are Sadhus sitting on the floor. I feel too big and white to go in there. It's fine where we are.

In the morning I wake at 5 expecting the train to be at Gorakhpur at 6 but it is 3 hours late. The morning is still lovely a mist covers the fields but it slowly gets hotter. At last we get to Gorakhpur straight away we get a taxi to the border. The driver drives very fast nearly hitting cows dogs busses cyclists rickshaws but being very careful where there are any potholes. Another 3 hours and we get to the border.

I really didn't want to stay the night in Gorakhpur or the vicinity and planned to go from Delhi to Kathmandu in a day and a half's travel. I had arranged for a car to meet us at the border and so we were met by our new trekking guide, Keran, and a young driver, a man called Susan. We drove for, I don't know, maybe seven hours and got to Kathmandu at nine thirty in the evening. After a couple of days sorting out trekking permits and hiring sleeping bags and down jackets we were off to Giri and the start of a twenty-eight day trek. We were headed for Namche Bazaar and then Gokyo and the hill above it, Gokyo Ri, from where we would be able to see Everest.

There are no roads in that part of the country and the main trail from Giri to the regional centre, Namche, runs at a right angle to the grain of the land, crossing high passes (two of them, I think, over 10,000ft) and deep valleys. It was hard work for us but much harder work for the porters who carried food stuffs, building materials and so forth up to Namche. These porters carried huge loads up and down steep slopes wearing cheap plimsolls. Some of them carried kerosene, which, being a liquid, sloshed about in containers on their backs. They were often young and sometimes female and came from very poor neighbouring areas. They carried little walking sticks that doubled as pack rests. On a steep slope they would stop regularly and prop their pack against these things to take the weight off their backs. Their progress was very slow. What was to us an adventure was to them, I believe, a living nightmare. We shared the trail with them but were in different universes. It felt wrong of course. But they were carrying goods up to supply the tourist industry without which they would have no work and be poorer.

One porter functioned as a sort of shop on legs. The outside of his huge pack was festooned with brightly coloured wools. We asked him if we could take his photograph and he stood up straight and proud for the camera. We bought some sachets of shampoo from him at a minute price.

I can't say much about our guide, Keran, or our porter, Take, because we never got to know them well. Keran spoke quite reasonable English but, like all Nepalis, was reserved, never asking us about ourselves or talking about himself and his life openly. Take had been with us on our first trek and we were pleased to see him but he spoke little English and was shy. They were both handsome young men in their twenties, quite small, with high cheekbones, narrow eyes and no facial hair. Keran talked to us in a friendly, casual way but something distanced him from us as time went by. For some reason he grew more reserved but I never understood why. Perhaps it was something that we said or did that was inappropriate in that culture.

Flic was carrying a sketchbook, of course, and also watercolours. She wrote and drew and painted every day. Here is some of her writing from that first part of the trek, the endlessly up and down route to Namche:

Went down to Bandar and found a quiet lodge. I painted and drew a crowd of children who wanted eyes noses mouths painted on their hands. Their clothes are grubby and so're their hands but they are all outside playing in the monastery garden along with monks playing interesting music and a man repainting the stupa.

Left Bandar at 7 am. I had had a terrible night not sleeping and a sore throat queasy feelings anxious dreams so next day didn't feel much like going far. I told Richard and Keran that I was exhausted and they decided to stop nearby in Kenja. The man there was protecting his bees by standing guard by the hollowed tree trunk with a stick and killing bad giant bees that wanted to kill his honey bees. He showed us his garden – growing ginger, curryfruit vine.

From Goyam we had to keep climbing to cross a high mountain pass. The rocks here are full of mica and its dust gets carried into the air and makes it sparkle.

Just over the pass were lots of blue gentians then down through pine woods and rhododendrons and thick lumpy moss distorting the shapes of trees, which were enormous. And there were maple trees turning orange. Past the forest the path straightened out we stopped to eat at a house but it was too smoky to eat inside with Keran and Tek. There were beautiful rocks – very big covered with Sherpa lettering. Then on through farmed land and cattle cows bulls yaks.

Jumbesi seems an amazing place so sophisticated and prosperous glass in windows paved streets Buddhist temple water powered prayer wheel and mill. The beautiful powerful river rushes along around rocks where people wash clothes.

All the water is polluted you can see pipes coming from the bottom of wooden toilets straight into the river. With no road it would be impossible to build a sewage works unless reedbeds could be used. So it isn't as heavenly as it seems – people can't have good health without clean water.

Down down down from Nunchello to where the crickets start to sing and people grow more food, over the long chain bridge over the Dudhcosi – the milk river which flows from a glacier, then along a bit through a very fertile valley growing yams and sugar cane, pumpkins, sweetcorn bananas pears chilli tomato cucumber tomato trees white radishes winter wheat millet potatoes. I felt quite hungry and we stopped and ate some food with some children – we peeled it with our fingers yams sweet potatoes, soya beans and roast sweetcorn and squash.

One day we came across some people with a freshly killed water buffalo. They covered it in dry grass which they set fire to in order burn off the animal's hair. It may well have been this same animal that we met with again several times in the form of a carcass cut up and carried in baskets (all uncovered and bloody, as Flic noted) on the backs of three porters. It grew smellier as time went by and we would overtake the porters to get well away from it.

We walked for ten days over this corrugated landscape seeing very few other trekkers and not coming close to the big snow-capped peaks. The days were good but in the evenings I tended to think about the future, about my ill health and the restrictions it placed on me. The truth is that my day to day life at home tended to be marred by the incapacities and discomforts of my illness. I could walk (sometimes with a limp, sometimes without) and I could look around at the world but very often I could do little more; my body just didn't co-operate. But now I was at the start of a wonderful adventure and it was stupid of me to be negative. And when we got to Namche and the big mountains things began to get truly impressive. I stopped dwelling on the future and became immersed in an amazing present.

Namche Bazaar is the trading and administrative centre of the Khumbu region. It is also a very popular tourist destination, at least for a certain kind of tourist. But it is more than 11,000ft above sea level, and sits in a steep-sided basin scooped out of a precipitous mountainside. And can only be reached on foot. There are no vehicles in Namche and there aren't going to be in the future; the landscape is too steep. Most trekkers and climbers fly to the airstrip at Luckla, two days walk away.

We stayed a couple of nights in Namche to acclimatise to the altitude and we walked up above the town. Here we were in the most dramatic mountain landscape we had ever experienced. To look at the summits around us we needed to crane our necks up and when we looked into the valley below we could see clouds halfway down. Such is the steepness and scale of those mountains.

This trip to Nepal and India was a big challenge and a big unknown. The trek was tougher than the Annapurna, and India loomed ahead. A certain fellow traveller by the name of Mr Parkinson made things more difficult often enough. And so it was that from the very start I decided that if we made it to the top of Gokyo Ri, at 17,500 or so feet, then the trip was already a success. But we took an indirect route to Gokyo through the vast dramatic landscape of improbably steep, snow-capped mountains and barren valleys populated only by yak herders and the occupants of isolated monasteries. The lack of oxygen made us walk slowly. The nights were very cold and we were sleeping with all our clothes on. But the beauty of the mountains sustained us; it made it all worthwhile. The day before we reached Gokyo we saw a body being carried down on a stretcher, as Flic put it: *completely covered so it must be dead.*

We walked up the final stretch of the Dudh Kosi valley to Gokyo at something like half a mile an hour, snow all around us and snow and ice underfoot at times. We passed some small, shallow lakes and finally caught sight of the sparkling turquoise water of Gokyo Lake itself. And then we arrived at the little cluster of trekking lodges and yak herder's huts that make up the village.

The following morning we got up at five and walked up Gokyo Ri. Near the summit we were walking three or four slow paces and then resting to catch our breaths. The view from the top was stupendous. Below us was Gokyo Lake, a vibrant blue-green colour, glistening in the morning sunlight. Beyond that the long grey ridge of glacial moraine fringing the glacier itself. All around very high mountains, masses of snow clinging to steep slopes. A deep blue sky and an astonishing clarity to everything, near and far. It's a challenge to properly describe it. You have to go there. Really, you must.

We were well enough acclimatised to spend over an hour on that summit and enjoy it immensely. It was a tough day: three and a half hours up and two down. I had a high altitude headache when we got back to the village but I didn't mind. In the evening we could clearly hear the voices of three Canadian trekkers in their room next to ours, separated from us by a thin plywood wall. They didn't know we were next door. *That English guy,* one of them was saying, *you know he's got Parkinson's? It took him three hours to get up to the summit but he did it. Now that's what I call ballsy.*

I understood that the expression *ballsy* was complementary; it implied that I had guts and determination. I look it up now in an online dictionary and find the word *courageous,* among others. Is that me? I'm not so sure. At the beginning of this chapter I described my unwillingness to commit to a friendship with someone who wanted to share their difficulties. It needed a different type of courage and I wasn't up to it. I'm just a person who is trying to make the best of a life that has its limitations. I have had the time and the money, and most of all the support of a loved one, to undertake a few moderate adventures. Alongside my difficulties I have had great good fortune. Not *ballsy* then. I don't think so. Looking back at the last few years I'm inclined to come up with a different word. I would describe myself as, among other things, lucky. I hope to be able to use that word for quite a while longer.

F is for Fort William (Scotland)

The first time I visited Fort William was with Phil, a school friend, whose life has since followed a straighter path than my own. We were taking a short holiday together in Scotland after finishing our A levels. He let his hair grow long that summer and I remember him standing under a sign in Edinburgh Castle that read *Way Out*. He wasn't way out for long and felt the pressures of conformity to a life in pursuit of material gain – *the rat race*, we used to call it. But wait, I'm assuming too much. Apologies, Phil, if you're currently building compost toilets in Tahiti or researching mind-altering drugs in the Ecuadorian jungle. And while we're speaking, do you remember staying in Fort William and walking up Ben Nevis? I can't remember it very well but I think we had a great time.

I was in Fort William another time on the way to a sailing trip among the firths, sounds and sea lochs of the west coast of Scotland. Out on the water I learnt about the way the sea flows back and forth and around and through and over the corrugated land. Great tidal races, eddies, currents and standing waves come and go under the influence of the moon. I learnt to study the air, the prevailing winds and the flukey breezes coming down out the hills and the marks they make on the water. And we navigated by land, taking bearings off lighthouses and beacons and hilltop cairns. That's what I remember of the trip – that increased awareness of the elements and their interactions. And the wild beauty and the cold and the rain.

7

The Road to Zagora Starts Here

It is sometime early in 1986. Flic, her father, Robin, and I are standing on the terrace of the Avon Gorge Hotel in Bristol under a grey sky out of which a fine drizzle has begun to fall. Somehow I have persuaded them that it is better to be outside, in the open air, despite the weather. Above us and to our right Brunel's suspension bridge crosses the gorge; to our left the land drops away and we can see the old red-brick warehouses and the terraced streets of south Bristol. Down below us the brown river flows between banks of grey mud.

Robin is wearing an agreeably scruffy old jacket, a bow tie (as always), and a lopsided smile. *This would be a good place, he says, addressing me, for a young man to ask a certain question of his girlfriend's father*. Flic is pregnant and I have written to Robin and Catherine (Flic's mother) to explain that while I'm not in favour of marriage I am very committed to Flic, our long term relationship, and our future child. He's hoping for something more. I don't take the bait but Robin doesn't seem to mind. And I'm pleased that he has brought the subject up with such charm and good humour.

Robin seemed to me in those days rather posh and a little intimidating, as were the rest of Flic's family. But I liked his *joie de vivre* and his sense of humour. In those things, if in nothing else, he was similar to my father who, when I introduced Flic to him, asked *does he snore?* as a cheeky way of finding out if we were sleeping together.

Flic's family are so different to mine in regard to wealth, education and social class, and the differences were very big for our parents' generation. They did, however, live through the same world war. They had extraordinary experiences of terrible times that our generation have been fortunate enough to escape. Robin was brought up as a Quaker and was a conscientious objector. He spent the war years in China, which was fighting Japan, working with the Friends' Ambulance Unit, as the Quaker Volunteer Service was known. Still a pacifist in his seventies he was proud of having been dragged away by police in the protests against the erection of a statue of Air Marshall Arthur 'Bomber' Harris, who had been responsible for the bombing of Dresden.

My father was an ordinary working class man who was a motorbike dispatch rider throughout the war. He hated the army and was nick-named the *static corporal* in honour of his failure to rise through the ranks. He found it difficult to obey orders and when he got promoted from time to time he soon suffered demotion for being where he shouldn't. He never saw the enemy and spent most of the war accompanying convoys of military vehicles in the UK. Sometimes he would slip away to visit my mum in London where she was working as a *clippie*, a bus conductress. A frequently told story has him following her bus on his army motorbike and waving to get her attention. She flirted with this seemingly unknown young soldier not recognising that he was her husband. At some point he took off his helmet and she got a shock, if not a disappointment. That was one of his few war stories.

My father did spend a little time overseas towards the end of the war. He was in newly liberated Holland where the people were hungry to the point that children were suffering from malnutrition. British soldiers, including my father, found themselves sharing their rations with the locals. Dad felt great sympathy for the Dutch people, was greatly respected by those he came to know, and made friendships there that lasted for many years after the war.

My mother spent some of the war years working on the

buses in London until she gave birth to her first child, my sister Pam. Flic's mother gave up her history degree at Oxford to work in the *Land Army*, in which women replaced agricultural workers who had become soldiers. My mum has been dead for many years but as I write this Flic's mum, Catherine, is still alive at ninety-four. She is the last in her family of her generation, marooned in the twenty-first century, a world so different from the one she grew up in.

Before Kit, our first child, was born Flic's parents drove down to Surrey to meet their future in-laws (out-of-laws?), my mum and dad. I choose not to be there; the embarrassment would have been unbearable. Robin and Catherine lived in what I can only call a *grand house* in Corsham, Wiltshire. Flic denies that it was grand. What can I say? Only that it stood in several acres of land and was big enough to house two adults and five children and still have the top floor (of three) rented out as a flat. It was, and is, a handsome Georgian building constructed out of Bath stone. I can't really imagine what Robin and Catherine thought of my mum and dad's council maisonette in Cobham. It consisted of four tiny rooms which added together might take up the space of the rarely used front sitting room in their house. Flic, again, wants to correct me. *Your parent's house wasn't so small, she says. It's just that the walls were very close together*. No matter. I know that my mum and dad liked and respected hers and I hope that the feeling was mutual.

The truth is that Flic and I started on the road to Zagora from somewhat different places. We have different backgrounds. My mum and dad were working class Londoners born and brought up in what we would today call poverty. Mum was the oldest of five children and she spent much of her childhood looking after her younger siblings (three girls and a boy) because her mother worked in a café in the day and did cleaning jobs in the evening. Mum left school at fourteen and went, as they called it then, into service, leaving home to work as a scullery maid in a grand house. It wasn't her choice, she wanted to stay on at school but uniforms were expensive and it just wasn't possible.

Dad was born to a young woman working as a servant for a middle class family. He was fostered and looked after by someone who he always referred to as *Mrs Kettle*. He never knew his father and, as illegitimacy was a source of shame in those days, had a tough start. He left school at fourteen too.

My parents had three children and lived in a council flat in south-west London, Dad working night shifts for London Transport. Then, in 1956, he got a job as a chauffeur to a rich architect, they moved into a tied cottage in leafy suburban Surrey and I was born. There was a ten year and more gap between myself and my brother and sisters and they all left home early and I grew up as a single child.

Flic and I had different childhoods. My playmates were the sons of architects and solicitors while Flic played with the kids from the council prefabs (prefabricated houses built during the war) and climbed over the wall into her own garden to scrump apples, not telling her friends she lived there. She went to a private nursery school, a convent school, and what might be called a *finishing school* in Oxford. I went to a good junior school and then a grammar school (clever kids only), in Kingston-upon-Thames. I see that already some of the differences are beginning to look like similarities. The truth is that while social class defined people from our parent's generation (imagine what leaving school at fourteen did to my mum and dad's confidence), it didn't affect us so much at all. I have never for a moment felt disadvantaged because of wealth or class. Those things are a sideshow, a source of interest and often enough amusement, that's all. The cultural differences between Flic and myself are mostly fun. Take, for instance, the subject of vocabulary.

There was a big wedding at Flic's mum's house recently and I was amused to see that the portaloos installed for the occasion had the word *toilet* covered up and replaced with the word *lavatory*. I can imagine Flic's oldest brother seeing the toilets, as I call them, and muttering the word *vulgar*, or, even better, *ghastly* – words I wouldn't dream of using. Sometimes the upper-middle classes make good use of the word extraordinary. It's pronounced like this: ex-STRORD-dinary, with a strong emphasis on a random syllable. Flic is one of six and their posh accent diminishes in direct proportion to their ages. So Flic and her younger sister Alice talk almost normally. But Anna, who is five years older than Flic, comes out with a highly accented GHAST-ly and even, on occasion, ex-STRORD-dinary. I don't mind. It makes me smile.

Other words? Well, *dinner*, is out of the question. What was it Flic was taught? *Only dogs and servants have dinner*. I may be exaggerating, *only dogs and children* I think it was. The correct word is, of course, *supper*. Just as *settee* is quite out of the question and *sofa* is right. *Lounge* is inadmissible and *sitting room* is the proper word.

The upper-middle classes also take delight in eccentric nicknames. Among Flic's friends and family you can meet with Twitch, Miney, Gog, Foff, Fluff, Feathers and many more. And Flic, short for Felicity, has been known in her family by that name from a very early age. In fact eccentricity is encouraged among such people, in great contrast to the *what will the neighbours think* mentality of my upbringing.

If we go back to my grandparents day the differences between our families are greater. My sisters both remember going to the dog races with my grandmother. Gran would bet on a greyhound, telling Margaret, my younger sister *you'll get that new coat I promised you if that dog comes in*. Margaret never did get the coat. My aunt Jean remembers, as a small child, collecting granddad's best suit from the pawn shop. Gran was a woman of high spirits with a zest for life that made her inclined to spend money that she didn't have. So it was that my granddad's suit was pawned during the week to provide some extra cash and then on a Saturday morning, after receiving Friday's pay packet, one of the children would be sent to get it back. This, like the dog racing, was meant to be a secret from granddad, or *Pop*, as we knew him.

I can just about remember my grandparent's house in Willesden, North London. I remember Gran rubbing my face with a flannel so hard, as if you weren't clean if it didn't hurt. And I just about remember the big family gatherings where we would dance *The Okey Cokey* or *Knees Up Mother Brown* and Pop would play the spoons. I'm not sure what Flic's family did on equivalent occasions but I've heard them sing Latin rounds.

I have in front of me now Pop's gold watch. On the back are inscribed the words *Presented by T Wall and Sons to E J Beale for good service 1939-1956*. That's right, sixteen years in the same job, an admirable achievement in those days when unemployment and the poverty that went with it were greatly feared. What a man wanted was a *job for life*. It didn't matter what is was, the noble thing was to stick it out and provide for your family.

And so it was that my father took up the job of chauffeur, driving a rich man up to London and back every week day for twenty something years. The man could have gone on the train, it would have been quicker, but to arrive in a chauffeur-driven Rolls Royce gave him a certain status. Not much of a job then; merely a rich man's status symbol. But Dad did what he had to do and was mostly happy. I remember Saturday mornings and him getting the Rolls out of the garage, washing and polishing it and singing and whistling as he worked. He would sing *I have often walked down this street before* from the musical *My Fair Lady*. Or Louis Armstrong's *What a Wonderful World*.

I once saw the film of Kazuo Ishiguro's *The Remains of the Day* with Anthony Hopkins playing the part of a butler in a grand house. He was brilliant, portraying the deferential, almost obsequious, manner that a man must adopt in such an occupation – a certain stiffness of movement, head bowed a little, face expressionless. How do I know this? Because I remember my father playing that role when he was with his employer. They spent a great deal of time in each other's company over the years but never spoke much and certainly not of personal things. After more than two decades of knowing each other my father's employer still called him *Collins* and my father in return used the word *sir*.

Of course people didn't open up about personal matters in those days in the way they do now. *Least said, soonest mended*, was one of a number of phrases used to say *we don't talk about that*. It's interesting to note that in Flic's family they were prohibited even from talking about not talking about things – at least in English. If an inappropriate subject came into the conversation they were told *ça ne se dit pas*, French for *it is not said*. In the bath they were told to wash those unmentionable places with the words *entre les jambes et sous les bras*. And in my family our parents Christian names were a well kept secret. I don't know how old I was when I came to know that they were called Harold and Winifred.

My father was *Harold* to his wife, *Collins* to his employer, and *Dad* to his children. But there was another name too. I have a vague childhood memory of hearing him addressed as *Cap* by old friends who came to visit. You might think that it stood for *Captain* or *Capo* but you'd be wrong. I have only recently learned that it was short for *Madcap*. Hmmm... not the name I would imagine for him but then my earliest memories are of him in his fifties. But wait, here's a memory and I believe it's true. On his seventieth birthday he rode his motorbike at seventy miles per hour no hands, and took a photograph of the speedometer to prove it. *Madcap* it is then. That's one of the ways that I'll think of him from now on.

I have spoken to both of my sisters about Dad recently. One sent some photographs that made me a bit lumpy-throated and tearful for a moment. The other sister sent these words (which also made me feel lumpy-throated and tearful for a moment too): *I would say that we were not worse off than our neighbours and Dad was always in work. We had clean school uniforms. A mum at home to care for us, a large extended family, wonderful Christmases and caravan holidays. Dad would be so proud to see us now. That illegitimate lad who with a bad start in life gave love, security and adventure to us.*

One of Flic's sisters started gathering a collection of stories of their father recently. He wasn't a madcap but certainly an eccentric with a great sense of humour. There is, for example, the letter, written in verse, that his niece, Christina, received from Rudolf Nureyev in answer to her fan mail. It included the words *I find my pas de deux les hard de deux thinking of you.* Some people believe that Nureyev didn't write that letter at all but that it came from a certain Robin Eden. When the residents of the new estate built at the back of Robin and Catherine's house looked out of their windows one morning and saw a tramp asleep on a bench, an empty beer bottle by his side, they phoned the police. The tramp turned out to be a stuffed figure, like a scarecrow. Again there are those who believe it might have been the work of a tall man wearing a bow tie who was seen in the vicinity earlier that morning. The name Robin Eden springs to mind. But who am I to say?

On the face of it my father and Flic's could not have been more different and so it surprises me to find myself writing about a couple of similarities. Firstly, I think that for both of them their activities in the war years will be remembered as being compassionate rather than anything else. That's a good thing to be able to pass on to our children. And they both retained a boyish sense of humour into their old age. I suspect that they were able to do this because they had the support of their wives, Catherine in the case of Robin and my mum, Win, in the case of my father, women who were each the emotional and practical backbone of the family.

Thinking about it now I wonder if the biggest difference between Flic and myself is that she was one of six and I was, in effect, a single child. My sisters left home early to get married and my brother was killed in a motor accident at the age of seventeen. So most of my childhood memory is that of an only child. Or, you might say, since my two sisters spoilt me and competed for my affection (and they still do), an only child with three mums. I guess that explains some things. Certainly Flic was brought up to share and to practice great tolerance. I wasn't.

My parents were ordinary people of straightforward kindness and integrity. Flic's parents were ordinary posh people of straightforward kindness and integrity. My mum and dad didn't try to make me follow a particular career; they just wanted me to be happy. Flic's mum and dad didn't try to make her follow a path either. Both of us were born to parents who were already in their forties, and we were brought up in comfortable, predominantly middle-class, leafy, small-town suburbia.

And so ends the chapter that included the words *Flic and I started on the road to Zagora from somewhat different places; we come from different backgrounds*. I really believed those words as I wrote them. Now I'm not so sure.

G is for Grindlewald (Switzerland)

I *am a killer, I kill only for money*, he said, holding a huge knife out in front of him. "But you are my friend," he continued, smiling. "I kill you for nothing." He was the Yugoslav cook in the hotel in Grindlewald where I worked for a couple of weeks washing up. It was his only joke in the English language. I was twenty years old and had set off from home with the intention of going to Lapland.

The hotel was called The Silberhorn, if I remember correctly, and it was run for Jewish visitors to the town, on kosher principles. I guess kosher is a symbol of an active commitment to a faith and a cultural identity. I have no idea if the persecution of Jews over the centuries has strengthened that commitment or if the strength of the commitment and the statement of otherness implied by it has led to the persecution. I try to respect other people's way of doing things but, in truth, kosher seems a bit daft.

The hotel kitchen had three different areas for different sorts of food and cutlery and plates and so forth were kept separate. On Friday we would make up lots of concentrated tea so that on Saturday, the holy day of *Shabbat*, it could be topped up with hot water and we wouldn't have actually brewed the tea on the day that God set aside for not brewing tea.

A fourteen year old boy who was working in the kitchen for the summer made friends with me. He was related to the management, was Jewish, and wore a little skull cap. When I left he walked with me to the station. Some local youths, seeing his headgear, called out names as we passed. It still goes on.

8

Not Lapland

I was twenty years old and didn't know what life was meant to be about. I had spent a few terms at a teacher training college; fallen in and out of love; worked as a forklift truck driver among other things; and saved some money for travelling. I was at home in leafy suburban Surrey, bored and lonely, unemployed, and longing for wild and beautiful places. I left a note on the kitchen table, *gone to Lapland*, and set off, first travelling by train to Paris – it seemed wrong that I had never been to this famous city that was relatively close by. I would make my way north from there.

Paris was a disaster. I was lonely and I didn't like the city that much. The first night there I went to a youth hostel and found it full so I ended up sleeping on a park bench under a plastic sheet to keep off the rain. The next day I looked at a map and saw the Alps not so very far away, wild enough and nearer than Scandinavia. I took a train some of the way and started hitching.

I remember now that my dream was to meet a young woman soul-mate in an exotic location and find myself settling down with her and of us leading some sort of unspecified meaningful life together. Reader, it didn't happen. What did happen is that I found the world to be a very beautiful and interesting place. I loved travelling and began to think of it as a life purpose. I would forget any ideas of material wealth that I might have had and live intensely. As I explained to myself, *experience* was to be the substance of my life, nothing else. I was, it must be said, a strange young man. I rejected the conventional life model of a settled career, a mortgage and so forth but I really had no idea what to put in its place. I was making it up as I went along.

As I travelled away from the city and into the hills I began to enjoy myself more. One of the first significantly beautiful places I stayed in was a village on Lake Neuchâtel, Switzerland. There was some sort of waterfront, perhaps a jetty, I don't know, a place where you could look out over the vast expanse of the lake, almost an inland sea. Above the village there was mixed farmland with arable crops and maybe hay meadows and certainly plum trees and vineyards. Then steep slopes covered in forest. Then, higher again, the summer pastures with cows grazing. A perfect landscape. I loved it.

I remember taking the little train up to Grindlewald on a steep rack-and-pinion railway line, standing on the little balcony (for want of a better word) at the end of a carriage, seeing the Eiger and the other big peaks and coming to understand the expression *it took my breath away*. I walked in a mountain landscape of outstanding beauty. And in the youth hostel I saw a well-paid job advertised and found myself washing up in a kosher hotel, working mornings and evenings, walking up the mountain a little way in the afternoons, seeing the moonlight on the Eiger from my bedroom window at night. I worked there for two weeks and then moved on.

I pottered about Switzerland, mostly on my own, sometimes with people I had met up with in youth hostels. One time I got benighted on a hill above a lake near Interlaken, slept in a barn, and ate so many bilberries for breakfast that I threw up. Above St Moritz I managed to scrabble up to a 10,000 ft summit on my own. There, with very cold hands, I attempted to open a tin of sardines, the only food I had with me. I failed and came down off the mountain feeling very hungry.

Then I decided to head for Greece. I walked out of St. Moritz in the wrong direction and ate a picnic beside a strange track that turned out to be the famous Cresta bobsleigh run.

Then I walked back through town and hitched in the right direction, towards Italy, getting a lift with a man who asked me to steer the car from the passenger seat while he looked at his map.

I arrived at a town in the Italian lakes on a Sunday afternoon feeling wary and timid. This country, I had heard, was more dangerous for the traveller. Crime was much more prevalent here than in other places I had visited. I hid my cheque card in the bottom of my shoe for safety and wandered about trying to find the youth hostel. There seemed to be a lot of signs to a place called *senso unico*, but I couldn't see it on the map. All the young men carried themselves with a certain *machismo*, a proud bearing which looked aggressive to me. Eventually I went up to one of these guys, a young man on his own who looked less scary than some of the others. He smiled and seemed sympathetic, understood my mispronunciation of *ostello della gioventù*, took me to a bus stop and put me on the right bus, explaining to the driver that he should set me down at the right place. The bus driver, I seem to remember, refused to accept payment. And these people didn't seem scary anymore; they were kind and helpful and I had got it all wrong.

It was in this hostel that I met an American who had just graduated from Harvard with a degree in classics. He was a fine violinist and carried an expensive instrument with him that he wouldn't let out of his sight. His ambition was to become a composer of stage musicals. I wonder now if he succeeded. His idea of travel was to buy a cheap car in Paris and sell it in Athens. And he needed fellow travellers to help pay for fuel. So he and I and another American and an Australian young woman set off together down through Italy. We stayed one night in Rimini and then carried on to Brindisi to catch the ferry to Corfu.

On the island we found a youth hostel in a rural location, with a cheap bar across the way and a beach nearby, accessible by a rough track. I bought a thick blanket in Corfu town and slept on the beach for a while, pottering about along the coast or in the olive groves, going to the hostel for meals. My violinist friend left for Athens and I moved up to the hostel. It was there that I spent the last of the money I had earned in Grindlewald. No matter, I would go into town and cash a cheque. I took out my cheque guarantee card and found that in the place on the back where my signature had been there was now the word VOID. I remembered that when I arrived in Italy I put the card in my shoe for, wait for it, *safe keeping*. This now looked like a mistake. The motion of my sweaty foot had rubbed out my signature.

I couldn't afford the small bus fare into town so I hitched. I walked around looking for something to steal but I had no idea how to go about it. Eventually I went to the hospital and offered to sell my blood, a convenient way of earning money abroad in those days. They checked my blood type and found that yes, there was a potential buyer, a relative of a patient in need of a transfusion. But I had competition, a German guy was also selling blood of the same type. The relative looked us over, the weedy little Englishman, the hunky blond German. He got his wallet out and negotiated a price with the hunk. I walked back to the hostel, hungry enough to try to eat cactus fruit along the way.

The next morning the proprietor of the hostel asked me where I was going so early in the day. I explained that I was waiting for a money transfer to arrive at the bank and in the meantime must go into town and sell my blood to pay for food. *No worry*, he said, *eat here, pay me when you have the money*. I ordered a large breakfast. This was a long time ago and I don't remember what I ate. But I have a feeling it tasted pretty good.

A few days later my money arrived. I was very happy but also ready to move on. I paid the kind youth hostel man what I owed him and set off for mainland Greece. On the way to Corfu town I hitched a ride on the back of a motor scooter. I had a big rucksack on my back and no helmet, of course, but the guy gave me a lift anyway. That was Greece in those days, the people very relaxed, happy, and kind to strangers.

Before long I was hanging out on another Greek island, this time Crete. I bumped into my violin playing former companion on the street in Heraklion. Then, as we talked, the two women we had gone to the funfair with some weeks before in Rimini turned up. I spent some time on Crete with a young woman from Vancouver called Carla. We walked down the Samaria Gorge and slept together (but not as much together as I would have wished) on the beach. She said she loved the sound of my voice in the darkness and that it soothed her into sleep. Hmm... And then we had different destinations in mind and separated happily and a little sadly too.

I travelled on but now, suddenly, I was lonely and homesick. I took a ferry back to Athens and a bus to London and home. My parents, who hadn't heard from me for ten weeks, were keen to learn about my experiences in Lapland. No-one in my family had travelled in such a way before and they were, I believe, a little bit proud of me. I knew that there were further adventures out there waiting for me. I had been very low before I left but now I believed (wrongly, of course) that I never need to be unhappy again. The world was a beautiful and exciting place. And it was good to be home.

H is for Harlem (U.S.A.)

I cycled through Harlem on a hot day in 2006 wearing the sort of hat that in America is only worn by old ladies. Not a baseball cap, like any other regular guy, but a sort of beanie hat, as worn by balding middle-aged Englishmen. It drew some unwelcome attention. A van pulled alongside me and a guy shouted at me in Spanish. Then a car and a guy speaking English, but in such a way that I couldn't understand a word. I think they were taking the piss in a friendly sort of way but I felt threatened. I *think* it was something to do with the hat.

This was part of a ride around Manhattan Island, thirty miles, most of it along the waterside on cycle paths. It was July and very hot. Stopping at red lights I felt the heat coming up off the tarmac like a furnace and the sun's heat from above like another one. The signs on some road lanes reading *Keep Clear for Snow Ploughs* seemed more than a little incongruous.

9

The View from the Bridge

I visited New York twice in the noughties, as we called them, each time for only a few days. The two trips could not have been more different: one a very happy family holiday, the other, a painful lonely experience.

In 2005, Flic and I went with our two teenage boys to the United States for a very short family holiday: six days in New York and four days driving from New Haven to Cape Cod and back. It was great.

On the first morning in the city we walked out from our accommodation on West 96th Street into Central Park. It was a sunny spring day and we were excited to be in this mythical city. We spoke to various dog walkers and wandered southwards until we reached a large reservoir and could see a marvellous view of the skyscrapers beyond. Then we walked out of the park and took a bus to a spot from which we could walk to the Empire State building. The queues went around the block so we jumped into a yellow taxi and drove down to Battery Park, the southernmost point of Manhattan Island. It was cool and clear and we took our time wandering around, looking out at the ships and ferries in the harbour, at Ellis Island and the Statue of Liberty in the distance. We bought food from a deli and sat outside to eat. We walked up to Ground Zero and looked at the damaged buildings around. The city was foreign enough to be exciting and yet we also felt very much at home there. I can't convey the excitement of being there in that city. I loved it particularly but I know that Flic, Kit and Peter did too.

On other days we hung out in MoMA and the Guggenheim; we walked across Brooklyn Bridge; we listened to a jazz band in the Natural History Museum; we took a ferry ride in the harbour; and we went boating in Central Park.

One evening we were walking back along the edge of the park and heard a strange noise in the trees. We went to investigate and saw racoons clinging to the branches.

We came across the Chelsea Hotel by chance. I knew the place had lots of literary associations (Jack Kerouac wrote *On the Road* there, Arthur Miller lived there for years, Dylan Thomas stayed there, so did Mark Twain, yes, the hotel is that old, loads more writers...) and, of course, famous musicians too (Joni Mitchell, Leonard Cohen), I could go on all day but I won't. Flic was brought up to go into hotels and ask for tea. We did. They don't serve tea in places like that but said we could buy some next door and bring it in. We talked to a man who lived there – a louche, slightly creepy, possibly gay, name-dropping, middle-aged guy who had once invited I don't know how many dogs to his pet's birthday party in the lobby. He took us up to the tenth floor in the lift and we walked back down looking at all the modern art.

Flic hadn't really wanted to go to New York but when she let slip something about being in love with the city I got the impression that the trip was a success for her too. She particularly enjoyed ice skating in the park at night. I still remember it as a very special family time.

I also remember a particular concern I had before the trip. It was that year that a friend pointed out to me that I was walking with a slight limp. How strange that she could see it but I had not been aware of it. And then, just days before we set off for America, I started limping badly. I was walking in the woods above the village one morning and really not enjoying it and I began to think that it would ruin our trip. At a particularly negative moment I wondered if I was going to lose the pleasure of this simple interaction with the world. I couldn't have guessed that I was at the start of such a terrible illness, a sort of intermittent creeping paralysis. And I would not have imagined that in the next few years I would walk, and enjoy walking, so very much, in places so very far away from home.

In 2006 I was writing a book called *The Garden Project*. A big part of the story was concerned with a particular type of outdoor theatre performance and I had to do some research. I read about something called *Gorilla Theatre* that took place in the public parks of New York in the summer. Then a letter came through my door offering the possibility of a writer's travel grant. I really wanted to go to New York again and this was an opportunity too good to miss. I applied, they gave me some money and off I went. Here's part of something I wrote on my return:

It's a hot and humid Saturday afternoon in July and I'm stand-ing in Fulton Ferry Park watching Boomerang Theatre Company get ready to perform. The park is small but spectac-ularly situated on the Brooklyn side of the East River, between the Brooklyn and Manhattan bridges. Big suspension bridges, they arch high above the water, framing a view of Manhattan skyscrapers. But now the view gets obscured by a freighter moving slowly upstream. I write her name in my notebook, Alice Oldendopf, and one word of description, ginormous. I hear big city sounds: the ship's engines; two bridges worth of traffic noise; one bridge worth of clattering commuter train noise (Manhattan Bridge is a double-decker – cars on top and trains underneath); tourist helicopters flying around the skyscrapers; jet aircraft higher up; a rock band practising in the warehouse behind me. I wonder how I'm going to hear the play.

Boomerang don't seem to be too stressed out and I'm able to speak to them. I explain to the director that I'm writing a novel set in a landscape garden in which a lot of outdoor theatre is performed. Five plays are embedded in the text, interacting with the outer story in all sorts of ways, with the boundary between the play and the world outside the play gradually breaking down. I tell him that I'm here in New York City to see some outdoor theatre, meet up with people involved in it, ask some questions. I suggest that he must have had some experience of times when outside events intrude on the play, the audience gets too involved, two worlds interpenetrate...

"No," he says. "Not really. I can't think of anything like that. The audience is always the audience and we do the play." A train clatters over Manhattan Bridge. "Of course, there is some extraneous noise to deal with. That's about it."

Now it's getting closer to two o' clock and kick-off time. I sit on the grass in what I hope will be the front row. A grey-haired man comes and sits next to me, arranges a take-out lunch on the ground in front of him, takes a paperback copy of this after-noon's play (King Lear) from his pocket and reads from where he last left off. When he looks up I have a chance to speak to him. I explain about my novel, the breaking down of the boundary between the play and the world outside... He's an aficionado – he's seen, he says, literally hundreds of outdoor performances in the city over the years. He must have some stories about the sort of thing I'm interested in.

"No," he says. "I can't say I've seen anything like that."

Oh dear. It seems that my imagination exceeds what can really happen. That's good in a way, it's how a writer should be. But I wonder about my trip here, to New York City, to see outdoor theatre and meet up with people involved with it. It's been very difficult to plan: theatre company's programmes always TBA (to be announced); other companies disappearing without trace; unanswered letters and emails; people who would be delighted to meet me but are unable to make it; the first play I go to see cancelled. And I'm not quite sure what it is that I'm searching for here. Maybe something that doesn't exist.

New York the second time was an experience but not a happy one. The first night was strange; I was exhausted from a very early morning start and jetlag, but I couldn't sleep. I got undressed, lay on the bed, got up and turned the air conditioning off, lay down, got up and turned it on again, tried to read, paced up and down, went for a crap, tried to read, went for a shower, tried to read, got up and shaved, packed my bag, read a sentence, wrote in my journal, went for shower, and so on. Really, something like that until 7am when I slept for an hour. I was lonely and homesick to an extraordinary degree.

On the flight out a big Hasidic Jewish man sat by my side with his back turned to me (as much as is possible on a plane) the whole way; I was staying in a cheap hotel with no public spaces for meeting and talking with other people; and the nearest outdoor space was a pier on the Hudson river, a gay pick-up place where I didn't feel I could talk to people without giving the wrong message. I was lonely and more than that; I was really frightened for my mental health. I was going to stay, I can't remember, maybe ten days. It seemed too much and I booked an early flight home.

Meanwhile I cycled around Manhattan Island in my now limping and sideways leaning style (perhaps it wasn't the hat, then). I took a ride on the Staten Island Ferry without wanting to visit Staten Island. I looked down from the Brooklyn Bridge on the neighbourhood Arthur Miller wrote about in *The View from the Bridge*. I dropped off a copy of my first novel in the bookshop that Michael Cunningham regularly visited for them to give to him, should he drop by. I saw fireflies as darkness fell in Riverside Park. And I saw three plays. Here's the description I wrote of the second one:

Now I'm at Shakespeare in the Parking Lot – The Tempest. I'm very early and have a chance to speak to the director, "I'm writing a novel in which..." The same question and the same answer, "No. I don't think I've ever seen anything like that." There's an hour to go before the play so I walk to the nearest park to eat my picnic supper. The park is incredibly crowded and with lots of activity, different sports and games overlapping each other, one game a strange New York thing that involves hitting a ball against a wall with bare hands – like squash without a racket. And I'm the only person there who isn't Chinese.

Back to the parking lot. It's a square space between low (for New York) buildings: many windows and fire escapes on one side; a bare windowless wall on another; bricked in windows on the third; a mishmash of signs (some in Chinese) on the fourth. No traffic right here but lots of not too distant background traffic noise plus the inevitable sound of police sirens. People are taking short cuts through the parking lot and through the set. I'm disappointed to see that there are plastic garden chairs set out for the audience and a distinct them-and-us organisation of space; I want to see site-specific promenade theatre where the play moves around, the audience follows, and the two get mixed up sometimes.

Half an hour to go. A more than half-naked and much pierced black man is on the 'stage' applying face and body paint (he later turns out to be Ariel). A group of actors behind some cars in the corner are chanting something. Other actors, or at least outgoing theatrical types, are in among the audience talking to friends. And a man close by is identifiable as a performer because of his visible pre-play nerves. Twenty minutes to go. A percussionist (bongos, drum-kit, all manner of cymbals and chimes, a vacuum machine hose that he whirls around his head to make a whining noise) has set up and is practising. As he warms up he gradually turns to face the audience and is now performing. Two sexy black girls start to dance. Are they in the play? No, I think they're part of the audience. I begin to like my plastic garden chair and I'm glad I'm not standing up; this thing ends at ten o'clock and that's three a.m. for this jet-lagged Englishman. Ten minutes to go. The sun is lower now and lights up only the top of the buildings. I'm still confused about some of the audience – are they really part of the play? They are certainly exotically dressed. A man wants to move his car and half of us must get up and move with our chairs. Then things are quieter as we get close to the start. I've been observing a mildly chaotic scene where reality is somewhat challenged. And I've seen a gradual transformation of a group of ordinary people into characters in a play.

The play: well, it's not brilliantly acted. Prospero is continually upstaged by Ariel and Ariel is upstaged by a woman passing through telling off her child in a loud voice. The audience grows larger as the play continues and there are people here now who would no way deliberately go out to see Shakespeare. Some of them are drunk and are as loud as the performers. They laugh in the right places, and in the wrong places as well. In fact they're doing it on purpose – they're performing too. There's a youth on a bicycle endlessly circling the parking lot, always turning his head to see the performance, not aware that he has become part of the audience and, for me at least, part of the show. I notice that there's a man watching from the driving seat of his car – drive-in Shakespeare? When the action slows I look around at the setting, at the big sign in the middle that says 4 hour parking limit, 25c per 15 minutes. There's an incongruity between the play and its setting but it adds something. The Tempest will never look the same to me again.

Why did I find the loneliness of New York so unbearable? Perhaps it was the as yet undiagnosed neurological illness that was making me crazy. I didn't use much of my experience in New York in the writing of *The Garden Project* but the few days that I spent in New York gave me some other ideas. Later that year I was in Morriston Hospital, outside Swansea, awaiting various tests including a brain scan and I started making notes for a novel that incorporated some of my New York thoughts. It was published in a small way a couple of years later under the title *The Quality of Light*. One of the central characters had just come out of hospital where he had been diagnosed with Parkinson's disease.

I is for Istanbul (Turkey)

A few years ago Flic and I travelled overnight to Istanbul from Cappadocia in central Turkey. The long distance buses in some countries are nowadays very luxurious, like flying business class; Turkey has some of the best, though not as good as those in Peru. Our bus did have a *flight attendant* I want to say, a smartly dressed young man bringing us hot and cold drinks. It also had little TV screens on the back of every seat, with a choice of channels and a pair of headphones for everyone. On the news we saw rioters in the streets of some foreign city, cars being overturned, chanting protesters being fought by police with water cannon. There was looting. There was bloodshed. We were curious and asked where in the world were such events taking place. Istanbul, we were told. We will be there in a few hours.

Have you heard the story of an Australian young woman who, some years ago, wanted to visit Britain? It was at the time of the *Troubles*, as they were known, in Northern Ireland and there were riots like the ones we were seeing on the bus TV screen. Her parents were strongly against such a journey, reasoning that the United Kingdom was too dangerous a place to visit. But, she said, *I won't be anywhere near Northern Ireland. I'm going to stay in Sussex*. Her parents looked at a map of the world. *Look how close it is*, her father said, *the violence could easily spread into Sussex*.

You haven't heard that story? Well, no – that's because I made it up. But you get the point. We had a great few days in a very large and mostly peaceful Istanbul. More recently we have had a great time in the war-torn but mostly peaceful Middle-East. Peace is very rarely reported on the television news.

10

The Right Side of Scary

On Gokyo Ri we were higher than we had ever been in our lives. In the lakeside village of Gokyo I overheard myself being described as *ballsy*. It was mostly downhill from there – but in a good way. After Gokyo Flic and I walked down the valley to an altitude where it was bearable to take off our clothes and wash. I had a shave for the first time in a while. Then we walked up another valley and climbed Chukhung Ri, moving at a similar pace to that achieved on Gokyo Ri. Then we descended until we reached Namche again. We checked in at a guesthouse with large south-facing windows. Namche, remember, is situated at a mere 11,500 ft above sea level. The sunshine poured into our room and it was a very great luxury to take off all our clothes. We amused ourselves for a while in the customary fashion of good friends who find themselves naked in each other's company.

The marvellous thing about trekking in Nepal is, of course, the altitude. The snow and ice-capped mountains are amazing in the very clear air. The way of life and the religion have a sparse beauty that is a product of the sparse landscape. The high places are wonderful, both culturally and physically. But it's so cold. You carry a down jacket and a down sleeping bag and sometimes you go to bed wrapped in both of them. The experience has to be short lived; very soon you crave warmth. And so our trek came to an end. We walked down to Luckla and from there flew in a light aircraft back to Kathmandu.

The flight was one of my happiest experiences ever. I know this because I remember that I could *feel* the smile on my face. Luckla airstrip is very short. The small, propeller driven aircraft don't so much lift off as fall off the end of the runway into the immense space between the mountains. Then they climb slowly and cross the corrugated landscape of the Himalayan foothills, negotiating high passes on the way. The land is mostly cultivated and the terracing makes beautiful patterns when viewed from above. Kathmandu airport was busy and we had to wait, circling the town of Barakphur a few times and looking down on the temples and market places. The landing was, for me, just the right side of scary, as I like to call it, but I as we left the aircraft I noticed the blanched faces of those for whom the flight had been just the wrong side.

Flic and I had walked for twenty-eight days, much of it at great altitude. We had enjoyed most of it very much and been deeply moved by some places and experiences. Mr Parkinson had made his presence known towards the end of the trek as Flic recorded in her journal:

Climbing up and up the next day, there is almost no flat land and I realise that I haven't seen a wheel let alone a car for a month. Richard is feeling low today as his left leg won't lift and every step is an effort however eventually he cries a bit and then gets angry which makes him walk so fast I can't catch up with him and then he feels better. It is wonderful here in Tsuryopka above Namche. Magical heavenly patch of earth.

Always before our travels there was uncertainty about my health and my ability to cope. Our trips have been much more than just holidays and more than just experiences. Each journey is a challenge. And once again the challenge was met and we had a special sense of achievement. But this trip had only just begun. Kathmandu, lowland Nepal and India lay ahead. First Kathmandu, from Flic's journal;

Saturday – a holiday for Nepalis who can afford it. We walked through dusty streets towards a tree-covered hill topped with stupas and gompas and prayer flags. We passed a small gompa where people were offering red colour, marigolds, flowers and winding string around a tree and lighting candles and praying. They put red colours on their foreheads and marigold petals in their hair.

We crossed a small river that smelt foul and had pigs rooting around the banks and ducks and chickens. We went through real streets and past real lives away from the tourist part of town. Lots of signs of Hinduism and Buddhism that are big parts of everyday life here. On the steps sat people begging for money and people selling things for other people to give the temples – leaf bowls, boiled eggs, marigolds, rice, sweetcorn. It was a special day for mothers and babies so one gompa had a long queue of people waiting to throw rice or corn in. There were statues of Buddha where candles burned and offerings were left. We were interested to see so many monkeys sitting, playing, defleaing each other, climbing and ganging up and rushing around eating the rice and corn left for the gods.

I talked to a man whose baby had a fever and he'd taken her to the hospital yesterday but today he'd brought her up here and 'look' he said 'her fever has almost gone'. The place was crowded but not many white tourists.

Some poor dirty children begging but mostly clean well looking children and their parents having a day out. One man was selling green parrots and budgies without cages. Another had apple-shaped balloons. There were monks there too from young boys to old men dressed in dark red with short hair and prayer beads and some with ipods. On the far side were great trees swamped with prayer flags blowing in the breeze. When the wind doesn't blow the air is smoggy and quite polluted but it's blowing today.

Two other memories of Kathmandu. First, the Garden of

Dreams, a colonial style garden that was created in the 1920s and recently restored. It is set behind a high wall by a busy street. There is an entry fee so it is quiet inside, a peaceful retreat from the noise and chaos of the rest of Kathmandu for those that can pay for it. I don't remember seeing any locals wandering around. Flic described it as a haven of trees, flowers, poetic quotes, water and expensive tea.

In complete contrast was a bicycle rickshaw ride back to Hotel Nature from Durbar Square, a genuinely historical part of the town where there are old courtyards and palaces and temples. Night falls fast in that part of the world and it fell heavily that evening as there were extensive power cuts in some parts of the city through which we were travelling. It was also rush hour with a chaotic mass of traffic in a state of inter-mittent gridlock. The combination was extraordinary. We travelled through near darkness among a multitude of other vehicles, some with lights on, many without, and passed busy shops and cafés lit by candles and stray light coming off the street. The bizarre shadows, the noise and bustle in the dark, the motionless commotion at jammed intersections, all together gave the sensation of being in some strange almost-nightmare, the allegorical dream sequence in a sinister art-house movie.

Then we went to Pokhara. I managed to get off the bus when it stopped outside of Kathmandu just in time to be violently sick. I was fine for the rest of the seven hour journey and then, when we arrived at a little lakeside guesthouse, other things happened. As Flic put it: Richard has a bad stomach but sorts himself out wonderfully in the dark toilet and changes his clothes. Wonderfully because Parkinson's reduces your movement and these bad tummy moments are more of a challenge than they might otherwise be. When we get home to Wales people always ask us if we got ill on our trip. Most travellers seem to get a day or two of stomach trouble in India or Nepal – some get more. We like to ask *did you get ill staying at home?* The answer is often yes, followed by a description of a week or two with flu and a bad cold to follow. We prefer to go away.

Pokhara is a sprawling unlovely city on a plain near the mountains. One corner of the town lies along the side of a beautiful lake and is heavily infected with tourists and tourism. There are hotels and gift shops in great numbers. But just where the town gives way to countryside there is a friendly village atmosphere and small places to stay looking out over the lake. That area is very special, a place we have returned to from time to time and one of the very few places we have visited where I would be happy to live. The lake and the hills around are particularly beautiful in the mornings and evenings.

One day there we took a boat out on the lake for something like five hours and saw extraordinary birds with – and we know this because we bought a bird book – extraordinary names. Best of all were the big brightly coloured kingfishers, more properly called the brown-headed stork-billed kingfisher. There were some extraordinary brightly coloured people on the lake too. On a small island there are some temples which people visit on holy days, holidays and special occasions (i.e. all the time). They are brightly dressed and pile into small boats for the trip across the water. Hinduism is fun, it's colourful and, like Buddhism, there is a reverence for places and landscape features (the River Ganges is the most obvious example).

We stayed a few days in Pokhara, visiting small scale tourist destinations like the bat cave and the Sita Gorge, renting bikes and pottering about the town and the countryside around both of which were full of interest.

We were cycling along a busy road on the opposite side of town from the lake when I noticed that each road to our left seemed to end abruptly in space, as if on the edge of a cliff. We went down one of these roads and found ourselves looking down a very steep long slope into a vast valley with a braided river winding about between a mass of boulders and gravel that, I guessed, was material carried down out of the hills in the rainy season. In landscape terms this didn't make sense, a deep valley so close to a big lake; there was something I couldn't understand about the geology of the area. But more extraordinary was the human activity: lots of people dotted about the valley bottom putting pebbles or gravel into plastic sacks and carrying them up the steep slope on their backs. It looked like ridiculously hard work, something like a torture or punishment, and it was clear that the people doing it were very poor and unsuited to the task. We saw old people who in our country would be enjoying their free bus passes and their gardens but here were condemned by their poverty to this grim labour.

Back in our guesthouse by the lake a young man, the son of the owner, wanted to take us to stay at his grandparents house on the terrai, the flat plains of southern Nepal. We would be near Chitwan nature reserve but staying in an ordinary farming household. Of course the guy wanted to charge us a daily guide's fee for taking us there and showing us around. Fair enough. The young man was called Eshaw and he had a slightly awkward but likeable manner as well as a catchphrase; he would show us *something a little bit different*. So we went off with him on the bus one morning and it was a great experience like he said, something a bit different.

Over to Flic now: the bus took four hours and then Eshaw took us in a taxi to his grandparents. Their house is built by hand and mostly of wood. I drew it with the grandfather and his friend sitting either side of me. Cows goats and cat and buffalo and ox. Sugarcane papaya mango banana coffee potatoes beans radish cauliflower rice maize in the garden. They had a wonderful way of making gas for cooking. Straw and dung from a small open barn next to the house was chopped with a special tool and dropped into a concrete lined pit where it made methane that was piped straight into a cooker in the kitchen.

This was a better version of *picturesque poverty*. Although the land was absolutely flat there was much beauty in the landscape: fine trees, a diverse range of crops and animals, simple but handsome buildings and none of the ugliness of urban areas – no traffic, no noise, no big new buildings. And the people weren't really that poor. Their lives were simple and their material possessions few but they had a healthy lifestyle, a friendly community and a clean environment. There were schools and young people seemed educated and spoke some English.

Close to the village there was a community forest, a sort of nature reserve owned by the locals. One evening we were walking by the entrance of the forest (it was fenced off to keep wild animals away from the crops) and a man came rushing over to us to warn us against going into the forest in the evening because two tourists had been attacked by a rhinoceros recently.

Eshaw's grandfather and his friend generally sat around outside watching the world go by. Flic was taken with them and had a chat with the grandfather with Eshaw translating. The grandfather was 89 years old and had been a Ghurkha in the British army in the Second World War. He had done some of his training in England and had parachuted into the jungle to fight the Japanese. His only regret was that he had served too short a time to get a pension.

Elephants are the big thing at Chitwan. We took an elephant ride into the forest to see wildlife and found it a disappointment. We went into what had been referred to as jungle but it felt like a wood in Buckinghamshire. I don't remember any major wildlife experience there. We also visited an elephant breeding centre and on another day Flic paid to *help* wash an elephant in the river. This is tourist stuff, not significant encounters with places and people different from ourselves. And yet it was worthwhile in its way. Flic wrote: from my window I can see an elephant under a shelter. On the way to the lodge we passed an elephant in the road. Amazing animals – so big and graceful, gentle and strong. They are wonderful. I feel in love with elephants.

Looking back now I can see the big difference between some of our more touristical experiences and the times when, as Flic put it, we went through real streets and past real lives. I'm thankful that we were able to do both.

In Nepal we had spent time in flatlands and highlands, cities and countryside. Nepal is a great little country. They managed to retain an independent sovereignty throughout the centuries of British imperialism. And they now have the charming habit of keeping their clocks fifteen minutes ahead of those of the massive country that surrounds them on three sides. I wonder if the great little country that I live in should keep a different time zone from its mighty neighbour. But no, Wales is to the west of England and would have to keep its clocks fifteen minutes *behind*. I won't suggest that. I don't think it would go down well at all.

J is for Jericho (Palestine)

In 1977 I stayed in the *Hisham Palace Hotel Youth Hostel*, Jericho, whose name echoed its steady decline from the glory days when it was frequented by the likes of the late King Hussein of Jordan. It was so hot in the night that I soaked a sheet in cold water and covered myself with it to cool down. I woke later, hot again, the sheet dried by the hot desert air and beginning to get damp with my sweat.

The proprietor was a man called Abu George, a charming anglophile who liked to tell the story of Montgomery meeting Rommel in the desert and finding that they were both whistling the same tune, *Lily Marlene*. He also told me about a fellow guest who I soon became acquainted with: a man called David.

David was from California, a business man with a crazy wife who thought that she was a reincarnation of Jesus. When she ran off with the hire car and all their money David was obliged to find work with a local construction firm – Palestinians who were building Israeli settlements in the desert. He was used to the LA heat, enjoyed the *camaraderie* of his workmates, and seemed to be having a great time. Sitting in the lobby in the evening with Abu George and David I felt that I was playing a small role in a quite well written piece of fiction – a BBC radio play maybe.

Other extraordinary people there included a Spaniard who spoke good Arabic and who convinced us that he worked for the French secret service. He took us to a wonderful oasis with cool water flowing out of the rocks into a deep pool. He put his few things in my bag and I discovered among them a cheap spy novel. I think it fuelled his fantasies.

I went back to Jericho in 2012 and it looked just the same: seedy, run down, characterless, and hot. But there was a new tourist attraction: a cable car running up to the monastery on the hill where Jesus had, apparently, been tempted by the devil. The Palestinian taxi driver who took us there stopped on the way and picked up two of his children and a grandchild and they had a day out with us.

11

Landscape and Memory-card

Flic and I moved to West Wales nearly twenty-five years ago and living so close to the sea was a novelty and a cause of excitement for a long time. We looked out at the water and at the curve of Cardigan Bay from many different beaches and clifftops up and down the coast. One time we were camping near Braich y Pwll at the end of the Lleyn Peninsula and we watched a sailing boat making its way through Bardsey Sound, the channel between Bardsey Island and the mainland. I wanted to be on that boat. A couple of weeks later I was given the chance to do just that – to join a crew sailing up the bay, through the sound and along the north coast of the Lleyn. We sailed for a few days and slept on the boat in harbours along the coast. I didn't like it. I spent many hours looking back towards the shore, barely visible through the summer haze. One day I borrowed binoculars to try to catch sight of a particular house that held very significant memories for me. I couldn't see it. But I came back with a title for a book, *The Land as Viewed from the Sea*. I spoke to Flic about it. *What's the story?* she asked. I had no idea. It was five years later that I started on the first chapter.

The book turned out to be the first of three novels dealing with, as much as anything else, the subject of landscape and memory; about perceptions of place and about memories attached to places. I wrote, in those days, by hand, more specifically with a fountain pen on A3 layout pads. Big sheets of paper, illegible writing at the speed of thought – those were the days before I had Parkinson's disease. I knew my imagination had taken flight when my characters said things that I didn't anticipate. But all the same I was rather taken aback when, towards the end of my third novel, one of my central protagonists, a certain Isabel Davies, came out with the words *places don't matter at all. People matter, it's only people that matter.*

To be fair I don't blame her. She had spent a lot of time in the company of people talking about psychogeography, or *psychoshit*, as she came to call it. But I'm afraid I can't leave off the subject. Sorry Isabel, if you're out there (but of course you're not). Here we go again.

It was William Faulkner who said *The past is never dead. It's not even past.* Memories live on in us and make us who we are. But I think different people have different ways of dealing with time. When I told my sister Margaret that we were going travelling she said *you will have such lovely memories.* Wow, what a great combination of living in the future and the past at the same time. You *will* have memories. Everybody has their own way of dealing with past, present and future but Margaret's is pretty special. I wanted to say that's not why we're going, we're going for the present moment, just for the being there. And it was true. But of course Margaret was right, we do have wonderful memories and that's why I'm writing this.

When we recover memories we give shape to them, just as the creative act of writing gives shape to our thoughts. At times like this I think of the year 1984. *Nineteen-Eighty Four* is the title of a novel by George Orwell that nobody reads anymore; a story of a future society under totalitarian government. When I read the book in 1975 the year 1984 was an impossibly distant future time, the stuff of science fiction. Now it's history.

In the real world 1984 was the year that Margaret Thatcher took on the miners and won. It was also the year that Jim O'Shaughnessy and I went to the Pickwick Fete. We turned up on bicycles and walked around with expressions of amusement and mild disbelief on our faces. Here was a posh garden fete in the grounds of a seriously grand house and here was our friend Flic, who, we now knew, was brought up in this house. Ex-STRORD-inary. I don't suppose I could have imagined then that 1984 was to be such an important year for me; the year that Flic and I started a life together.

I met Jim recently at Pickwick and reminded him of our first time there. He told me about his memory parcels. Jim has his own take on landscape and memory. He stores up memories of particularly special places and times so that he can return to them in moments of difficulty. Psychic reservoirs of good feeling that he calls memory parcels. I think they have got him through some rough times.

There is a wonderful book called *Landscape and Memory* by the historian Simon Schama. It is a history of Western society's relationship with place and an assertion that our response to landscape and the natural world is culturally determined. That is to say that when I or you are moved by a particular place or landscape it is because we were brought up that way. I was strongly resistant to this idea when I read it.

Then I was in the Ystwyth Valley, here in Wales, doing a botanical survey of an old meadow surrounded by conifer plantations. Conifers, as we all know, are bad news; they are alien species of little value to native wildlife. The plantations are monocultures, completely lacking in biodiversity and a blight on the landscape. A man who was, I guess, on holiday came along and talked about how lovely it was there. It reminded him of pictures he had seen of wild places in Canada. I looked up at the scene; the little River Ystwyth flowing down past the meadow, the tree-clad slopes on either side, and suddenly it was beautiful. In a moment my idea of that place had been changed. And I understood a little about how our perceptions of places are constructed, not as instinctive as I had imagined.

Flic and I spent a few hours walking along the cliffs between Borth and Aberystwyth recently. The sky was fairly clear and the sea was a deep dark blue, not mud coloured near the coast and grey further out as it can be so often in Cardigan Bay. I hoped to see seals or maybe otters in the water and perhaps six members of the crow family flying by (yes: rooks, crows, magpies, jackdaws, ravens and choughs are common enough along this coastline and the last three are a pleasure to watch being aerial acrobats). But it was not what we saw but our ways of seeing that left an impression on me.

It started when we decided to have a spell of deliberate silence rather than intermittent chatter and see how it felt. We often walk a little way in silence but this slightly more prolonged spell of not talking and not even thinking of talking had an interesting effect. It was as if a switch had been thrown somewhere in my brain and the flow of information redirected. Quite suddenly I could see much more. On the water there were cloud shadows and cloud reflections, patterns made by the wind, changes of colour, and the lines of waves refracting as they met the shore. The sky was pale against the horizon. There were grasses and flowers along the clifftop that I hadn't noticed before. Then I had another change of perception.

There was one spot where a valley came down to the shore and the hillsides folded against each other in a handsome pattern. I reached into my pocket and got out my camera, framed a well composed view and pressed the button. A message came up on the screen; no memory card. I put the thing back in my pocket, irritated that my son had borrowed the card and not put it back. Now I became aware of how in recent years I have got into the habit of looking for photographs, framing views in my head. It has become my way of looking at landscape. And now, in the absence of memory-card, I began to see differently.

I wondered if Flic, as an artist, found herself looking at the landscape for paintings. As if on cue she looked up at a patch of woodland on the edge of a hill and said *if I was painting that wood I think I'd...* and so forth, something about painting a dark colour underneath a light one and scratching through to it. It was turning out that both of us had constructed ways of seeing.

We carried on with our walk, talking now and pointing things out to each other as we went along, something we've always done. Did I say always? No, there have been times when this is impossible. When we were in India there was just too much to see. Whatever fascinating things I noticed as we walked down the street there were an equivalent number catching Flic's eye at the same time and it was impossible to share them all. India is sensory overload. And we have been to plenty of other places where the beauty and interest in our surroundings is too much to take in and too much to point out. That's what I like about travelling in foreign places. You live intensely in the present, in a landscape untouched by memory and where everything is brand new.

K is for Kathmandu (Nepal)

Hotel Nature, where we stayed in Kathmandu, is in the tourist area of Thamel. But go through a little alleyway at the end of the street and you come onto a busy road in an ordinary (read extraordinary) part of town. Some of the lorries that passed up and down the road were beautifully hand painted. The bicycle rickshaws were decorated with bouquets of plastic flowers. A barber shop sign there included the words *New Barbar Shop. Hair Caurley, Facial Bliching.*

And it was a short distance down that road that we saw a little band play at a wedding celebration. There was an outsized rhythm section beating on various drums; an oom-pah-pah brass section playing really out of time; and a handsome, charismatic leader improvising over the top on clarinet. He was the only one whose clothes fitted. As the crowd gathered to watch I moved to the back where I could see over people's heads and not get in anybody's way. Did I just say that? Yes, I'm a tall man in Kathmandu. Flic was given a chair to sit on and a random baby to hold. We were both happy.

12

Travel, India, a Short Guide

It is December 2008 and we are on the second of our big trips. We have finished making friends with elephants in lowland Nepal and fly from Kathmandu back to Delhi. We have spent only twenty-four hours in India so far. Now the fun begins.

Delhi is a city of great contrasts. We visited the Lodi Gardens, a public park with a formal layout of exotic (to us) trees and lawns dotted with handsome stone mausoleums dating from the fifteenth and sixteenth centuries. It was a quiet place in which a few amiable stray dogs, green parakeets, and middle class locals hung out. Some people engaged in a peculiarly Indian form of mock exercise: an ostentatiously brisk walk punctuated with spells of heavy breathing and arm waving. No-one attempted anything as vigorous as jogging. But there was yoga, as Flic observed: *one man made me jump when he leaned over, stuck out his tongue and roared, other people sit in the lotus position and meditate, or lie with their legs in the air.*

In another part of town we passed by a camel market. I say passed because a young guy came up to us with a mildly threatening manner as if encouraging us not to hang around. The market was situated in an open space among the rubble of demolished buildings and surrounded by other derelict and ruinous buildings. There was rubbish everywhere; there were pushcarts and cycle rickshaws and lots of young men coming and going; and there were the camels, decorated with coloured sashes and tinsel and strange seemingly hieroglyphic patterns drawn or painted on their sides.

Flic saw: *people sleeping on the pavements, and pushcarts full of oranges, papaya, bread, boxes, cows walking alone in the traffic, ox* carts being driven. Masses of clothes hung in the middle of the road and in trees drying. We walked down Chadni Chouk, a busy street, people selling food, fruit and veg stalls, jewellery, clothes, women with babies begging, bicycle rickshaw drivers ask us over and over again if we want a ride.

On our second day we visited a large mosque where we were allowed, if we paid a small fee and took our shoes off, to climb a minaret and look down through the smog-filled air to the dirty streets. Then: we walked from the mosque to the old railway station down more narrower crowded streets stepping over piles of rubbish and pools of black water past sparkling jewellery shops. We made it to the station crossing a great road. We tried to use a pedestrian crossing bridge but when we went up we could see the other half had fallen away so we came down again.

In the station I queued to buy railway tickets for the next day. We loved Delhi for a whole morning but now, a day later, we were ready to move on. I was constantly jostled by the man behind me and was ready to turn and confront him. But I looked across to the next queue and saw that everybody stood not just close but actually *physically touching*. Physically touching! I can sense my Western distaste for close contact with strangers coming through. But this was India and if you weren't pressed up against the person in front somebody would push in.

On the way back to our hotel I saw a large billboard advert with the words *Keep Delhi Young – Exercise Daily*. On the street below there were two skinny men pushing a very heavy barrow of bricks up a slope. They may not have been able to read but they were on the job.

Before we leave Delhi here's Flic's description of what turned out to be typical Indian street food: On the corner of the road is what I first thought was a bakers but it's more like a fryers, there's a huge vat of bubbling boiling oil and a man stirring it and everybody's buying fried battered pakoras samosas poori. Opposite is a fruit shop with custard apples and pomegranates and coconuts, pineapples and all kinds of luscious fruit. I ate a persimmon and a custard apple.

The next morning we went to the station to get our train to Jaipur, in Rajasthan. We were very early as we were advised to be. A helpful man looked at our tickets and said that there was a problem. He took us across the road to a travel agent. Now I had read about scams at railway stations and so I was sceptical but we went along with it more out of interest than anything if I remember correctly. In the office a man shook his head at the letter W on one of our tickets. He said it was for *waiting* and only valid if someone else cancelled. He made a show of looking at the computer and then made a phone call. He said the train was full but he would sell us tickets for the one at five in the afternoon. I had lost interest by now and we went back to the station and got on our train. I had the ticket with W on it and very much enjoyed the view from the *window* seat.

In India they have the caste system and a much stratified society and it's no surprise that the railways have ten classes of railway travel, if you include the various sleeper classes. We travelled AC chair car, with AC standing for air conditioning. It didn't cost much and we were surprised to be given a free English language newspaper and a cup of tea soon after we set off and then, also in the price, a substantial breakfast at eight o'clock. The windows were dirty but it was fine to open the carriage door and stand in the doorway watching the world go past. Flic saw: semi-desert with big sand dunes and thorny looking trees. Wells with people collecting water in bright saris, people ploughing the land with mattocks, some camels pulling carts, flat roofs with men in white clothes.

We arrived in Jaipur and found ourselves choosing to travel in a tuk tuk driven by a very handsome young man dressed in white robes and hat. He introduced himself as Imran and strode off across the car park with his head held high while we struggled behind with our rucksacks. When we told him we were from Wales he laughed and said, in his strong Indian accent, *very funny people Wales people, they talk very funny*. He took us to our unpleasant hotel and we arranged to see him later for a tour of the city.

Jaipur, the pink city, is painted a foul orange colour, is unbelievably dirty and busy, and looks like it has been hit by an earthquake – it hasn't, it's just in an advanced and ongoing state of decrepitude. Imran took us through the old city and on to a promenade by a shallow lake complete with seemingly floating palaces. We walked for a bit and Flic, when I was looking the other way, was on the receiving end of quite a few male stares.

The city turned out to be foul and fascinating and in our few days there we saw palaces and forts and colourful birds and glimpses of ordinary life too. The most amazing of the historical buildings was the Jantar Mantar Observatory. It consists of a number of weird abstract architectural forms that were once used to chart the movements of the sun, moon, stars and planets for astrological purposes. There is, for instance, a huge sundial with a pointer about twenty-five feet high. It's built of stone, as are most of the bizarre structures there, and has a staircase running up to the top.

Stepping out from the observatory into the street again we were met by half a dozen forceful vendors of guide books. The charming expression *in yer face* gives a fair idea of how these guys operate and how stressful it is to deal with them again and again. Tourist touts, rickshaw drivers, shoeshine boys and beggars young and old and a whole lot of vendors of things you don't want are in yer face in large numbers in some parts of north India. It's really stressful.

How do you deal with them? In the worst places you keep moving and don't look at them – in fact in the very worst places don't engage with anybody, just move on. My theory is that these guys are forceful and rude because they are desperate. I don't know their circumstances but I imagine they have families to feed at home and are struggling to make any money at all. So here's another strategy – be firm, by all means, but be sympathetic. If you are aware of how tough these men's lives are it makes them more bearable and it comes over in your body language I think. They are less confrontational.

Being on the street in some parts of Rajasthan is hard work. As Flic said: it feels sometimes as if I've been dropped into a parallel universe or other world or a game where I don't understand the rules. I keep making mistakes and almost being hit by motor bikes, bicycles, being butted by cows with painted horns, treading in cow dung. Flic never quite got the idea that cows in India require a certain amount of respect and will take a swipe at you with their horns if you pass by too close.

But being on the street is what it's all about. For instance: we saw an amazing wedding procession. A tuk tuk with a generator providing power for tall lanterns held on peoples shoulders, a band playing and dancers followed by two horses wearing silver and gold drapery, children dressed up on their backs and fireworks exploding regularly.

I remember seeing an elephant or two dressed up for ceremonial reasons – perhaps that was for a wedding too. As well as the occasional elephant or horse there were many other animals playing a part in daily life in Jaipur. In one part of town there were herds of small black pigs rooting around in the piles of rubbish. We found out later that they weren't feral but owned by people, members of the sweeper caste. There were cows, of course, wandering everywhere, making their way through the heaviest traffic. Some people kept goats. There were camels for riding or for towing carts and donkeys as beasts of burden. There were monkeys on the rooftops and swinging from electricity cables. And there were rats coming out of the sewers onto the street in broad daylight.

Before we left Jaipur we spent a few hours pottering about

by the lake and saw lots of wonderful birdlife. Our little bird book gives the names. There were lily-trotters, stilt legs, red-vented bulbuls, mynah birds, golden-backed woodpeckers, feral peacocks and, best of all, the hoopoes that have the habit of raising their crests when they landed. And they were easy to see, much tamer than birds in Europe.

My son, Peter, is in India as I write this (as noted earlier). He emailed me recently asking about staying in hotels. I found myself emailing back, under the heading *Travel, India, a Short Guide*, the following message:

There are 3 types of hotels in India: the cheap ones that Indians stay in (glitzy, modern, lots of tinted glass and cockroaches – at 3 am some guy starts shouting for his mother-in-law, she's a heavy sleeper but one of the grand children wakes up and starts shouting back, the grandchild's mum starts telling it off and that sets off next door's dog, that wakes the couple next door and she says "it's all your fault, I should never have married you" to her husband several times over until he wakes up, at which point you realise that the sound like that of a barking seal was him snoring, it's now stopped and at last you can go to sleep – or can you?); the cheap ones that Europeans stay in (not glitzy, quieter, much much quieter); and expensive ones for both Indians and Europeans. Some towns that don't get foreign visitors only have the expensive and the seal barking ones. Indians are, of course, wonderful people but they don't have the be-quiet-you'll-wake-up-the-neighbours thing in their culture. Good luck.

What I should also have said is that he should take the hotel with the best rooftop view in town. When we arrived in Pushkar this is exactly what we did, though not on purpose. The bus was met by a number of men with pushcarts ready to help people with their luggage and find them somewhere to stay. Here the atmosphere seemed relaxed and amiable, quite different from the aggressive hustling of Jaipur. And so it was easy to allow ourselves to be led to Hotel Everest with its wonderful rooftop.

You've no doubt got the idea now that life on the street is hard work for a visitor to north India. There is so much to see and so much to bump into and sometimes a lot of hassle. But up on the roof you can relax. You are still in India but it's down there, at arm's length instead of *in yer face*. And there is the view.

From the roof of Hotel Everest we could see much of the town and some of the surrounding countryside. One of the disappointing things about north India as we experienced it is the quality of the light. We had spent twenty-eight days walking in the Himalayas where, in late autumn, the sky is an amazing deep blue, the air is very clear and everything is sharply defined. Here, in India, it was always hazy, with moisture or pollution in the air. But in the early mornings the low sunlight gave, for a while, a dreamy beauty to the landscape.

Pushkar was surrounded by yellow-grey hills of rock and sand with sparse semi-desert vegetation. On one side of the town was a high ridge and on the other sides were small conical hills, at least two of them topped by small temples. The town itself had no high buildings, just the usual Indian brick and concrete flat-roofed houses with some more ornate larger buildings that might have been temples. The houses were painted, as Flic described it: a cool harebell blue. The temples were white apart from one which was day-glow orange.

There was the usual rooftop human activity, people hanging out washing or preparing food, and there were also lots of boys flying kites, practicing in advance of a festival. The kites were very light, made of paper and with a single string. They could be flown in the tiniest breeze but it took a great deal of skill to get one airborne. This we know because Flic bought one from the hotel owner's son. They are inclined to self-destruct in the branches of trees and on buildings and are very cheap, disposable, and bought ten at a time.

The other occupants of the rooftops were the monkeys, both the red macaques and the big grey langurs. The langurs were very handsome with black faces, hands and feet, silvery grey fur and tails longer than their bodies. They were not easily intimidated by humans and every rooftop had one or two sticks kept handy to beat them off. They were not frightened of children and if there were monkeys on the roof children kept away. We had to keep the door to the roof closed or they would come into the building. I spent a lot of time watching them.

We walked up two of the little hills on the edge of Pushkar and had two quite different experiences. On the first one a group of local boys harassed us asking over and over again for money and refusing to go away. It was a very unpleasant experience and they failed to arouse any sympathy from us because they were aggressively rude and didn't look particularly poor. The other hill had a temple on the top and we walked up in the company of friendly pilgrims with whom we shared the heat, the exercise and a sense of *camaraderie*.

From Pushkar we had a day out travelling by bus to nearby Adjmer. The people there were mostly unpleasant. Flic describes it well:

we walked through the park and a boy dived towards Richard's feet and started brushing his shoes. Everyone seemed interested in us. We left the park to go to the ruins, ending up in small streets, gutters full of foul water, horrible bristly pigs and dogs and rats, people begging, one small alley led to another until there was one that we just couldn't face going down, so smelly and dirty. Everyone we passed seemed to want something from us or be laughing at us. Our way back to the bus station was better: we walked back down an interesting street full of shops. Bowls of rose petals and marigolds and gold embroidered cloths were being sold, shoe shops selling glittery pointed toed sandals, jewellery shops, butchers with live hens under the counter and plucked ones above, tea shops, cafés with giant woks of boiling oil and floating pakoras, jalebi shining in honey, more giant woks with gas flames below boiling gallons of milk reducing it to sweet gunge to mix with coconut and blackened pots on bricks of fried foods, puri, gulabjumun.

Before we left Pushkar we rented bikes for the day and cycled out into the countryside. There was scrubby semi-desert but there were green areas too. We passed by large fields of marigolds and rose bushes, grown just for their flowers and petals, used for decorative and religious purposes. Small trucks went by carrying people dressed up in turbans, pointed shoes, sarees, as if off to a fancy dress party. Went past some groups of school children who were horrible. Asking for pens, trying to grab our bikes and slap us, one boy got hold of my bike rack, Richard shouted at him and he let go. It felt like a racist attack.

And now it's coming back to me – how we loved India and hated it too. I think our first experiences were tough. We weren't always happy and sometimes we were counting the days, looking forward to our flights to Kerala, in the south, where people were said to be friendlier. Before we went south we experienced two more Rajasthan cities, Bundhi and Udaipur, where we spent Christmas and New Year respectively. But India is tiring and we need to take a break. After a while we'll forget the hassles and miss the noise and colour. Then we'll be drawn back. Really, it can happen.

L is for Lucca (Italy)

When our first born son, Kit, was two years old we went cycle touring in Tuscany. We averaged fifteen miles per day, cycling very slowly up the hills and slowly down too, because there was so much to see. Kit had a special child seat on the back of Flic's bike where he was strapped in and could fall asleep and he had a tiny little seat on the crossbar of my bike where he had to lean forward and hold onto the handlebars. He was a chubby, dreamy little boy and was happy watching the world go by. And then, at the end of the day, we would check in at a cheap hotel and he would bounce up and down on the bed, full of energy, in contrast to his mum and dad, who were exhausted from a day's cycling. It was spring, sunny after a period of rain, and everything was fresh and green.

We cycled along the top of the city walls in Lucca. Then we came down into the town to buy food for a picnic. We bought a tub of green gunge; it looked nice but we had no idea what it was. It tasted great and we found out the name of it later – *pesto de genovese*. Now you can buy it here.

In those days we lived in Bristol. We both worked part-time and both had days at home with Kit. I used to take him out around the city on a bicycle, usually Flic's bike, that had a more comfortable seat for him. We went to places like the botanical gardens at Leigh Woods or the park at Brandon Hill. It was a very special time and I feel very lucky and privileged to have been able to spend those days with him, a young child, excited by every new day. As a parent you get a vicarious pleasure and see the world afresh through the eyes of your children.

13

Difficult Times

My worst moment ever. A hot sunny afternoon in the summer of 1989. A tiny patch of garden next to the car park at Morriston Hospital, Swansea. Flic has come out from the ward in her nightdress and sits on a bench. She is both physically and mentally very weak after suffering a brain haemorrhage. I have to go to the car to get something and I leave our four month old baby Peter on her lap and four year old Kit by her side. When I return I find that she hasn't been able to hold Peter and has dropped him on the ground. He is crying, she is crying and Kit is crying too.

Three weeks into our new life in Wales Flic had got up in the night and collapsed in the bathroom. She was rushed to hospital in Aberystwyth where she remained unconscious and semiconscious for a few days. Then she was taken to the Morriston. Two weeks passed before a young doctor called me into an office and told me she had a brain tumour. He was awkward, seemingly untrained in the job of breaking bad news and said that it could be one of a number of things. I had to keep asking questions to get a less vague diagnosis. Perhaps that's the way they do it, to lead you to the devastating news gradually and when you are ready to hear the answers you ask the right questions: *Is it cancer? Yes. Is she likely to die? Yes. Quite soon? Yes.*

I went back to Flic's bedside and we joked and laughed a little, as you do when things get really bad. She was still very weak and, as far as I remember, I didn't bring up the subject of her diagnosis. I drove back down the M4 to Wiltshire thinking that here, on the motorway, I had to keep it together. This was not the time or the place to go to pieces. There were my two children to look after. And then I had to break the news to Flic's parents. And so it went on, emotional breakdown was not an option. Others could burst into tears but I had things to do and I just had to hold on.

They discovered that Flic had a very rare, fast growing cancer called choriocarcinoma and whizzed her up to Charing Cross hospital in London. There she had brain surgery to remove the tumour. I remember going to the post operative ward and mentioning that they were bringing the chemo up to start her on it immediately. They didn't believe me. One of the nurses admitted later that they thought she would die. They started introducing the chemo through a tube that they had inserted into her brain. The cancer was very fast growing but very easily treated. It was a kill or cure moment, the most likely outcome being a further haemorrhage and death. It was then that she contracted meningitis...

I have to tell you that now I have come back to this short chapter, knowing that there is so much more to tell. But I can't say much and you can guess why. Time travel is not always an enjoyable experience. Other grim memories of those days? Yes, a few. Peter was in the children's ward for a couple of nights at the start. Then I went and got him. I went into Boots in Aberystwyth and bought a baby's bottle, powdered milk and sterilising tablets. Then the three of us travelled around staying in different people's houses, three cardboard boxes of clothes in the back of the car labelled: Richard, Kit and Peter. We went to the hospital to see Flic; we went to her parents' house and stayed there; we came back to Wales from time to time.

Flic and I still owned a house in Bristol and had difficult tenants who would not pay the rent. Meanwhile the awful landlady of the house we were renting in Wales told me off for things like sticking a photo of Flic to the wall and damaging the wallpaper. I remember one awful day hanging out in a dirty park in London while Flic had her second lot of brain surgery, not knowing if I would see her alive again. Maybe that's enough.

Reader, she survived, that's the important thing. There was a time when it looked like she was not going to regain her mental faculties and I would have to look after the three of them. But Flic did make a complete recovery and we drove back to Wales after her last dose of chemo in February 1990.

Now we were a happy family of four living in a beautiful part of the world. And it was good. Family life was very fulfilling and rewarding. But planet mum is a very different place from planet dad and I can't say that Flic and I were close. There were more difficulties to come. I loved my family but it didn't stop me from loving someone else for a while. I wrote a novel and, when it was shortlisted for a major literary award, was famous for a few weeks. Somehow Flic and I endured. The years brought us closer to knowing and understanding each other. And then I was diagnosed with Parkinson's disease.

One of Flic's first impulses was to run away. She didn't. And here's the strange thing: I suspect that we have been closer and happier in our relationship in the last few years than at any other time.

Together we brought up our two boys and gave them as happy a childhood and start in life as we could. We have been lovers, friends and travelling companions off and on for nearly thirty years. There have been good times and bad. There have been times when we have had two very different ideas about the state of our relationship. Now, alongside the other roles, Flic is becoming a carer. Someone who looks after the needs of a person who can't look after themselves. Maybe it's OK. The children have grown up and she gets some fulfilment out of looking after me instead. She tells me that my vulnerability makes her feel closer to me. When she wants to get away I can get a friend to stay and help – she can still have some independence.

From my point of view, however, it's not ideal. If you were to ask me about the things I have lost since being ill I would name independence as the most important. And, while I think of Flic as the ideal (well, let's say very, very nearly ideal) life partner or travelling companion, I begin to lose confidence that she might feel the same about me. There are big time self-esteem issues for someone with a disability. And so it is that I dream, from time to time, about Flic going off with some other guy. Dreams tell you about things going on in the more hidden parts of the mind. Sometimes it's stuff you need to know, sometimes things you would prefer to remain hidden. I suspect that for anyone suffering from a newly acquired disability loss of self-esteem is a big issue. I don't know what anyone can do about it.

M is for Madrid (Spain)

We were in Spain visiting friends in March 2012. Everywhere we went the light was pure and clear and there were strange dark patches and lines on the ground. Next to a tree, for example, there would be a perfect representation of the trunk and the spreading branches and the twigs marked out on the pavement. I took photographs of these horizontal facsimiles and noted that they moved and changed shape during the course of the day. I had some memory of seeing such things before but it seemed to come from a long time ago. Then I understood; they were *shadows* and were associated with sunlight, something we had not experienced in its pure form for a while. Certainly the whole of January and February had been cloudy in Wales, sunshine and shadows a distant memory. How nice it was to be in Spain.

And right next to our hotel in Madrid there was another miracle, the *jardin vertical*, a garden growing sideways out of the gable end of our building. It was by the entrance of an arts centre called *Caixa Forum*. We went in and looked at the temporary exhibitions and we also walked around the corner and visited the *Museo del Reina Sofía*, famous for housing Picasso's *Guernica*. Madrid has a handful of big time art galleries and some fine architecture. But what I remember best of all was the clear light, the early spring sunshine, and the wonderful shadows.

14

Distant Relatives

We are back on the second of the six major adventures Flic and I have had since the onset of my debilitating illness. Rajasthan has been extraordinary but tough, too unpleasant too often. Until Bundhi, that is. I recommend Bundhi as a place to stay. It has all the colour and life and foreignness of a north Indian town and the usual compliment of palaces and forts. But it is just a little off the tourist route and people are easier going, both the townsfolk and the people in the countryside around. They are friendly and helpful.

Here are a few words I wrote while we were in Bundhi:

6 am. Up on the hotel roof. Still dark, a tiny slither of old moon rising, two Muslim calls to prayer, then a third. Lights on, a radio somewhere, lorries on the main road, people are starting their day. A man chases monkeys off his rooftop as he did yesterday. A red-faced monkey sits near me for a while before moving on. Others are climbing down the walls of the fort and the palace and making their way into town. A bell rings somewhere for puja.

8-ish. The sun is up now and a Canadian man called Phil comes onto the roof and says 'Merry Christmas'. It sounds so out of place here that I laugh out loud

9-ish and onwards. A tiny (they're all tiny), colourful-sari-wearing woman walks down the street carrying a tin bowl of dried cow-dung on her head. Another carries firewood. She has bare feet. Motorbikes pass by, brass vessels fixed fore and aft carrying fresh milk into town. In the market place people sell piles of clover for giving to the sacred cows that are standing nearby patiently waiting. People sell big cheeses – but no, Flic is offered a taste of one and it's some sort of sugar. Others sell marigold garlands and rose petals for religious offerings.

Maybe 10am. Stop in a little chai shop for a glass of sugary tea. The proprietor shows Flic a blue-painted cupboard inside of which is a shrine containing a photo of himself and a man in a loincloth, a mirror and some pctures of Hindu gods. Skin-lightening cream sachets hang overhead. The man sitting next to me points to the proprietor, an ordinary enough looking man, 'Guru', he says. He does some stuff with his hands that I guess is a blessing. A little way down the street a goat has a word painted on its side in Hindi script. Pigs feed on a pile of rubbish. There are cows with painted horns and a crippled beggar by the side of the road.

11-ish. Now we're by a lake with enormous kingfishers, herons, stilts, lily-trotters, egrets and lapwings. Green parrots in the trees. Professional laundrymen beating clothes on the water's edge. And a young man whose limited English includes the words 'Santa Claus'.

1 o'clock. Lunch of Indian junk food in a public park. Bulbuls and mynah birds perch on the seats waiting for crumbs. Palm trees and bougainvillea. Two drongos. Grey babblers with fierce blue eyes. A view across the lake to the palace where Kipling wrote Kim. The café plays Bollywood hits. A tractor passes by, dressed up in tinsel (but not because it's Christmas – they're always like that here). It tows a trailer carrying about 20 men and women. The guys are on their way to the Improbable Turban of the Year Show. A family come over to look at Flic's drawing.

3.30 Back in our hotel room for a siesta after walking back through the part of town where every house is painted blue. A holiday atmosphere, perhaps it's a special day here too. People are politer, less demanding, friendlier here in Bundi than in other towns. It's busy, noisy and squalid but it's beautiful in places. The palace is gorgeous: fanciful architecture, delicate stonework, extraordinary murals, all in a state of decay. There are huge wild bees nests hanging under the arches on the south side. When it's a little cooler I will go to the internet café and type this up.

I rarely made notes or kept a diary when we were traveling; there was just too much to put down. And I don't think I got around to typing up those Bundhi notes and sharing them with people at home. And I never told anyone about my close encounter with one of the palace bees.

The palace on the hill above Bundhi is owned by the local maharaja, the kind of guy who maybe had the first Rolls Royce in Rajasthan and counts Prince Charles among his personal friends. He now lives down in a smaller, less ostentatious palace in the town and the old palace has been neglected for many decades. He recently opened a large part of it to the public and we visited it twice. The murals are amazing. Imagine rooms decorated from floor to ceiling, and across the ceiling too, with patterns and illustrations of mythical, historical and religious scenes that have been hand painted with the kind of detail that you would expect in a miniature. The windows are without glass and the rooms are open to the elements leaving the paintings to decay gracefully.

There are also the courtyards and terraced gardens to explore. It was here that I found myself being quietly scornful of a fellow tourist making an unnecessary fuss when a bee came near him. A little later I was on my own in the gardens when a huge bee got inside my t-shirt and I panicked. A distinguished Indian couple came around the corner and found an Englishman, naked from the waist up, kneeling on the ground and beating a t-shirt with a sun hat. They turned and walked the other way.

We stayed eight days in Bundhi, at first in an old guest house of tiny rooms and winding staircases that was run by two softly spoken effeminate brothers who liked to fly paper kites from the roof. Then we tried a place owned by a man called Geeto who was pleased to tell us a little about his circumstances. He was 24 years old and had an English girlfriend of 43 who lived with him for some months of the year. She had bought the house for him. We met him in the street riding the motorbike that she had also bought him and carrying a parcel, a present that she had sent from England. Best of all was the fact that, as he told us, she loved sex. In northern India young unmarried men are generally doomed to celibacy. Geeto considered himself to be the luckiest man in town.

Then we stayed in a cheap hotel called Kasera Paradise. It was situated below the palace and it overlooked the old town. The rooftop was a great place to watch the morning commute of monkeys coming down from the hill and into town to forage, a place to watch sunset and sunrise, to get away from the cacophony and hullabaloo of Indian streetlife, and to meet interesting fellow travellers. We liked it there very much.

One day we rented bikes and cycled out into the local countryside. We stopped in for chai in a simple café where a man wearing a hi-vis saffron turban and bizarre wrap-around legwear made fun of me for having no moustache. We cycled further and saw large fields of roses and marigolds grown for decorative and religious use. We saw camels grazing on the scrubby trees and children herding goats. At one point in the ride there was a bump and my bike seemed to be going more slowly. I looked over my shoulder to see a smiling young lad who had jumped on the rack for a free ride.

One morning a tuk tuk driver casually engaged us in conversation on the street. He said that the real life of India was in the countryside and not the towns. We found ourselves employing him to take us on a village tour on which we met with friendly, colourfully dressed locals who showed us a little of their way of life. We saw corn being ground in a quern and a village potter at work. In these villages people seemed to have a nice mix of traditional and new (mobile phones and TVs, for instance) and a reasonable quality of life. We were to visit much poorer villages in other parts of Rajasthan.

After Bundhi we stayed in Udaipur, a handsome town and an upmarket tourist destination with a palace on the lake converted into a posh hotel.

Some snapshots of Udaipur:

- We see tiny donkeys being used as beasts of burden, each wears panniers full of bricks and they struggle along to a building site. And then there's one who has broken free and running off. Yes, maybe there's a children's book in this – *The Donkey Who Ran Away*.

- *And other stories* because here is a tuk tuk rounding the corner, only two passengers sitting comfortably in the back – a man and a large billy goat.

- We watch the tuk tuk car chase from the James Bond movie *Octopussy* (filmed in Udaipur) in a rooftop restaurant. They show it every night.

- We have rented bikes again and on an uncharacteristically quiet stretch of road a car overtakes us and skids sideways to a halt. It goes on, turns, passes us again and does another handbrake skid. We turn around and head back towards town. When the car passes again a pleasant enough looking young man leans out of the window and says *take no danger*. We translate this as *we didn't mean to scare you, we're only having fun* and carry on with our ride.

- It is on that same bike ride that we pass two puppies in the road – the live one eating the dead one.

- We are watching the sunset over the lake from the rooftop of our cheap hotel. The monkeys on the palace

ॐ roof nearby sit in a row watching it too.

In Udaipur airport Flic takes out her sketchbook and makes drawings of the security staff standing nearby. They catch sight of her and come over, smiling, wanting to see their portraits.

From Udaipur we flew to Thiruvananthapuram in Kerala, the land of the many syllabled language of Malayalam, or, as I called it, *Malayalamalorum*. The distance between Udaipur and Trivandrum (as it's often more conveniently called) is about the same as that between Stockholm and Madrid. India is a big country and the differences in culture, way of life, language, climate, vegetation, and everything else are even bigger than those between European countries like Sweden and Spain.

Flic's diary sketchbooks are wonderful off and on. There are times when I can't say it better. Here are some notes from our first days in Kerala:

Spent all day yesterday travelling – getting to Trivandrum at midnight. Triv seemed too hot to stay in so we headed to the beach. Palm trees galore, I've never seen so many and coconuts, husks piled up for fuel, green ones tops chopped off and a straw for coconut and water drink. Watched fishermen in long boats made from tree trunks unloading octopus and fish and where there was a gap in the killer waves we swam in the warm sea. There was a strange tribe of pale people in trunks and bikinis swimming. I realised I was one of them. The beach at 5 o'clock was completely different to what it had been at 10 in the morning. It was much more fun with crowds of brightly dressed Indians. We met a fisherman called Philippe (there are lots of Christians here from the Portuguese) who is going to take us out on his boat tomorrow morning.

Went for a walk through palm trees and new houses, a bit of beachurbia? Went to meet our fisherman. The boat was four tree trunks – solid and long and stable. We had snorkels and dived and swam around. The water was a bit murky but we saw some extraordinary weird fish and Richard got threatened by an eel. There are big fishing boats and about 30 men take them out. There is a huge hullabaloo when the boat is dragged out of the sea, so many men pushing and pulling and yelling to each other. The men here wear lungi which is a skirt which they wear rolled up or down.

Went out for another walk up the coast and had a serious coconut experience. A man first climbed a tree and cut down two large green coconuts. Then he smashed the husk off by pounding it onto a spike so I had a smallish nut inside covered with whitish fibre. Then he cut the top off so I could drink it. Richard had a couple of turns trying to climb the tree and gave up. I didn't even try.

Yes, coconut palms, a warm sea, friendly people. But it felt too much like a tourist resort there and we moved on to Varkala. There are two Varkalas: the Indian town of that name and the Varkala where the foreigners stay – a leafy tourist suburb on top of the cliff overlooking a beach. It's nice there but I was very disappointed. This was not India, it was more like Greece in the 1970s. But we stayed a few days. It was there, in Varkala, that I read the words *sorry we trashed your house* and *we'll fix the window* on my younger son's facebook page. The boys, desperately missing their parents over the Christmas period (hmmm...) had taken to partying and had achieved a certain level of success. They had begun to talk of us as their *distant relatives*. We didn't worry. Kerala at its beachurbian worst was still lovely and a whole lot lovelier than west Wales in January. We were having fun in our own way too. We tried to rent bikes.

I thought my new year's resolution would be to be less impatient but then I thought no – it's impossible. I can't be. But in India it would help, no-one does anything straight away. Every shop has a sign up claiming to do lots of things but it means that they know, or have a relative who knows, someone who might do these things.

We see a sign *BICYCLES FOR RENT* so we ask – can we hire two? The man wobbles his head from side to side and lifts his eyebrows. 'Bicycles' I say, pointing to one. 'Five minutes' he says. I get irritated, 'don't you know if you've got them or not?' 'Five minutes you wait,' he says. Another man comes out. 'Please can we rent some bikes?' 'Yes, yes,' he says. 'Just five/ten minutes.' 'Why?' I think or ask. He says he'll phone and two bikes will be brought here if we just wait 10 minutes. 'Well maybe we can walk to where the bikes are – is it far?' 'No, no. Not far, five/ten minutes' walk straight on.' He points out the direction 'just before the helipad, he says. 'Five minutes' walk.' 'OK,' I say, 'we'll go and find the bikes. So we walk but after two minutes the road divides and we're not sure which way is straight on. We pick the left and walk for half an hour and decide to call this a walk and try again tomorrow.

We did rent bikes eventually and we cycled to relatively idyllic, moderately unpeopled, coconut-palm-fringed beaches and swam in the Indian Ocean. Then we moved on.

We stayed in Kollam, where we saw: a large modern church with open sides and Indian Christians just as fervent and devout as any Indian Hindu; buses with no glass in the windows; and a puppy dog being attacked by kites. Then we took to the backwaters.

The backwaters are a series of lagoons, lakes, rivers and canals stretching parallel to the coast for much of the length of Kerala. They were formed naturally but have been improved on to make hundreds of miles of navigable waterways passing through a countryside of paddy fields, coconut palms, yams, banana trees and so forth. There are all sorts of exotically-shaped, brightly-coloured fishing boats and ferries and canoes on the water as well as exotically-shaped brightly-coloured birds in the sky above. From Kollam we went out in a boat to be shown how coconut husks are made into coir matting. And then we went to Alappuzha (Allepey).

What we saw. Kollam > Allepey ferry trip. 400 rupees, 8 hours:
   like Surrey on one side
   palm trees on other
   piles of rubbish plus scavenging birds
   bright painted fishing boats
   Chinese cantilevered nets
   men in dugout canoes with paddles and nets
   giant sexy statue of liberty, Indian style
   more fishing nets on bamboo cranes
   silver flying fish
   Brahminy kites
   coconuts being harvested
   concrete bridges
   kingfishers
   pale pink temples
   women in saris with black umbrellas
   children waving
   cormorants on posts
   cashew nut flowers
   billowing clouds
   waving village people and builders
   washing lines
   the sea

We also passed some huge pink apartment blocks which turned out to be the ashram of Ammachi, a big-hearted all-loving all-hugging woman guru with a great international following. Flic wrote: she hugs people for hours on end, which could be misinterpreted. Ammachi actually hugs individuals quite briefly but she hugs a lot of people, sometimes dealing it out for three or four hours non-stop.

In Allepey we stayed in a guesthouse run by two giggly young men. There was a Jain temple on the other side of the street and one of the guys tried to explain a little of their religious practices. He said that the Jain people were *all vegetables* and wore a cloth over their mouths to *stop the insects coming out*. I believe he meant to say that they were vegetarians and wore a cloth to stop the insects inadvertently going *into* their mouths.

We ate one evening in a dark café that served large quantities of meat, some of it beef. We had chicken and chapattis and icecream for thirty pence per head and ate, as the other customers did, with our fingers, cleaning up afterwards at the wash basins in the corner. We noticed that the women diners were segregated into a room at the back. I guess it was a Muslim establishment.

On the beaches at Allepey we saw dolphins in the sea and spider crabs on the sand. In the morning the town beach was decorated with shallow scrapes containing human excrement. We didn't swim there.

Kerala really was so different to Rajasthan. Men went bare headed and wore rather smart newly washed and ironed shirts. Below the waist they would wear a *lungi*, a skirt which could be let down to ankle length in the cool of the morning and doubled up to knee length in the day. They were forever fiddling with their lungis. People were much more amiable down here, waving happily at passing tourists and not hassling. The vegetation was tropical and lush. And it was hot, far too hot for us really. That's why we took to the hills, Kerala's Western Ghats.

We stayed in Kumili where there's a wildlife reserve in the centre of which is a lake. We took a boat trip out on the lake and it turned out to be an unforgettable experience. We arrived before seven in the morning at the gates of the reserve in order to be among the first in the queue for the boats. We bought our tickets and waited in a tuk tuk for the gates to open. Then the fun began. Engines roared, the gates were pulled back and the jeeps, cars and tuk tuks rushed into the park, everybody racing to get to the boats first. There were signs saying *drive slowly*. We drove fast. There were signs saying *no overtaking on bends*. We overtook and were overtaken on bends. It reminded me of *Whacky Races*. We arrived at the lake and, after queuing again, made it on board a double decker tourist boat. There were signs (written again in English because visitors from the north can't speak Malayalam or Tamil and the locals don't know much Hindi) saying: *Quiet please, No Singing and Dancing, No mobile phone music*, and suchlike. As you might imagine there was mobile phone music, and shouted conversation, and laughter, and some singing and dancing, punctuated by cries of *shhhusssss, you will scare away the animals*. Which was right; we did see the occasional wild deer disappearing into the bushes or over the horizon. I guess you could say that we did see wildlife but not as we anticipated. Indian people on holiday are noisy and joyful and fun-loving. And they are always noisier than we are. It was in Kerala that I first saw bicycle rickshaws with bells fixed to the forks of their bikes and strikers on the spokes of the wheels so that the bells ring *continuously* as they ride.

One of my best wildlife moments ever was in Kumili. Just as we were leaving our hotel overlooking the jungle I glimpsed what I thought to be a large number of birds passing overhead. We quickly went up onto the roof for a better view. The sun had set and the sky was tinged green. We looked out over the small town in one direction, the jungle in the other, and wild hills all around. Above us flew hundreds of bats the size of crows, not whizzing around catching insects but all flying steadily in the same direction. They were on their evening commute from feeding grounds to roosting place. We watched for maybe fifteen minutes, wave after wave of them silently beating their way through the still air.

We went on to Munnar and made friends with a couple called Mark and Claire. We talked with them in a café one evening and arranged to share a taxi ride with them the next day. We were going to see wild elephants. Now a curious thing about Parkinson's is that I lose the sense of where the right hand side of my body is and what it's doing. I was riding in the middle of the back seat with Flic on my left and Mark on my right when I looked down to see that my right hand was resting comfortably on Mark's thigh. I laughed and took it away. Someone said *what are you laughing at?* and I explained. *Oh, I didn't notice*, Mark said. Claire turned around from her place in the front seat. *I think he liked it,* she said. We've been friends with them ever since.

After watching elephants through Mark's binoculars and visiting some tea plantations we travelled on with Mark and Claire to a town called Kodai Kanal. We stayed in a hostel perched on the edge of a great steep scarp and with views over, as Flic put it, mountains and clouds and mountains poking through the clouds. Kodai was high enough to be very cold at night. On the edge of town were big houses set in woodlands with names like *Loch End* and *Roseneath Cottage*. It looked more like Surrey than India. And what had been a hill station set up by missionaries was now popular with Indian tourists. That's more fun, of course, but for us there is one drawback: at the most wonderful viewpoints, at least those that are easily reachable, are stupendous amounts of rubbish, most of it plastic containers and wrappings from take away meals.

Now we were running out of time. We had to get to Mumbai for our flight home. We bussed overnight to the handsome port of Kochi, watched the boats coming in and out, looked at the cantilevered fishing nets, bussed to a nearby beach and swam, saw crows gathering around in distress as a dog tried to eat one of their compatriots and saw sixteen neatly dressed schoolgirls get into one tuk tuk. It felt too hot but still, after fourteen weeks away, the days felt rich in new experiences and we were almost but not quite ready to go home.

Then, early one morning, we set off by taxi to the airport and a flight to Mumbai followed by a night flight back to the UK. Our last day in India was spent in one of the most populous urban areas in the world, a city of twenty million souls.

It was only a few days earlier when we had been with Mark and Claire that we had a typical Indian taxi driver experience. We were travelling along a road that dropped off a plateau into a valley side with fantastic views. *Can we stop here for a minute, please,* someone said. No answer from the driver, we carry on full belt, losing height, losing view as we go. *We want to stop, please. Stop here. Can we stop here? STOP,* and other variations on a theme made no impression at all. He turned and smiled briefly and we hurtled along.

If you want things to be like home, then stay at home could be the motto of the experienced traveller, or, more simply, *they do things differently*. And so it was that we sat in silence in the taxi that wouldn't stop and waited patiently for one of the best views in the Western Ghats to pass away into memory. Then we stopped. It was a marvellous spot with a splendid view and a little place to buy tea and something to eat. It seems now, on reflection, to be likely that the little café was owned by the taxi driver's best friend's brother-in-law and that the driver earned a little commission for taking us there. There is often a brother-in-law. And taxi drivers don't always take you where you want to go.

When we arrived at Mumbai airport we had much of the day to fill before we catch our evening flight. The last few hours of our never-to-be-repeated, trip-of-a-lifetime journey around India and Nepal. We asked a taxi driver to take us on a tour of the city.

We drove, at first, through a very ordinary city passing banks, hospitals, hotels and such like. The traffic was very heavy and we moved slowly enough to write down some of the things, mostly adverts, that we saw written in English. *Fight Hair Fall* was one of my favourites. *Business without advertising is like winking at a girl in the dark*, may not work so well in wink-free India, even with the explanation *you know what you're doing but she doesn't*. And there were two things that were written, as it were, for me, or for someone in my situation, suffering from an increasingly awkward and uncomfortable neurological disease. First, on a big placard outside a church, *The Most Useless Emotion is Self-pity*, and an ad for mobile phones that said *Make the Most of Now*.

We drove and drove and the morning seemed to be passing by without us getting anywhere. We tried to get the driver to stop but he spoke very little English and drove on. Then he phoned his brother, who spoke more English, and we explained that we wanted now to stop and have some lunch. That was how we came to eat at Mumbai's McDonalds. Then we drove on. Our driver was a very nice smiley guy with very dark skin, almost black. Like any big city Mumbai hosts people from other parts and this guy was from Chennai, way down in south India.

Our destination, we discovered, was the Taj Mahal Hotel on the sea front. It had been the scene of a dramatic terrorist attack a few months before (when we were in Nepal) and now was on the tourist trail. There wasn't much to see, just a few bullet holes in the stonework, but we walked along the prom and then took a boat out into the harbour with the other visitors, all of whom were Indians. People took photos of us as if, Flic said, we are the unusual ones. And Flic made friends with a man from Sri Lanka and his Indian wife who let her hold their baby.

We were taken to the famous Chowpatti Beach and to a park with topiary animals and to a Jain temple. Then we tried and failed to get our driver to take us to the airport. He was very proud of his adopted city and showed us a huge road that was under construction stretching out to sea and back again on concrete pillars; a ring road that would alleviate some of Mumbai's traffic problems. He insisted that we come back to the city in 2010 to see the completed Sea Link, as it's now called. We agreed to come back but we knew it wouldn't happen. We asked if we could go to the airport as our flight time was growing closer. He took us to another beach, hot and crowded with brightly dressed people and vivid coloured stalls selling fruit and juice and icecream, Flic describes it. We walked among the crowds for a little while and watched the sunset before asking again if he could take us to the airport. He agreed. He had shown us as much as we could fit in and we had enjoyed our day out with him. Now it was time to go home.

N is for Nuweiba (Egypt)

I don't know how many hours we waited in the port of Nuweiba, on the Red Sea coast of Egypt, for the ferry across to Aqaba. It wasn't run as a convenient passenger service but for the transport of huge lorries which took an unforeseeable amount of time to load onto the boat. Outside of the steel shed that was the waiting room we were invited by some Jordanian guys to join them and eat a share of their lunch. There was both roast chicken and boiled eggs in the same meal making it a sort of *mother and child reunion*, as Paul Simon would have said.

We had been staying in nearby Dahab where we went out one day in a glass bottomed boat to look down on the reefs and the tropical fish. After we had stopped for a while to do some snorkelling and had started on our way back to the shore I noticed a local man who was out for the day with three of his children. They were dressed in *Western* clothes but he wore flowing robes and a head cloth. He nodded to me and said the words *Alan Shearer*. At least that's what I heard. *Alan Shearer*, there, he said the name again. I woke at four o'clock the following morning with the name sounding in my head followed by the words *Newcastle United* and the image of a black and white striped football jersey. What was this all about? Oh yes, the boat had been surrounded at one point by black and white stripy fish. And the Egyptian man spoke to me in the international language of football. Unfortunately I'm not a fluent speaker.

It was a couple weeks earlier, on the opposite shore, that Flic had another typical traveller's experience. We were staying by South Beach, Aqaba, when she decided to walk along the shore alone as the light faded away after sunset. *Be careful*, I said, as

she set off. It took some time for her to return and I was
worried. And, of course, the inevitable had happened. She had
been stopped, invited to eat some food with a Jordanian family,
and came back with no appetite for supper whatsoever. *But I
told you to be careful*, I said.

15

Africa

It was a cool summer evening in 2001 and here, in our living room, we had lit the wood-burning stove for the benefit of our guest, Joseph Sekiku. He was a short, chubby man with a round head and black skin, in truth more of a milk chocolate colour, which was a novelty to us here. And he was that colour all over; I knew that because he hitched up his t-shirt (and Flic's jumper, which he had borrowed) to scratch his ample belly. He wore a big smile on his face as he said the words, *Richard, when you come to Africa...*

Joseph had been telling us the story of the journey he made from Kampala, in Uganda, back to his parent's home village, Nyakasimbi, in north-west Tanzania. Joseph's father was a doctor who been educated by the British and had gone to live in Kampala where Joseph was brought up. Joseph's father was killed by Idi Amin's soldiers when Joseph was fourteen years old and now, as a young man at university, Joseph wanted to go back to his roots, to the village where his grandparents and aunts and uncles lived. Kampala to Nyakasimbi takes less than a day by car now but in those days, twenty-five or so years ago, the roads were rough, public transport limited, and people didn't travel that way, into a very poor part of Tanzania.

Joseph's story included sleeping outdoors amid a group of people heaped up together to keep warm and being given a lift by a nun of whom he was very suspicious. His difficulties included not being able to speak the local languages or even Swahili, only English and Luganda. When he reached Nyakasimbi everybody recognised him and he could see his family resemblance in the faces around him but he couldn't communicate – only a few older people spoke English in Nyerere's Tanzania. And when it came to bed time there was no room for him at all; he had to sleep with the goats.

Joseph came from an urban middle-class background and sleeping with goats was not something he had expected. He laughed with horror and delight as he told us the story. But what he was most aware of was the poverty. Here, in rural Tanzania, he witnessed a standard of living way below that he had experienced in Uganda. And these were his people. He decided that he would help them.

It was a few years later, after he had completed his degree in agriculture, worked for a while, and learnt to speak Swahili, that Joseph returned to Nyakasimbi. He bought some land, found himself a sturdy, intelligent wife and settled down to become the one man NGO who now sat in our living-room giggling and laughing as he talked. He had addressed a meeting in the nearby town of Machynlleth, met the children in our local school, and sat with me on the hill above the village, looked out across the fields and said, *is it true that some farmers here have their own tractor?* Now he looked at me, smiled, and said, *Richard, when you come to Africa...*

The story of our connection with Joseph Sekiku Mtabazi began two years earlier when Flic worked in a nursery school in Machynlleth. She came home one day with a letter from Africa asking for help. Joseph had been to Machynlleth a year or two before when he had taken some courses at CAT (the Centre for Alternative Technology). Now he wanted a link between his community and ours and he wanted a nursery school teacher to go out there. A conversation took place between myself and Flic that may have included the words, *when are you going?* and (in an incredulous tone of voice) *what? me?*

Flic applied for a grant for her airfare and was scared for the best part of a year and then got on the plane, stopped being scared, and spent three weeks visiting schools and various projects that Joseph had set up. She was on the receiving end of a great deal of hospitality, kindness and good humour. It was difficult for her get a clear idea of Joseph's work; she was, as she puts it, *overexcited*, in a world so different from anything she had experienced before. I think she was brave to go out there alone, to be met at the airport by a man she didn't know. I know I would have found an excuse for not going.

When Joseph came to Wales a year later he still had the idea of a link between communities with a support group at this end. He wanted me to go out there next. I would not have to be brave like Flic; I knew Joseph and I knew about the wonderful time she had out there. But I needed more of a concrete reason for going, something I could contribute.

I took Joseph to meet my friend Bob Shaw out in the woods south of Aberystwyth. Bob is an expert on green woodwork and woodland management, a countryman and naturalist, a visionary, and is one part tree and one part human being. If you saw lichens growing up his leg and moss in his beard you would not be surprised. We showed Joseph a pole lathe, a simple device for turning green wood into chair legs and tool handles, among other things. I explained that it was an outmoded thing, not practical for the twenty-first century, just for hobbies. Without hesitation he said that it was to him *appropriate technology* and it could be useful where he lived. I thought I had better go out there and make him one.

The last part of the drive from Entebbe airport, outside of Kampala, to Nyakasimbi, was along a typical African red-dirt road; the sort of road I had seen in Flic's photos from Tanzania and an aspect of my romanticised picture of that part of the world. So when we arrived I just set off alone down that road, to get a feeling of the real Africa. I only intended to walk a couple of hundred yards or so. What happened is that one of Joseph's sons, a twelve year old called Simeon, came and walked with me. It was a remote spot in a very poor part of a poor country but Simeon spoke some English and he took me off away from the road and down through the verdant farmland until we came to a place where a man and wife team were weeding a crop of beans growing between the trees. The man looked at me and burst out laughing, a good natured infectious laughter of pleasant surprise at seeing a white man turn up unexpectedly in his field. We stood and laughed and smiled at each other for a while, sharing no words of each other's language. Simeon introduced us and explained that the man was his uncle, Joseph's brother-in-law. The man and wife then took me a short distance to their home. I was their guest.

They lived in a hut of maybe two rooms, built of poles and mud with a roof of banana leaves. There was no furniture, just mats on a swept earth floor. The only decoration, if I remember, was a single random page from a magazine stuck on the wall. They fed me freshly harvested pineapple – or was it mangos and the pineapple somewhere else? I don't know, I just remember the laughter and spontaneous hospitality. It was good.

I had brought with me to Africa a rough plan of how to make a pole-lathe, a few tools, and a certain amount of scepticism. When Joseph and I dropped in at a timber merchants to buy some square sawn pieces of wood, there, in the corner, was a perfectly good electric powered lathe. The pole-lathe was surely a white elephant. But on our way to Nyakasimbi we had picked up a friend of Joseph, a softly spoken young man called Aloysius Gonzaga. He was a carpenter by profession and he seemed genuinely interested.

Aloysius and I worked together making this simple piece of equipment, not a true pole-lathe but one powered by bungee cord as the pole would have to be seasoned to retain its springiness. Then he made a perfect cylinder out of a piece of jacaranda wood using a hand adze rather than an axe. He fitted the wood onto the lathe and quickly made a pestle for pounding grain. He was pleased and explained that electricity and electric lathes were expensive but here was a cheap alternative he could use in the workshop with his trainees.

I liked Aloysius Gonzaga. When we were in Joseph's house later on in the afternoon there was some weird African status thing going on that meant that some people in the room were given a beer and others sat empty handed. I was in the first group and Aloysius in the second despite the fact we had just spent the best part of the day working together. I found an extra glass and shared my beer with him. I received a letter from him when I got home saying that he had made several bungee-powered lathes. And before I left Nyakasimbi he gave me the jacaranda pestle. We don't pound much grain here in Wales but I'm pleased with it and it sits on my desk as I write this.

When Joseph picked me up from the airport he had two of his children with him: Jeff, a skinny little four year old with lots of energy and intelligence and a cheeky grin to go with it; and Comboni, a sleepy toddler somewhere between one and two years old. Joseph was good with children and made friends with children in the village here in Wales. At home in Tanzania he would often take one or two of his kids along with him and had looked after all five of them when his wife, Isabella, was away on a course. But his family life was complicated and needs some explanation.

Joseph split his time between the village of Nyakasimbi and the town of Kayanga where he had an office. In Nyakasimbi he lived with his wife, Isabella and their children, Simeon, Lawrence, Dorothy and Jeff. Isabella was a strong, handsome, capable woman who could carry a plastic jerry can full of water up from the stream on her head, could work in the fields or in the house all day long, and who could deal out large amounts of both love and discipline to her children as appropriate. In Kayanga he lived with his second wife, Eliot, a beautiful, vain, sleepy young woman with coffee coloured skin and the sleepy Comboni as her only child. How did the two women get on and how did they feel about it? I can't even guess. The children came and went as children seem to in Africa, always looked after somewhere within an extended family.

I am *friends* with two of Joseph's boys, Jeff and Simeon, on facebook. They were both likeable, intelligent children and I expect that they are turning into capable young men. I can't imagine that they remember me and I don't have so very much in common with them. The last time I looked at Simeon's facebook page he was pretty keen on sexy white women, fast cars and Jesus, if I remember correctly. Now I check again and see a handsome young man, a graphic designer by profession, looking very community spirited and very happy. As for Jeff, he's *just chillin...*

There is so much I could write about my two and a half weeks in Africa. I was taken around by Joseph to meet people and see projects that he had initiated. Some looked good to me; others I was doubtful about. It did seem like there was grant money available to start new projects but not enough to keep them running. Joseph was therefore always scratching around for new ideas. The priority had, perhaps, become ticking the boxes in a grant application form rather than meeting the needs of poor people. But Joseph was a good man with his heart in the right place and at least some of what he did was worthwhile and successful. And for me it was a special experience to be travelling around with Africans and staying in their homes.

On the way back to the airport Joseph took me to a game reserve. We drove out with the warden through the long grasses and scattered trees and caught an occasional glimpse of something with horns. Then we went to the river and watched hippos messing about. We passed an airstrip used by wealthy South Africans when they fly in to hunt. And then we came across some locals hunting with spears illegally. They hid and slipped away but their dog put its feet on a termite hill and stuck its head up to see what was going on. The warden raised his rifle and with no hesitation shot it dead.

A better memory to finish on. I sometimes walked around the town of Kayanga on my own. The children there would call out *m'zungu, m'zungu* in greeting, smile, run up to you and take your hand to walk along with you for a while. That's what they do when they see a white person, a real stranger. I liked that.

O is for Omorushaka (Tanzania)

I was driving with Joseph Sekiku through a town called Omorushaka when he remembered that a friend's wife was in hospital there and we stopped to call in. She was sitting on her bed recovering from a major operation and looked rough. Her husband looked pretty shaken and I empathised with him very much; I had been in that situation, seeing the person you most care about suffering from a life-threatening illness. I must have given him a sympathetic look, we certainly didn't say anything as we had no language in common. Or perhaps I looked worried, remembering how it was when Flic had cancer. When we left the ward he took my hand. We walked down a long, long hospital corridor like that, holding hands all the way.

16

I felt it touch my face with its whiskers

Now we come back to the recent travels of Flic and Richard. Times of hanging around at home feeling, off and on, too ill to do anything much, certainly too ill to think of another adventure. And then one day I would feel good, we would talk ourselves into doing one more special trip and I would buy some air tickets. Then I would feel rough again and be certain that we couldn't go. The days would pass and my condition would improve, worsen, improve, and we would get on the flight. Once out in some foreign place the same pattern would continue. Days when it seemed too much, too dodgy to be so far from home and so dependent on both Flic and my medication. Days when we were having the time of our lives. Always the certainty that this would be our last adventure. Until next time.

In 2010 we went to India and Nepal again and visited some wonderful places. We started with Agra. The Taj Mahal is the big thing in Agra; it's big and it's beautiful and it's visited by large numbers of tourists (most of them Indians) and I'm not going to write about it here. I'm going to quote from Flic's journal:

We took a tuk tuk to Agra Fort to visit the bazaar. When we got there we weren't sure which way to go so we got out our guide book which was a mistake. As soon as you look like you don't know where you are or what you're doing men gather around giving advice and offering to help, very cheap, so we put the book away and walked off purposefully probably in the wrong direction. A rickshaw driver followed us and we gave up our independence and climbed into the vehicle. He cycled off proudly as if we were fish he had caught.

He took us up a very crowded street, the air choked us, so full of fumes, there was almost a complete jam of traffic and I thought why are we here, it's not fun, traffic jams are horrible and we've just paid to be in one. The driver reassured us that he would take us to the old bazaar. The street was a bit like hell and we weren't moving. After a bit we found that he wanted to take us to some shops where he would be paid 20 rupees commission. We decided to pay him the 20r and get out and walk, it felt better.

Large rolls of cloth and plastic sheeting and tarpaulins were being sold, then great amounts of leather and wooden shoe lasts, some of the leather was cut to shape, there were piles and piles of it spread out on the ground. I smelled honey further on and there was a sweet shop, squares of coloured sweets like Turkish delight, halva and coconut ice in piles on counters. Then the smell of flowers – more marigolds. Dark kites circle overhead among the black power lines and grey sky and crows.

Then a pile of rubbish being eaten or sorted by cows, pigs, dogs and an old man. Later plastic was being graded and stuffed into big sacks by women. Children paddle in the stinky gutter. I feel a bit sick. Being rich and foreign we can get into a tuk tuk and be driven out of this place.

And that is how it is; you can dip one toe into a sort of hell and then pull back and go away. It comes back to me now, the foul intensity of street life in that town. There was very little beauty, only from time to time something religious, a temple or a gaudy shrine with a multi-armed and multi-eyed goddess clothed in purple and scarlet. Near the Taj a man took us to a shrine with Krishna, Shiva and a portable television set showing the test match against Sri Lanka.

It was cold enough in January for us to wear jumpers and coats. Locals tended to wear a blanket around their shoulders rather than a coat, even when riding a motorbike. We saw a goat dressed in a pink jumper, two scarves and a sack across its back against the cold. It also wore anklets on its front legs to enhance its beauty. There was one place on the river bank where we warmed ourselves for a moment:

We were stopped by a sight of piles of ashes and a crowd of people carrying bodies to be burnt and put in the river. They made bamboo and marigold and tinsel lids to put over the corpses. Dogs lay sleeping on the warmed up stones after the fire's ashes had been swept away. People were wading out into the river carrying a small bundle, I wondered if it was a child. We warmed our hands over the warm ashes of a corpse. Death is not taboo here.

Another memory of Agra: we had eaten supper in the garden of our guesthouse (well wrapped up against the cold) and were talking to other travellers. I went into our room to get something. There was, as there often is out there, a power cut and I searched about in the dark for my head-torch. I was having increasing difficulty moving and eventually was unable to do anything other than sink to the floor, where I lay, unable to get up for a while, listening to the conversation and laughter outside.

I browse through Flic's journal for this, our third and final of six once-in a-life-time adventures and I can find plenty of Parkinson's moments: Richard thinks he's too ill to cope with this; Richard went to lie down feeling ill; after lunch Richard is too ill to go out so I draw and read until he feels better – that sort of thing. And as always there are new, unanticipated symptoms to get used to. For instance one day I found that my tongue had started the habit of moving around my mouth of its own accord, rubbing against my teeth and pushing into my cheek. It's doing it now as I write and I'm used to it but the first day it started was unpleasant. Sometimes, of course, the symptoms are more than unpleasant – they are scary and I want to go home. Until, an hour later, I feel fine, because that's how it is with Parkinson's. It is not a boring illness.

Flic's experience of the illness was second hand and she could wait out the tough moments knowing that I would feel better and function better quite soon. Meanwhile she could get out her sketchbook and draw and paint, sometimes attracting a crowd of people wanting to look over her shoulder or be in the picture. There is very little reserve among people in India. If they want to use their few words of English they do. But perhaps I'm talking about the men. The women were quieter. Only when in a big family group at some tourist spot or pilgrimage site they would come and ask to have their picture taken. And one of the fascinating things for Indians visiting such places is the presence of foreigners with their pale skins and ridiculous clothes.

Our next stop was Fatehpur Sikri, a typically fantastical small town with a full complement of extraordinary historical buildings and colourful street life. It's somehow off any major tourist route and it's a relaxed, friendly place. The high street has an amazing number of small shops and tiny stalls. Walking along the street are a mixture of men in dull Western clothes and men and women in more traditional dress, the guys with turbans and the women in traditional hi-vis day-glow saris and shawls. They carry bags of vegetables and suitcases and heaven knows what else on their heads. I have a photo of a group of women in front of me that I took in Fatehpur high street and they are dressed in: lime green and blue; lemon yellow with white patterns; blue and orange; saffron and pink; blue, lime green and yellow; and, finally blue with yellow spots. They wear, as Flic describes it: *jewellery dangling from ears, noses, necks, and toe rings and have painted soles of their feet.*

And then there are the vehicles: strange, seemingly home-made trucks, the cabs open to the weather and the engine likewise; tractors and trailers, bicycles; lots of motorbikes with two or three or four or, in one case, five passengers; bullock carts; horse-drawn carts; push carts and tuk tuks. There are no ordinary cars. And there are the usual animals on the street: cows, pigs (including a sow with piglets) dogs and more.

We bought chai from a little stall where the owner sat cross-legged and we watched the street life for a while. Then we walked along and things got busier and then more colourful. Busier because in a narrow part of the street the traffic, mostly people on foot, reached gridlock. More colourful because we were called over to see a Hindu ceremony.

It was a small scale affair with the atmosphere of a village fete. There was a stage with a band of musicians and something like a pulpit, the whole thing vibrant in orange, yellow and pink draperies and festooned with marigold garlands and framed ultra-kitsch pictures of Hindu gods. There were only twenty or thirty people attending and most of them were old ladies and children but the man who had called us over was young and earnest, a pleasant born-again Hindu I guess. I wanted to take photographs but wasn't sure if it was alright so I handed him my camera and he went around snapping for me. We were sat down and given tea in disposable clay pots and the guru came and tried to speak to us. It seemed that his only word of English was purification. Then he spread out his long hair and put dark glasses on like a rock star. I was chosen to go forward and pass him a marigold garland and then he sang and chanted and preached. I like the way Hindus encourage you to join in. It's a daft (to me) but joyful religion.

Fatehpur Sikri has a huge mosque, an uninhabited palace and an abandoned ruined city on the hill above the town. They were built by a Mughal Emperor in the sixteenth century but only used for a few years because of lack of available water.

And it has a railway station: At four o'clock we walked out to the station – completely empty apart from a cow, a peacock and three peahens. Nice to get some space and quiet, only the mooing of the cow.

And a tourist office with a sign that reads *How can you visit Fatehpur Sikri*. As Flic observed in her journal: There is a lot of trouble with syntax.

While we're on the subject of use of language I'm going to quote from my blog:

DoorMatry or VIPRoom cum Toilet.

We have just arrived in Phalodi and found something like a hotel. Some English written up outside but no-one who speaks English around yet. So here I am, next door at a printers/computer place while Flic waits for the manager. We have a choice of rooms ranging from DoorMatry (yes, that's what it says) to VIPRoom cum Toilet. We might be VIPs at five pounds for the night. Enough now. I'll see how Flic's getting on.

Blogging was a new traveller's past-time for me, something that was to continue over the next journeys. I don't function well in internet cafés so my posts most often were short. All the same it became a preoccupation for me; as I wandered around various countries on a number of different continents I would compose amusing (I hoped) titles, a sample of which will be coming your way.

We didn't stay in the *VIPRoom cum Toilet* in Phalodi. We went to Ossian. We were on a bus going somewhere else, I don't remember where, when it stopped by a small town in the desert with, at its centre, a hilltop temple. It looked interesting and we hurried to get off the bus. There, awaiting us, was a young man who wanted to take us to a guest house. He told us pretty soon

that he was of the Brahmin caste (as Brahmins generally do –
though no-one else in India tells you their caste) and, although
he was poorly dressed he had a certain dignity and grace in his
movements. He led us through scrubby trees and palms with
much rubbish and with pigs scrambling about into sandy back
streets and to a handsome large, though single storey, house. It
turned out to be a marvellous place to stay.

The house was owned by a Mr Singh who just rented out
two rooms on a fairly informal basis. Mr Singh was well
educated and both he and the house gave the impression of
faded grandeur, of having come down in the world but having
still maintained one's dignity. He told us that the house was
three hundred years old. It was built of stone and stretched
around two courtyards: a small more private one that was the
scene of domestic tasks (the women's area) and a larger courtyard surrounded by stables and with big gates opening onto the
street (the men's courtyard). Opposite the gates was a raised
and covered verandah with a bedroom and bathroom at either
end. It was grand but it was very cheap and the beds were a
little bit small for two so we took a room each.

The verandah was a fine place to be, the stone pillars that
held up the roof were ornately carved with leaves and flowers,
the walls decorated with sculpted plaster and framed photographs of illustrious family members. We would come from
our private rooms and sit overlooking the courtyard. There
were curiously high feed troughs (meant for camels) and the
rooftops around were regularly visited not by monkeys as is
usual in India but by peacocks. The Brahmin turned out to be
our cook. He would bring food to the veranda and he and Mr
Singh would sit disconcertingly close to watch us as we ate. I
wrote on my blog:

*It is very quiet in the night here. The quietest place we have
been in India. But at 5 a m there are Hindu hymns broadcast*

*over loud-speakers for half an hour, then quiet, then the Muslim
call to prayer at 6, then drums and trumpets that maybe come
from the Jain temple. The proprietor of our 'guest-house' is not
Hindu or Moslem or Jain but a Sikh. He prays at home. 'Wealth
or poverty, good fortune or bad,' he says, 'it is God's doing.
What else can there be?'*

Flic gave her own account of the day beginning. In her
sketchbook she drew and watercoloured a patch of red
sandstone wall, a scrubby tree with a peacock roosting, and in
the background the many domes of the Jain temple. She wrote:
I woke up early and watched the dawn and in a tree dark shapes
became peacocks that woke up slowly and eventually flew down to the
ground. As the sun came up I heard a man give a great shout. Earlier
there were other noises, calls to prayer and a puja bell ringing.

We visited the Jain temple complex with its extraordinary
architecture and stone carvings of voluptuous figures and
animals. It is a place of pilgrimage and related business opportunities: rows of bright stalls outside the temple but nothing for us,
all is to offer to the gods at the many shrines: coloured string,
sweets, incense, marigolds, coconuts, bangles, tinsel, fairy lights,
photos of gods in flashing gold frames.

Our young Brahmin friend was dismissive of Jainism as it
was a young religion like Buddhism, barely 2,500 years old.
His religion, Hinduism, is recorded to have been around 4,000
years ago with its origins going back further still. He was proud
of his high caste destiny and the limits it placed on him: no
drugs, no alcohol, no meat, no eggs and no marrying until
you're twenty-five.

Ossian is a handsome town but very small and there's not
much to do or see there. We rambled about a while, took a short
camel ride into the desert, and moved on.

We went to another desert town, Jaisalmer, the most westerly
of all the towns we stayed in while in India. Of all the

Rajasthan towns Jaisalmer seemed to us the one most dominated by tourism. The old town situated inside the castle wall had become a tourist shopping mall. We did the tourist thing and took a trip out to villages and into the desert to spend the night under the stars. I remember that while Flic spoke to a village woman I counted twenty-five bracelets on one of her arms. I remember sleeping and mostly not sleeping on the hard sand and how very cold it was in the night. And I recorded in my blog the words that came to me as I woke from a curious dream: *I felt it touch my face with its whiskers.*

After Jaiselmer we travelled to Jodhpur on a *super, deluxe tourist bus* which stopped every mile or two along the road to take on more and more village people who squeezed up against us and beside us and pretty much on top of us. Jodhpur had the usual (marvellous) forts and palaces and a lot of tourists and also the extraordinary day to day life of an Indian city that you can experience just by walking down the street and looking around you. We had some interesting encounters.

One morning we went out by tuk tuk to the edge of the town and walked in a barren, rocky piece of countryside for an hour or so. We came across some builders doing some renovation work on a temple and the foreman, I guess he was the owner of the firm, wanted to talk to us. He was a self-educated man with a great passion for knowledge and an interest in the world. He was very keen on the internet and travel and was saving up to visit London. His English was good but his pronunciation was pretty rough. Still we managed to talk about nano-technology, stem cell research and reincarnation. He was a Hindu, of course, and a believer in the God Shiva and managed to explain that the symbolism of his religion included references to the atom and the whole universe. For him the contemporary scientific explanation of the world and a belief in the existence of supernatural beings fitted together without any problem.

And one late afternoon we set off on foot to visit a little temple perched on a pinnacle of rock that we could see from our hotel rooftop. We had trouble finding it but had a good view of ordinary Jodhpur life on the way. In most parts of the world people don't sit indoors in the evening watching TV like we do; they're out on the streets socialising. So we saw lots of activity including a few cricket games. People are poor in the north of India but here, in Jodhpur, the feeling wasn't of desperation. They were struggling but they quite enjoyed the struggle. Only a small proportion of the population are hopelessly poor. For most there is a good chance of making some sort of living and finding some sort of fulfilment in life. Of course they deserve better things; better access to clean drinking water and healthcare and education and opportunities. But India is not a country full of miserable people suffering abject poverty. There is, amongst over things, a joyful energy about the place.

That's how it felt to us that evening in Jodhpur. And, as we were in an area where tourists never go, people were interested in us and friendly. My heading for the day's blog was *Shaken*. The fact was that I have never shaken so many hands in a short period of time.

We reached the temple on the rock a little before sunset and two young lads, ten or eleven years old, took us in and led us past candle lit shrines and up the series of metal ladders that went to the top. We had climbed up maybe 100ft above the little houses at this end of town. It was, some might say, only just the right side of scary. I took a photo of the boys smiling big smiles into the camera, their arms around Flic as if she was a special auntie or big sister. And then we watched the sun set beside Jodhpur palace and the light fade over the chaotic mass of streets and houses that make up the blue city.

P is for Paris (France)

We were in Paris for a few days on our way back from Morocco at the end of our last big trip abroad. It had been raining and the River Seine was full of swiftly flowing grey water. There were tourist boats and commercial barges making their way up and down stream, their bow waves spreading and slapping against the concrete river banks. We walked from our accommodation near the Botanical Garden down to the Île de la Cité and back a few times and I was aware of the strange miracle of constantly flowing water. For in Northern Europe the rivers run every day of the year whether it has been raining or not. Perhaps it has been fine and dry for three weeks across northern France during a hot summer spell. The river still flows. How weird is that?

Pretty weird if you are an immigrant from north Africa. In Morocco we had seen dried up water courses fill after rain and then empty to nothing a day later. In so many of the drier places we have visited rivers are seasonal or occasional things. Our rivers must seem beyond explanation to someone from those countries. What we have is groundwater. It flows out of the rocks into our rivers and streams along their entire length every day of the year. We can drink it, swim in it, transport ourselves and our goods on it, and write songs and paint pictures about it. Groundwater makes our landscapes, developed our economies, and enriches our culture. I've never thought about it before.

17

Meetings with Remarkable People

Back to 2010. We travelled from Jodhpur by train to Delhi, by air to Varanasi, and by bus to Pokhara. I'm going to say a little more about Delhi and Varanasi in a later chapter. You'll see why. This chapter is about Pokhara and our trek to ABC, Annapurna Base Camp. But there's a place we stopped on the way that deserves a mention: Lumbini, the birthplace of the Buddha.

My sound of one hand clapping is louder than your sound of one hand clapping. That's what the array of Buddhist temples in Lumbini seem to be saying. There are temples built by Buddhists from Thailand, Korea, China, Myanmar, Japan, Sri Lanka, Nepal, India, and Tibet, among other places. They are surreal, grandiose edifices, each one in a different style, all seemingly trying to out-compete the others. They aren't made from local materials and sit uneasily in the landscape (the artificially landscaped landscape I should say). More than one of them looks like a giant wedding cake. It is, in short, the Birth Place of the Buddha Theme Park. By the ruins of what archae-ologists have identified as an ancient monastery there are a dazzling superfluity of prayer flags. And there are air condi-tioned tour coaches carrying affluent pilgrim/tourists from the different Buddhist countries around the site.

We were trying to find something to eat when a Buddhist monk complete with shaved head, purple robes, sandals and twinkling eyes came up to us and asked Flic, *Are you looking for something?* He smiled and waited for the profound ambigu-ity that his words carried in such a place to sink in. Flic, well versed in the subtleties of Zen paradox, paused before replying, *No. I am only looking*, she said.

By way of contrast we went on rented bicycles out into the countryside nearby and came across a sort of Hindu (I guess) garden fete. A large number of other bicycles were parked up and village people were enjoying themselves. There was a tall pagoda made of bamboo and coloured paper. Some men were dancing to the accompaniment of singing. Fun for everyone, Flic observed in her journal.

We made our way from Lumbini to Pokhara via Tansen. You know about our bus journey from Tansen as it was extraordinary enough to qualify for best-bus-journeys-of-all-time status and made it into chapter five. From Pokhara we set out trekking again; this time to Annapurna Base Camp.

This was our third trek in Nepal and maybe one too many. Certainly one too many for you, reading this, and so I'll just say a little about it. It was a short trek and didn't lead along ancient trading routes but merely through some very beautiful steep hill country and then up a bleak valley to a spot where there was never a base camp but there is a grand view of the Annapurna range, ice and snow slopes rising to stupendous high peaks all around. Not a trek too many then but lacking in the cultural encounters of our other treks and different in a number of ways.

One difference was that, as it wasn't a trade route and didn't lead anywhere, the path didn't have the usual traffic of donkeys and yaks and porters carrying goods. There are wonderful suspension bridges in Nepal. They have generally been made with help from outside; the engineering and the money to build them comes from abroad (although such bridges were built in the Himalayas hundreds of years before we had them in the west). They are foot bridges, no wider than is necessary for a fully laden donkey or yak to pass across, held up by steel cables hung from concrete stanchions. Sometimes the wooden decking is in a bad state of repair, with holes through which you can look down perhaps fifty, perhaps a hundred feet, to a rushing river below. But you know it's safe; if a mule train or a number of yaks have crossed without the bridge giving way then you know it can take you. But here, on the ABC trek, there were no beasts of burden to test the bridges. We had seen a bridge in the Everest Region that had given way when the huge rock to which it was anchored had slumped forward. We could choose to be a little nervous crossing the bridges here if we wanted to.

Another difference is that we were trekking in the early spring and there were still huge amounts of snow on the high slopes, deep snow to trudge through near the base camp, and the probability of the path being closed by drifts or avalanches. On the way up we met disappointed trekkers coming down having been unable to make their way through the snow. We crossed a recent avalanche at one point but we were lucky enough to be among the first trekkers to reach base camp that year. Outside one lodge we spent part of an afternoon shovelling snow away from the entrance – very hard work at that altitude.

On this trek I was a year further along the Parkinson's road and now had difficulty putting things in and getting things out of containers; particularly squishy things like clothes and sleeping bags into squishy containers like rucksacks. Imagine being Flic. You've walked all day beside a guy who keeps asking you to put his jumper here or look for his hat or find something from the bottom of his rucksack and all the time it's in his pocket. The snow was deep and your feet are cold and wet (why didn't he tell you to get new boots?) but when you mention it he says, too smugly, that his are dry. You are now exhausted, cold, and suffering the discomfort of high altitude but you've arrived at the lodge and you can lie down for a while and rest, maybe later talk to that handsome young

Australian guy who you met in Lumbini (what a great coinci-
dence that he should be here too!). You're just settling down in
your sleeping bag, all warm and cosy, when you hear a voice,
Flic. You ignore him for a bit, pretend you didn't hear. You're
just dropping off to sleep and he starts again, *Flic. Flic, can
you help me with something? Flic?*

Hmmm... perhaps I wouldn't choose me as a travelling
companion. On the Annapurna Base Camp trek we saw fresh
snow leopard tracks in fresh snow. We had fabulous views of
Machupuchare, the fishtail mountain. We met interesting
people along the way. But there were times, it has to be said,
when we weren't as good together as we might have been. And
I was saddened by that.

When we got back to Pokhara we slowed right down. We
stayed in a guest house by the lake again. It was there that we
met some remarkable people, including Jules and Nigel; they
were staying in the room next to us. Jules was a life-loving,
come-to-the-cabaret type of person. An all-singing, all-dancing
good time girl, a great traveller, a JAP (Jewish American
Princess) but not of the east coast variety – she comes from
California. She was, I guess, in her fifties and still in posses-
sion of much *joie de vivre*. She and Nigel met some years ago
and became friends and casual lovers for a while. Still great
friends they were spending a few weeks together by the lake at
Pokhara before returning to their homes in San Francisco
(Jules) and Thailand (Nigel). They were friendly neighbours to
us and fun to be with. Nigel was the more remarkable one.

On the balcony that we shared with our new friends there
was a plaster statue of Ganesh that Nigel was decorating with
acrylic paint in bright garish colours. He said he was an artist
but I don't think so; I think it was just colouring in. But he
loved doing it and people passing by complimented him on his
work. Ganesh was monstrous, having the head of an elephant

and the body of a human, only with more arms. Nigel, on the other hand, looked OK, was tall and gaunt, suntanned; doing well for his sixty eight years. He was Jewish too but was brought up in England. He became, as his parents would wish, a sensible professional man, a Harley Street dentist. He told us straight away that he liked to (putting a special emphasis on this word) *smoke*. Somehow he had given up dentistry and become a grower (of marijuana, that is) in Amsterdam and then a dealer in LSD. He got caught and was lucky to spend only a year in prison. He lives now in Thailand and Amsterdam on the remains of the money he made in teeth and drugs.

Nigel was charming, sort of modest and self-confident at the same time, friendly, open, relatively carefree. When I first overheard him talking to Jules I thought there were two men present; a well-spoken Englishman and an urbane American. He has never lived in America but has managed to acquire an adrift-in-the-mid-Atlantic accent.

Nigel smoked a lot of hash. We suggested to him that it masked the ups and downs of life and took away some of its richness. *What ups and downs?* he said, without a smile or any hint of irony. He was meant to have a lover waiting for him back in Thailand, a Korean woman who he had rescued from an abusive relationship. But she had returned to the old boyfriend in Nigel's absence and the man wrote to Nigel and told him so. *It's not important*, Nigel said. And there was his friendship with a high-caste (Brahmin) Nepali woman who had separated from her husband. She came to the balcony and told Nigel that the husband was jealous and making trouble. She wanted Nigel to take her away with him but he wouldn't and she left in tears. *It's all OK*, he said, or at least implied.

He was a great womaniser whose speciality was kindness and caring. But he remained, somehow, unconnected, a free man, untouched by the consequences of his actions for other people. But he seemed badly shaken on the afternoon of the day that he heard the news from Thailand and also received the visit from his Nepali *inamorata*. His voice retained that mid-Atlantic confident tone, he seemed calm, spoke reasonably. *It doesn't matter*, he said. But I thought that his face showed signs of emotional stress. He looked distraught.

In the evening Nigel looked happier again. He bounced back; I admired him for that. He had finished painting Ganesh and was busy wrapping up small lumps of hash (were there thirty of them?) in layer after layer of clingfilm so that he could smuggle them into Thailand. Before leaving for home he would swallow these parcels and then in the days that followed he could retrieve them, unwrap them one by one, and carry on with his comforting habit. I imagine that if you asked him about himself and his life he would say it was fine and he would more or less be telling the truth. *What ups and downs?* he would probably say.

There was Jules and there was Nigel and there were other visitors to the balcony. Dmitry, a beautiful and crazy Russian ex-heroin addict. Franz, a stilt-walking accordion player from Bavaria. A Korean man (I can't remember his name), in dreadlocks and leather jacket, the son of a wealthy industrialist who had once made a present of 500 chickens to a local village, got chatted up by one of the women there, and punched on the nose by her husband. There were probably one or two more but I can't remember them all now.

One day we set off with Jules and Nigel to go to a village in the valley beyond the lake. They were fun to be with. Jules chatted up a young man whose jeans were held up by a very flashy belt with an elaborate buckle. She insisted on taking a photo of the buckle which involved a period of time focusing the camera on his crotch. He didn't seem to mind. And when we passed the *Hungry Feel* restaurant she commented that she had experienced one or two of those in her time.

The real reason for our journey was that we wanted to ride on the roof of the bus, something we could try here on a short trip down a country road but wouldn't be tempted to do on a long journey over mountain passes. It was great, and would be one of my favourite bus journeys of all time if it hadn't been over so quickly. We travelled along the edge of the lake and into a wide valley of agricultural land, some of it newly sown with rice. There were water buffalo grazing, each one with a white egret as a companion. We passed by our favourite banyan tree with its fantastical aerial root system. We stopped to let cows and chickens cross the road. We squeezed past a bus coming the other way and greeted its load of rooftop travellers. And the ticket vendor climbed up onto the roof as we drove along and sold us our tickets. These are things that just aren't going to happen on the bus from Aberystwyth to Machynlleth. A good time was had by all; except for Nigel who as a bony sixty-eight year old found it distressingly uncomfortable when the tarmac road gave out and we bounced along a rutted track.

We got off at the village and walked a little way down the valley. Jules and Nigel asked the inhabitants of a seemingly random house if they would cook us some lunch and we wandered down to the river while we waited for it to be prepared. Nigel sat down and indulged in his customary habit. Flic took out her sketchbook and drew a picture of the village on the bank opposite us. Perhaps it was there that Jules had the idea of commissioning a picture from Flic. It turned out to be a view from the balcony that we shared with them. I believe that it's still on the wall of Jules' house in San Francisco.

It was in Pokhara that we had the chance to celebrate *Holi*, the Hindu festival of colours. It's a national holiday for Nepalis and people are out on the street. Bottles of coloured water and little plastic bags of bright coloured pigment are for sale and children, teenagers and some foreigners enjoy throwing it at each other. Flic enthusiastically attacked small boys and ended up covered in colour herself. When it got too much we rented a small boat and went out onto the lake. It's nearly always calm and beautiful out there and we spent a lot of time on the water during our stay in Pokhara.

The lake is particularly beautiful in the mornings and evenings. Early one morning I walked out along the shore and managed to rent a boat from a lakeside guest house. I paddled out into the mist and waited calmly for it to clear and reveal the view of the hills and the snow-capped Annapurnas in the distance. I was the only person on the water and it felt magical, just waiting for the mist to clear. But the mist didn't clear and it stopped feeling magical after a while. When I got too cold I paddled back to the shore.

Back at the guesthouse I had time to write a piece to put on my blog:

We can look down from our hotel balcony onto a network of tiny terraced fields. Two weeks ago, before we went to Annapurna basecamp, a man was ploughing them with a simple wooden plough (small enough and light enough to be carried in on his shoulder) and a pair of oxen. The fields are so small that the animals are constantly driven into tight turns at the corners and headlands. Somehow they manage – the man controls them with a long stick and a number of wordless grunts and cries.

Then yesterday he ploughs again; this time followed by his wife who dribbles a line of seed (rice, wheat, barley? we don't know) from her hand into the open furrow. They work all day and only when they are nearly finished does it begin to rain.

It rains a little, eases off, rains again. Then, at dusk, the storm begins. Massing clouds, high winds, thunder, lightning, and a torrential downpour. Somewhere behind the clouds the sun descends and sets and the sky turns from orange to sickly yellow to dark grey. At first we see only the pale impressions of lightning and long after hear distant thunder. Then the storm comes out from behind the hill and great wriggles and forks of electric light flash in the southern sky, facing us directly as we sit on the balcony. Sometimes it is loud enough and bright enough to make us enjoyably scared.

There are four of us sitting in a row on cane chairs, shouting and cheering against the noise of wind and rain on banana leaves and tin roofs. The storm lasts maybe two hours, moving eastwards and lighting up the lake before disappearing behind further hills.

There is an incongruity here – the medieval ploughman surrounded by modern hotels and curious tourists. Sometimes it seems like we are time travellers. But we met a nice man running a trekking lodge in the hills who had travelled a little, spoke good English, and had one foot firmly in the 21st century. When the lodge closes for the monsoon he returns to his family on the Terrai (in the flat south of Nepal) and ploughs his land with his own oxen. He was a handsome young man, high cheekbones, brown skin, a ready smile and a Nike hooded sweatshirt. It seems like he occupies two times zones, one past and one present. But that's not really how it is. He is just a Nepali living in Nepal and it's not the UK, it's different here. Much of it is beautifully different.

Q is for Quito (Ecuador)

On the way to Quito we met two people who had been robbed there, one of them beaten up a little in the process. In Peru we had a bag stolen from us and also met an Englishman who had been robbed at gunpoint on a night bus. That's South America for you. So we walked about the beautiful city of Quito in fear, not enjoying it as we should, seeing the shady characters staring from shady doorways as much as we saw the handsome buildings and green spaces.

We visited a neo-Gothic basilica, a huge church on a hill in the centre of town. The outside featured anteaters, iguanas, turtles, pumas, monkeys and pelicans carved out of stone. Inside we found that we were allowed access to all sorts of areas normally hidden from the public. We walked along a wooden gangway that ran the length of the building in the roof space between the curved ceiling of the nave and the v-shape of the roof above. It led to a series of stairways and ladders that took us outside of the building and onto more ladders leading up a flying buttress and onto a spire. At the other end of the church we went up spiral staircases inside the tower and saw a large clock face from the inside with the numbers back to front. At the top of the tower we were more than 300 feet above street level and had an amazing view over the city.

We visited a museum housing the works of Oswaldo Guaysamín. They were very impressive and powerful large paintings depicting, among other things, the struggles of the South American people. It was a special place; my favourite art gallery in the world.

We also saw a man in the park demonstrating the medicinal uses of a sort of giant (6 inch long, and fat too) slug/snail.

But we didn't see the volcano that stands above the city, it was covered in clouds. Volcanoes and clouds spend a lot of time in each other's company in Ecuador.

18

Me and my Monkey

This chapter is about three places and one river. Our last few days in India were spent in Rishikesh where the Ganges flows out of the mountains and onto the plains. On the way there we stayed by its tributary, the Yamuna, outside Delhi, and also spent a few memorable days on the Ganges at Varanasi, the holy city.

It occurred to me that the river is the link that ties these places together in my story. But I look at a map and see that the drainage basin (why isn't there a more poetic word for this?) of the Ganges is massive. The outflow of the lake at Pokhara, the Marsyangdi and the Kali Kandaki rivers around Annapurna, the snow-melt and ice-melt of the Everest region, the Yamuna river that flows past Delhi and through Agra, all flow into the Ganges. Half the places we went to in India and *all* the places we went to in Nepal are in the Ganges catchment. It's big.

On February 3rd, 2010 I wrote this blog post:

Train from Jodhpur to Delhi, 10pm > 11am overnight sleeper. A man snoring like some blobby monster or a pig drowning or maybe a walrus. Loud, varied, continuous blubbery wet snoring. There are 64 people in this 3 tier sleeper carriage; one awful loud snorer, 63 plotting murder. Fortunately he gets out at Jaipur at 5am.

We arrive in Delhi and stay at the Tibetan colony, north of the city. Monks with maroon robes and shaved heads. A rooftop view of allotments running down to the river, scrub and reedbeds and woods on the far bank. We go for a walk across the Yamuna River on a pontoon bridge. The water is black, the colour and very nearly the consistency of used engine oil. Completely opaque. It smells bad. In the woods on the other side we see deer.

From the rooftop in the morning I see a three-quarter moon reflected in the putrid river. A sickly beauty. No, just sickly, I think.

When we looked down on the Yamuna we saw roughly built shelters of poor people close to its banks. In the very hot weather of summer the smell must be... but I don't think there can be a word for it. The foul Yamuna flows into the Ganges. And further downstream at Varanasi 200 million litres of untreated human sewage enter the river every day. But the Ganges is, to Indians, both pure and purifying. Not symbolically but literally pure. That's just how it is.

We flew from Delhi to Varanasi. Looking out of the window to the north we saw strange clouds with unlikely shapes to them. They were not clouds but mountains as high as clouds, their peaks at an aircraft's cruising height. The Himalayas.

Outside Varanasi airport we were told that there was no bus to the town; we needed to take a taxi. A few minutes later we were in a taxi in heavy traffic, surrounded by buses going our way. Never mind. The taxi took us to Assi Ghat and we found a very cheap hotel overlooking the river. We climbed up onto the roof and took in the view. I think we knew that Varanasi was a foul holy city on a foul holy river. Nobody told us that it was beautiful but it is; viewed from a rooftop in the morning or evening light it's a magical place. From Flic's journal:

It took a while driving through crowded streets to get to Assi Ghat. There we got to the river, a great expanse of water, grey not black, sandy opposite shore, even a beach. Beautiful old buildings line the shore, it's peaceful and quiet, we walk along with our rucksacks until we find a hotel with the right specifications – a rooftop restaurant and view over the river. The room is a bit grotty but it's got a loo and shower room. As we got up so early this morning we both fall asleep.

Next morning I woke feeling excited and we got up early and went out along the ghats and walked as the sun rose over the boats, people praying in lots of ways, pouring water over their heads, burning incense, doing yoga, lots of beggars. We went along a street, people sitting on sacks being given ladlefuls of green mushy food on newspaper plates, they eat with their fingers, right hand only. Others sat behind baskets of vegetables, cabbages, radishes, potatoes, holding out their dark dirty hands. People are desperate to sell something – hand massage – they grab your hand as you pass, haircut? Some are having their heads shaved, long hair falling to the ground. People will do anything. Some guy covered in white paint, looks like a Westerner, swinging a candle-holder all lit, dancing, standing on one leg in the dawn.

On the same morning walk I made a note of seeing marigold vendors, beggars, outdoor barbers, copulating monkeys, washermen and washerwomen, holymen, fishermen, conmen, goats, cows and water buffalos, corpses on funeral fires, people bathing, and boys playing cricket.

There are more than eighty ghats stretching perhaps for a mile along the river bank. They are stone embankments with steps leading down to the river and are designated either for bathing or cremation. At the bathing ghats pilgrims perform ritual ablutions, ducking their heads and scooping up palmfulls of water, holding them up to the sky and muttering prayers. At the burning ghats corpses are brought down on decorated biers and carried several times around a great pile of wood before cremation. There is a constant traffic of corpses and mourners and timber being carried onto the ghats. Behind the ghats are temples and shrines, hotels and cheap accommodation for pilgrims.

We spent our few days walking up and down the river bank,

being asked a thousand times if we wanted a boat ride and hassled by beggars and vendors of postcards. Other people, often children, sold little leaf boats bearing candles and offerings to be set on the water. We took a ride in one of the rowing boats two or three times, crossing the river to look at the muddy, sandy beach on the far shore, looking at the city from the water, or simply when we were tired to be ferried back to our hotel.

Varanasi is India at its best and worst, at its most extraordinary and colourful and at its dirtiest. There is no end of hustle and bustle and hassle. After a few days we had had enough. We went to the station and got a train towards the border with Nepal. We loved and, it must be said, hated India but we would never regret having spent time there. We decided that we would not be coming back again.

Some weeks later we were staying by the lake in Pokhara and still had a little time left before catching our flight home via Delhi. I suppose we began to get bored. We went back to India and stayed by the Ganges again, but this time alongside a very different stretch of the river.

My blog post for March 6th, 2010:

Rishikesh. We got here last night after a 15 hour journey from Kathmandu which included the dodgiest taxi ride in the dark that you can imagine. We were forced off the road twice by oncoming cars. Loads of vehicles had no lights at all. There were lots of water-buffalo towing cart-loads of sugar cane to the distilleries, camels looming, unlit, out of the dark, huge lorries and overloaded buses and more. But now we're here and it's fun as Hindu holy places tend to be. There are Sadhus and lots of devout but jolly Indian pilgrims, some tourists and some Western holy-hippies. The Indian tourists stare at us and we try not to stare back. The Ganges comes out of the mountains and onto the plains right here in front of our eyes. People bathe and shiver in the glacier-melt-blue cold water and scatter petals and feed monkeys and so on...

On the edge of Rishikesh a suspension footbridge called Lakshman Jhula takes you across the river to a small area of houses and temples and cheap hotels squashed between the river and a steep slope clad in jungle. We stayed here, in a simple guesthouse right on the river bank. Upstream there were a few buildings and then only the hills, the trees and the river rushing among rocks and sandbanks. Downstream we could see a large multi-storey temple that looked like it was built in the sixties or seventies, other smaller temples, and the bridge, busy with pilgrims, a few tourists, one or two motorbikes, some monkeys and the occasional cow. Opposite us the bank was steep and sandy. A hermit or holy man lived there in a rough shelter built against a boulder. A tattered flag by his hovel was blown downstream in the early mornings as the wind came off the hills; then the wind changed direction and the flag flew the other way for the rest of the day.

We found that we could explore up the river and find places to swim. The river was powerful but there were little beaches and small areas of still water among the rocks. Locals had painted signs in English explaining that the half-naked foreigners sunbathing and swimming in their holy river were a source of deep offence. On the other hand young men would come out from town on motorbikes to stare at the Western women. We tried to go a little further upstream away from other people.

The first time we went to swim there I found that my illness made it too difficult to get changed; I didn't have enough control of my arms and legs. It was a hot afternoon and I wanted to swim like everyone else. It was the first time this had happened to me and I felt bitter. But the next time we were there I found that I could get my clothes off. That's how it is with Parkinson's; you can do things but not necessarily right now. You have to be patient.

We explored further upstream one day searching for a waterfall on a tributary of the river. We talked to a charming woman who came originally from south India but lived in Canada. She had trained as a dentist but had moved into alternative therapies. She sounded so convincing for a while but I never did follow her advice for the treatment of my illness. It involved drinking my own urine. *It is a gift from God*, she said. Credulity is not one of my strong points.

There are a great number of beggars in Rishikesh. Our idea about people poor enough and desperate enough to spend their days at the side of the road with their hands out is very simple. We give them money. Still it was difficult to carry enough small change to get us through the day and we couldn't give to everyone. But one morning we were walking along a shady path under the trees in a quiet area downstream of our accommodation and we met a personable young man with only one leg. We sat down with him and listened to his story. He had been involved in an accident and was now unable to find work. He explained that he was saving up for an artificial limb and told us how much it would cost. We, of course, handed him some money, the equivalent of five pounds or so. Five pounds! That's very big money in India. We realised afterwards that he only needed to meet people like us two or three times a week to live quite comfortably. He was on to a good thing and I think he was quite unlikely to ever buy that new leg. It would be the loss of his livelihood.

We took a trip from Rishikesh to Mussoorie and stayed a couple of nights. Mussoorie is an old hill station and as such is pretty weird. It's a town developed by the British colonial rulers as somewhere to escape from the heat of the plains. The main promenade is known, to this day, as the Mall. It is said that there were signs along the Mall bearing the words *Indians and Dogs not Allowed* during British rule. Now it's not a place that is attractive to foreigners like us but is very popular with Indian tourists and so, and this is the weird twist, all the shop signs are in English. More than that, and weirder, is the fact that cafés sell the most appalling English food. We had the worst sausage, egg and chips imaginable.

We walked around looking at the hazy views of the distant Himalayas and at the amusement arcades and souvenir shops. We stopped to watch a march of young Tibetan women. There is a small expatriate Tibetan community here and in other towns nearby and it turned out to be *Fifty-first National Tibetan Women Uprising Day*. I got my camera out but it seemed wrong to take a picture. This was serious. The women were mostly sturdy teenage school-girls, impassioned, chanting slogans in English and Hindi, *China, out of Tibet, China, out of Tibet*. Both Flic and I were moved in a way I can't explain. Later on we wandered into an aquarium and then through the exit into the foyer of a large restaurant in the same building. The marchers came up and stopped outside, facing us as we looked out of the window. They were chanting again, looking stern, almost angry. It took us a moment to understand. The shouts grew louder and I realised that we were standing in the entrance of a Chinese restaurant. We left, quite quickly, and by another door.

We stayed in Mussoorie in a cheap hotel; a timber building with a corrugated tin roof, like many of the buildings there. After we had moved from our lilac and chocolate coloured room to another with similar paintwork but no mouse nest in the wardrobe we had an encounter with a monkey. Flic had returned from the local bookshop with a book entitled *Being Indian*. She told me that she had slipped quietly past a couple of monkeys on the balcony and I was concerned that I had left my shoes out there. We opened the door and there were my two shoes, one where I had left it, the other in the hand of a small brown monkey standing at the end of the balcony. I acted swiftly, grabbing Flic's new book out of her hand and throwing it at the monkey. He dropped the shoe and made off up onto the roof with the book. It took some time to get it back. The guys running the hotel chased around on the roof for a while and eventually found the book abandoned on the terrace at the other side of the hotel. I guess the monkey had read that one before.

We took a bus out to Kempty Falls. Flic wrote: I wanted to go on a tour bus to some waterfalls. Richard warned me that it would be awful but I still wanted to go. Richard felt very ill but he came on the bus with me. The waterfalls were ruined in an Indian way. There was concrete everywhere, lots of shops and disco music. I remember the bathing and boating pools, the later complete with plastic swan-shaped pedalo boats, and also the concrete dinosaurs and the disco music, played loud enough to be heard over the sound of gushing water. We walked down and down away from the crowds in an effort to find somewhere quiet to swim on our own. We got away from the people but not from the rubbish. It was, as I predicted, awful. But the natural beauty was so comprehensively wrecked that it was interesting and almost fun. The Indians leaping about like ten year olds in the water were certainly joyful and daft in a way that adults in other parts of the world can't match. And there were other waterfalls around Rishikesh that weren't spoiled. We went to one of them another day.

On our way to Rishikesh in the dark Flic and I had been on the last leg of a very long journey. We were very tired and dropped off to sleep from time to time. Late at night we dreamed that we were passing along the edge of a town so festooned with coloured lights as to be beyond belief or imagination. If there was a city of one hundred funfairs this was it, here, in India, on the road to Rishikesh, in our dream. *How unusual*, I hear you say, *that two people should dream the same dream.*

Simultaneously! I admit that it seems unlikely but there can be no other explanation. Imagine the Blackpool lights ten times over, no a dozen times, twenty times over. Could there really be such a place on the plains of north India?

Well, okay, there is Haridwar, the seventh most holy place in Hinduism, and the gaudiest, glitziest holy place in the world's gaudiest, glitziest religion. The place where on January 14th, over a million pilgrims bathed in the Ganges at the start of the three month long bathing festival, the Kumbh Mela. Perhaps that was it. When we got back from Mussoorie the pilgrims from Haridwar were visiting nearby Rishikesh in increasing numbers as we got close to another of the big-time auspicious bathing days when the river would turn to nectar.

We decided to go to Haridwar, but not on the busiest day. It was March by now and India was getting hotter and hotter. The thought of those crowds in that heat was too much. Meanwhile Rishikesh was getting more pilgrims. They came from all over India and we could recognise some of them by their dress. There were certainly some from places in Rajasthan that we had visited. And there were others dark enough to be from south India and of a caste that traditionally wore red baseball caps. Some of the pilgrims went barefoot. Some of them carried their belongings on their heads. They were happy people, seriously devout but having a good time too. They didn't mind when Flic asked if she could take their pictures.

On the day before the big-time bathing day we visited Haridwar. The river there is much wider and faster flowing and somewhat canalised. It doesn't have the natural feel of Rishikesh or Varanasi. Along the concrete banks and across the bridges chains hang into the water for people to catch onto if they get carried away by the current. On the way into town we passed huge billboards advertising a host of different gurus. We went to see the enormous marquees where they speak to the faithful and the fields of tents put up to accommodate everybody. We saw lots of police and stewards in hi-vis jackets, lots of devout pilgrims, of course, and quite a few Sadhus in orange and saffron robes. Imagine a dozen big evangelical revivalist meetings taking place in a tacky holiday resort but with more people and more colour and more heat. That's Haridwar. We didn't stay very long.

On one of our last mornings in Rishikesh we set off to visit the ashram of Maharishi Mahesh Yogi where the Beatles stayed in 1968. We walked past the multi-tiered concrete temple with its pilgrims pacing around the balconies ringing bells, lighting candles and saying prayers. We walked past the sculptures of six-armed figures standing on crocodiles and black faced, tongue-rotting, cross-eyed squat monsters, as Flic described them, adding the words, how can people worship these? We walked on past cripples and beggars and pilgrims and a Western woman trying to befriend a rather large monkey. We carried on past the tourist shops and the bathing ghats and the little corrugated tin shacks on the edge of town.

Eventually we came to the place where the Ganges broadens out and flows shallow among rocks and over pebbles. On one bank the land rose gently to the main new part of town. On the other bank was a steep hillside covered in sub-tropical forest, almost jungle. At the very edge of this wilderness we found the derelict ashram, fenced off with netting and barbed wire. We discovered a place where we could scramble over the fence and went in to explore.

The main buildings were flat-roofed constructions of concrete and brick with zigzag balustrades along the balconies and yellow paint peeling off crumbling plaster. It looked like a 1960s holiday camp, abandoned long ago and overgrown with trees and flowering shrubs and creepers (in fact Ringo Star had described it at the time as a spiritual Butlins). Dotted around and about were little two-storey circular concrete buildings faced with pebbles. They looked like tacky copies of the stone beehive huts of monastic settlements on the west coast of Ireland. There were monkeys in the trees, exotic insects in the air, and through gaps in the vegetation we could see the blue-grey water of the Ganges flowing past below us. The place was seedy, defunct, atmospheric and almost beautiful. We clambered about and explored for quite a while. I liked it there.

I tried to imagine it as it had been, with the charismatic guru casting his spell over rich, spaced out rock stars and celebrities. Lennon, McCartney and George Harrison with their acoustic guitars, being taught to fingerpick by Donovan, and coming up with songs that would eventually appear on the White Album and Abbey Road. Songs with titles like, *Why Don't We Do it in the Road, Sexy Sadie and Everybody's Got Something to Hide Except Me and my Monkey.*

R is for Rotterdam
(The Netherlands)

I was twenty-one years old and travelling back from Israel, where I had stayed on a kibbutz. I had been out there for four months, mostly working on the banana plantations. I had found myself a girlfriend there (or maybe she found me) and now I stopped off and stayed with her in her home town, Rotterdam. She had left Israel a couple of weeks before me and was now living at home with her parents and working in a baker's shop. She wasn't really my kind of girlfriend, Rotterdam wasn't my kind of town, and I don't think her parents liked me. I was there for two weeks I think and I had to amuse myself while she was at work. *Don't bore yourself*, her little sister said; making the verb reflexive and putting the responsibility on me.

I tried not to bore myself. I borrowed a bicycle, explored the town and some local countryside, and fell off three times. Once when the wheel slipped in between the tram lines. Then again when a sudden gust of wind came out through a gap in the buildings and caught me unaware. And then I forgot that you had to back pedal to brake and tumbled off the edge of a dyke.

It was late September and the beginning of autumn. I loved the feel of the westerly wind on my face.

19

A Short Intermission

My sister, Pam, once said of me: *Richard lives like there is no tomorrow.* Well, as it happens, there is no tomorrow. My future outlook is bleak and I should do what I can now. But the truth is that I have always been a cautious man and her words were way off the mark. What she was referring to was my tendency to change my job from time to time and not follow a career path. I have had, it must be said, a quite a few over the years. I would like to tell you about some of them.

One of my first jobs was in a builder's merchants with the unlikely name of *Gridley Miskin*. I was a forklift truck driver of the dreamy, contemplative type. I always carried a classic novel in the pocket of my donkey jacket and when I had the yard tidy I would park up behind a huge stack of bricks and read Zola or Hardy or DH Lawrence. Once I turned the truck over by carrying too big a load too high. I jumped clear but the truck was damaged. They didn't give me the sack.

Later on I gardened for the rich and famous in my home town, Weybridge, in Surrey, for a while. I met Cliff Richard's dog but failed to recognise the famous man on the other end of the lead. I trimmed the roses and swam in the pool of the comedian, the late Dick Emery, and also tidied the gardens of two of his ex-wives (I believe he married five times). And when I worked for the National Trust at a landscape garden nearby, my boss (who was getting on a bit) told me that he had to eject a young long-haired man who wouldn't leave at closing time. *Don't you know who I am?* the man had asked, good naturedly. *I didn't know him from Adam,* my boss told me. *George something, Harris was it, Harrison, I don't know. Have you heard of someone called George Harrison?* I can't remember what I said in reply.

Quite early on in my career I achieved one ambition – that of being paid to go for a walk in the countryside. On a mixed farm in Sussex where I worked my first job of the day was to walk around the fields checking that the livestock, the cattle and sheep, were OK. Four legs pointing at the ground, good; four legs pointing at the sky, bad – as George Orwell might have put it. My sister, Margaret, visited at lambing time and was amused to see me carrying a shepherd's crook. *You look like something out of a nativity play she said.*

Some of my farm worker memories are not so happy. One cold March I did a month of night shifts as a lambing assistant on a farm here in west Wales. The farmer was a brutal Englishman who had a fascination for breeding animals but a particularly unsentimental attitude towards them. If I remember rightly he ran over one of his dogs when it wouldn't get out of the way quickly enough and then had to shoot it. He didn't seem upset. In the evenings I would drive an old Land Rover up to some fields on the hill to check the mountain ewes that were lambing out of doors. On the way I often stopped at a telephone box to phone my girlfriend who lived in Hereford. I remember snow blowing in and around my feet where a window pane was broken at the bottom of the door and I remember the particularly mournful sound of a telephone ringing far away in an empty room. Empty, I might add, because she was out having fun with another young man.

So much for country farms; I have also worked on a so-called *city farm* in Kentish Town, London. It was really a community project and my job title was stockman/youth worker. I was in charge of one cow, seven goats, four sheep, two pigs, a goose called Maverick and shed full of chickens. I got on well with local kids and took school groups around. And I got most of the animals pregnant, not personally I might say, but by taking the goats and sheep to be *served* (that's the farming euphemism) and by getting the AI (artificial insemination) man in for Ermintrude the cow.

It was a strange thing for me to live there, in the city, far from any wild open spaces, but I used to go up onto Hampstead Heath at the weekend. I once took Ermintrude with me; she was very tame and was used to being led around on a horse's head-collar. We walked down to Gospel Oak, stood by the zebra crossing and waited for the traffic to stop. It was a summer's afternoon and a few people were sitting outside the pub. One or two of the guys looked at me and the cow and then down at their glasses to see if there was anything wrong with the beer. Something, somehow, was not quite right. I led Ermintrude up onto the heath and drew a few more stares. After a while a police car drove up one of the broad tarmac paths and stopped nearby. The policeman wound down his window and spoke to me: *Excuse me, sir. Is this your cow?*

My sister Pam has a memory of my time on the city farm. I had borrowed a billy goat for the purpose of *serving* my female goats; they would then have kids and give milk – the whole purpose of a dairy animal. I had to take the billy back to a farm in Essex and the only available vehicle was a minibus. I filled the vehicle with a random selection of people who were hanging about the city farm: one or two rough-or-ready folk who were doing community service with us having committed minor offences, drug dealing, housebreaking and so forth; and some kids (two-legged ones) who had been excluded from school for being too high spirited to conform to petty rules like not hitting the teacher. We turned up at my sister's house in nearby Bury St Edmunds without prior warning and piled into her kitchen. We left the billy goat in the minibus but after an hour in its company we smelled so strongly that we might as well have taken it into the house. She had been baking and was pleased to offer us tea and cake. A good time was had by all. Pam reminded me of it recently. *I've never forgotten that day*, she said.

My worst job ever? Possibly when I was staying on a kibbutz in the seventies. It was an agricultural community and I worked in the banana plantations on the flatlands below the settlement, in the orchards of apples and pears on the hills close by, and once in their commercial rose gardens. But sometimes I was required to work in the broiler houses, catching chickens and boxing them up to go to the slaughter house. We started at midnight, when the birds were asleep, and worked until we had caught the required number, something in the thousands, by which time it would be early morning. Then a breakfast of roast chicken, a freshen up in the kibbutz swimming pool, and bed – at the time when everyone else was getting up.

My best job ever? It was my last one, teaching practical skills at the agricultural college, then part of the university, in Aberystwyth. I worked with the legendary Bob Shaw (you might remember him being described as one part man, one part tree in chapter fifteen) and the multitalented Geoff Oldrid (fluent in French, Spanish and Scouse among other things), two of the best work companions you could hope for. We taught drystone walling, hedgelaying, fencing, a little carpentry and suchlike to enthusiastic (that's what we told them) countryside management students. In the fifth year of the job I was getting clumsy and awkward and I was limping badly at times. I struggled to hide the symptoms of what appeared to be a neurological disease but I really couldn't carry on. I was sad to leave that job but I thought that other opportunities would arise and that life moves on. And so it has, with both disappointments and achievements. There is a long list of things that I can no longer do and, believe me, being unable to work is not the worst one.

I have interrupted the story of our travels here because I felt the need for a break – a short intermission. It is hard for me to go from India to Peru in a couple of pages or a couple of hours. The truth is that eighteen months separated Rishikesh on the Ganges from Lima on the grey Pacific where we started our next big trip. We were here, at home in Wales, where we have lived for twenty-something years. This book makes my life and the life Flic and I have lived together sound like one long traveller's tale. But at the heart of our story is our time as a family here, in a small village in the countryside and close to the sea.

We moved here from Bristol where I had a poorly paid job digging holes and filling them in again; commuting from the city to the countryside and planting trees and doing other estate work. I applied for what must have been the worst paid job ever to be advertised in the *Guardian*: estate worker on nature reserves in west Wales for the then Nature Conservancy. Yes, digging holes and filling them in again but for less money but in a beautiful place. They gave me the job and we moved out here with a new baby making us a family of four. Our lives were disrupted by illness (you remember Flic's cancer in chapter thirteen) for seven months and then we settled in Wales properly.

It has been a wonderful place to live and a great place to bring up children. Some of my happiest memories ever are of family days out in, for example, the Rheidol valley or by the Mawddach estuary, and of weekends away in Pembrokeshire or the Lleyn peninsula.

And in the eighteen month intermission between great foreign adventures Flic and I, when my health has allowed it, have walked and cycled and sometimes paddled (in kayaks) very happily here. Recently it began to feel as if those days out were to become a thing of the past. I felt sad but at the same time very pleased that we had done so much while we still could. But last week (as I write this) with Flic's help, I was on my bike again and enjoying the landscape around Dolgellau, Barmouth and Cregennan Lakes. Phew...

Wales has been the place we come home to and that's been good. It seems different each time and, I have to admit, can look a little grey in winter if you have just returned from India. But it seems pretty good at other times of the year: in the summer of 2006 I returned from an unbearably hot New York, and later from an unbearably hot Barcelona, to a cool green Wales and it felt like the best place to be.

Coming home from abroad does make things look different. I remember arriving back in Britain after just a few weeks in Tanzania and Uganda and catching a bus from Heathrow to Bristol. I travelled down the M4 in the dark. There were just lights, hundreds of lights: white ones travelling in one direction and red ones in the other. No people. No people on foot or on bicycle or in little roadside shops. No people standing chatting or nursing babies or herding goats. No children playing. Only the lights hurtling along like some vision of the future: a science fiction movie in which the world has been taken over by machines.

And Wales after India is similarly unpeopled. Stand on a hill here and you can look over well-tended farmland, healthy-looking animals grazing, hedges trimmed, farmhouses and outbuildings dotted here and there. It all looks so organised but so empty. You might walk for some hours and see no-one, just a single tractor in the distance. Where have all the people gone?

I come from the south-east of England where people must be among the unfriendliest in the world. Speak to a random stranger in my home town and you get a look that says, *do I know you?* So rural community life in Wales seems particularly good. I am, it must be said, a bit of an outsider here as I have been everywhere else; it's part of my nature. Perhaps a little more so having tried to learn the language and failed. And I am aware of the cultural differences between the English and the

Welsh. Here's something, for example, that I find strange. The new summit building on Snowdon is engraved with the words of the distinguished poet Gwyn Thomas:

O'n cwmpas ni y mae camp a gwae hen, hen genedl.

All around us are the grandeur and the anguish of an old, old nation.

To me, as an outsider, this is difficult to understand. They are curious words to use to describe one's country. Grandeur I'm fine with, it's the combination of age and anguish that gets to me. I can think quite easily of twenty-five other nations (they are listed in this book) who would never chose those words to describe themselves. Then I think some more and guess that Thomas's anguish is about the continuing loss of the Welsh language, *yr hen iaith*, and the culture that goes with it. I can try to imagine, but can never really understand, the enormity of this loss as experienced by some Welsh people. There are only a few times when I have had just a little insight into how this feels.

I remember a tiny incident that I experienced some years ago in the doctor's waiting room. A local man was speaking quietly to the receptionist, a rather loud, middle-class English woman who had recently moved to the area. *Dafydd Williams*, she said, *Dafydd, what a strange name, how do you spell that?* Poor Mr Williams spelled out for her one of the most widely used Welsh Christian names. *Can't find your records at all*, she continued, *have you just moved in?* The man replied with quiet exasperation, *I have lived here all my life*. I could imagine him muttering under his breath the words *bloody English* and I sympathised. He was feeling ill and it was not a good time to experience his language, culture and sense of community disappearing from underneath his feet.

The very nice man who tunes our piano described his first

meeting as a local councillor and his dismay at finding that he was obliged to speak English, not Welsh, the language in which he best expressed himself and which was the first language of his family, friends and the community he grew up in. I didn't tell him that I had recently heard an Englishman say, *the Welsh language, they only speak it to be bloody minded.* Of course, as the Italians speak Italian and the French speak French, only to be bloody minded. Enough said.

I must admit that I sometimes find Welsh culture more inclined to look inward and to the past than that of the countries that I have recently visited. I prefer to look to the future, towards change and renewal. But I'm happy here in Wales. There's nowhere else I would rather be.

S is for Skopje (Macedonia)

Iwas twenty-one years old and travelling to Israel to work on a kibbutz. I didn't know anything about the country, I just wanted to stay abroad for a while. I could have flown all the way but then I would have been certain about arriving at my destination. I preferred uncertainty, the possibility of the unexpected, so I decided to hitch to Athens and get a boat or plane from there. I was in a country then called Yugoslavia, hitching from the coast to Skopia, as it was called then, and on to Greece. But the area was too beautiful and I had to stop and spend a day walking in the hills. Then I set out from the small town where I had stayed the night and started walking down a road signposted for Skopia.

I intended to hitch but there was almost no traffic at all. I walked and hoped and was passed by the occasional donkey or motorbike. The road surface deteriorated as it looped up into the mountains. Still no traffic. I guessed then that this was not the main road or was an old road that had been replaced by a new one. Then a car came around the bend and stopped. It was being driven by a German woman determined to travel on the most minor roads from her country to a destination in Greece. She was very surprised to see me on that road and she gave me a lift.

We wound up into the mountains through a wild, little-inhabited landscape, high enough for there to be patches of snow on the ground even though it was April. Then down to Skopia where people were celebrating the birthday of President Tito. I think they had to; he was that sort of president. Someone said that the country would go to pieces when he died. There would be bloodshed. I couldn't understand it. It seemed peaceable enough to me.

20

A Very Short Story

No-one can say that we're not decisive. I believe that we decided never to go back to India a few times and changed our minds; one time returning within weeks. But that's India for you. Then we decided that we wouldn't be able to travel again; my health was far too variable. And as for South America, we thought about it more than once and decided, more than once, not to go there. Then we booked return flights to Lima, in Peru, with the intention of seeing some of that country and a little of Ecuador and maybe Bolivia. We were to be away for fourteen weeks. *And why South America?* I hear you ask. Well, we liked to tell our stay-at-home friends that we were stuck in a rut, having been to the Indian sub-continent three times in a row. We needed a change.

Reasons for not going to South America:
- a) too much crime, some of it violent – what if my medication got stolen?
- b) we couldn't speak Spanish
- c) flights cost a fortune
- d) my health was getting worse

Action to be taken:
- a) leave some spare tablets at the first place we stay and carry two weeks' worth in zipped pocket at all times
- b) learn Spanish
- c) spend money
- d) it's now or never – go to South America ASAP.

From my blog for Saturday, 3rd September, 2011:

8.30 in the morning, at Casa Ana, a friendly damp guest house in a cold grey dirty city. Lima is grim but we are excited and happy somehow because we are off again on an adventure. And because we had a good flight yesterday.

It took about 26 hours from Casa Catherine [Flic's mum's house] to Casa Ana – Pickwick to Heathrow to Sao Paulo to Lima. The last bit was brilliant. We flew right over the continent. First there was countryside: irregular patterns of woods and fields and scattered settlements, a bit more like Sussex than Brazil. Then, after a sleep, we looked down on huge square clearings in the forest, regrowth or primary forest, I don't know. Then, much later, steep hills turning Into snow-capped mountains – the Andes. And then the sea, much sooner than we expected and so close to the mountains. But no, there's a further shore and we realise that it's a very big lake, hundreds of miles long – El Lago Titicaca. More mountains then a hilly high-altitude desert, uninhabited, uninhabitable, seemingly endless. Then a blanket of cloud like a sea against a shore with the real sea, the Pacific, underneath. And Lima.

The worst thing about Lima is the grey sky. The city lies under thick, low, unbroken cloud for eight months of the year. The second to worst thing is the crime. And the city is grim and grimy and heavily polluted and not very friendly. It doesn't have really fine architecture or museums. It does have the parks, gardens and beaches of Miraflores but we stayed in a very ordinary, dull area called Breña. Lima was just a way into what turned out to be the most beautiful country I have been to. And while it's my least favourite city in the world we did have a few interesting moments there.

Just down the street from Casa Ana we asked for a café and were taken into a room in an ordinary building where some women sat round a table making sandwiches. They gave us pork and omelette sandwiches with tea. Flic reported:

a beautiful young man with high cheekbones and a wide smile tried out his English on us and we tried out our Spanish. We didn't get very far. It turned out to be a co-operative which had a small shop and a statue and an ice-cream box and maybe other businesses. They were so friendly and interested in us. The young man asked us why were we in Lima? It was a hard question to answer.

Then I had an idea of going to a suburban seaside destination called *La Punta*. A few taxi drivers refused to take us there but eventually one agreed. It was a pleasant enough middle-class area on the edge of a desperately poor and crime-ridden district called Callao. We wandered along the shore and took a ride out in a little wooden boat with an outboard motor. We passed among some very expensive yachts and saw pelicans on a breakwater. That was it. Then we tried to get back to Casa Ana. We couldn't find a bus and when we asked a taxi driver he took us to a police station. A policeman then came on the bus with us into Callao where we should change busses to get to our destination. He was a very gentle, friendly guy and as we waited for our next bus he pointed out various rough-looking youths that came by and told us how dangerous they were. He seemed nervous. After a while the right bus pulled up we said goodbye to him. I imagined that he too might have asked the same question. Why were we there?

We got out of Lima the next day riding on an immensely comfortable double decker bus in the upstairs seats above the driver. I've mentioned this bus journey before. It was awful and wonderful in parts. It took us an hour to get out of Lima and then we travelled up the coast, a huge bleak ocean on one side of us and a vast desert on the other. Meanwhile the

Australian couple next to us bickered and various unpleasant movies were shown on a screen above our heads. We turned inland and the landscape became lumpy and green and then hilly and greener and then, to the soundtrack of foul swearing from the movie being shown, we travelled across immense plains between snow-covered mountains and eventually arrived in Huaraz.

We stayed at *Jo's Place*, Jo being an expatriate Englishman who married a local woman. I guess I had better quote from Flic's journal on our first morning there:

Now a beautiful sunny morning, 8.20. At 6.30 when we got up it was freezing. The mountains were silhouetted by the early morning sky and framed in the arched windows. This room is square and blue with black beams and shiny brown floor. It's the highest room in the hotel and there's a spiral staircase up from the kitchen area below. Hundreds of cockerels crowed in the dawn. I've got a hint of altitude headache and had very lucid dreams.

The lock on our door doesn't work well so we've had to climb in through the sliding window. We managed to stay up 'til 11pm making love and going on the balcony to smoke and talk. Richard feels very ill, backache from carrying his pack. He can't sort out the sheets and blankets and I heard him crying in the night. I feel so sorry for him but I think he's really brave doing all this. If we had stayed at home it would have been worse, we have had an exciting time already. I am covered in bruises from climbing in and out of the window.

The town of Huaraz was almost entirely destroyed, with much loss of life, by an earthquake in 1970 and now consists of low, modern, ugly, brick and concrete buildings laid out in a grid pattern of dirty streets. But we were there for the surrounding mountains, the *Cordillera Blanca*. On our first morning Jo suggested a route for a short walk that would get us acclimatised to the altitude. *But there's one thing I have to tell you*, he said. *I have to say this. Sometimes people get robbed at gunpoint up there. They're not bad guys, the robbers – once they gave someone some money back when he complained that he didn't have enough for a beer. But I have to tell you...*

We set off through the streets of Huaraz towards the cemetery from which a path winds up onto the hill where there stands a huge, blue, concrete cross. The town wasn't without interest; there were plenty of *campesinos* in town – the country people who are of native American blood and who speak Quechua (pronounced *ketchwa*) as their first language.

We saw women, both young and old, dressed in colourful, knee-length skirts over colourful layers of petticoats over leggings, with more brightly coloured layers above. They wore a sort of trilby hat but with an extended crown, like a stovepipe, set at a jaunty angle. And they wore a piece of cloth strapped around them so that it hung over one shoulder; it looked decorative but no, one young woman carried a baby in it. And then, further down the street an older woman had no baby but a gas cylinder on her back. These *campesinas* were extraordinary looking but not good looking. Not to us at least, with their squat sturdy bodies under extraordinary clothes. But the younger ones walked with their heads held high; *they* knew they looked good.

The *campesinos* were noticeable but actually a minority. Most people there were dressed in ordinary dull clothes. And everybody was short and stocky and had thick black hair. We must have looked strange to them but no-one interacted with us; they were a reserved people.

I never did get my bearings in Huaraz and I certainly didn't that first morning. We zigzagged back and forth when the streets didn't go in our direction. The sun came out from between the clouds after a while but had climbed so steeply that it didn't give much indication of north and south (close to the equator in September the sun doesn't incline either way but goes straight overhead). When we came to an intersection of wider streets we could see the hills around. They were steep but not high and were covered in grey-brown parched grasslands with patches of pine forest. Only in one direction could we see snow covered peaks. And in the opposite direction we could see the big cross on the hill that we intended to climb. It wasn't getting any closer.

I didn't feel well and I was limping badly, my right leg dragging as I walked. It was also beginning to get very hot. And, unsurprisingly, the thought of setting out towards the possibility of robbery at gunpoint didn't help. We took maybe an hour to walk across town and then I had had enough. We struggled back, getting very lost on the way.

The next day we set out early and took a taxi across town, thinking we would be on the hill before the robbers had got out of bed. I wrote in my blog: *Fabulous walk this morning. Up to the big cross above the town and then on to high pastures where we saw great views of the mountains with snowy wastes and glaciers. Closer to us some wildlife we'd never seen before including a black humming bird and some big grasshoppers that changed colour when they moved onto different vegetation. On our way down we met a man with five cows, a few sheep, a couple of donkeys (as well as the one he was riding) and a big smile. We dropped in on the market in town that sells cow's hooves and pig's heads and various unidentifiable animal parts as well as guinea pigs both live and dead (skinned) among other things.*

I chose not to describe the aborted trip of the day before. But here's a little more of Huaraz from the blog: *We go on day trips (and longer trips) to the mountains but we are staying in town. It's a fascinating place. I saw a man cycling down our road with a basket of freshly harvested green barley and wild flowers in front of him this morning. And just now we saw women selling bundles of something like clover and an old lady in traditional dress (very colourful, weird hat, etc) carrying green barley on her back. It must be donkey fodder. Flic wanted to buy vegetables to cook for this evening but the stuff sold on the street is unrecognisable – great long hard bean pods, for example. And we realise that we can't work out what is being sold to feed humans and what is for animals. Yes, it's nice and different here. Many women in traditional dress. More street dogs than you can imagine. One or two people doing their washing in the river. Marching bands and fireworks all the time. And a strange lunch.*

We went into a sort of café across the road, walked through to the covered space at the back and found a cock-fighting ring. The young waiter enthusiastically invited us to tonight's fights, starting at six o'clock. We really couldn't understand the menu or the waiter but I ordered a plate of rice with plantains and fried eggs and a plate of spicy raw fish on beans. Flic had a harder time ordering. After much deliberation she agreed with what the waiter suggested – and a had a good helping of 'nothing for me I'm not hungry thank-you'. It took some time for us to realise.

One of our walks took us up to a very high pasture where we were accompanied by a dog for a while and then met an old woman who wanted to talk with us. She was dressed in purples and red but with a sort of man's style almost-cowboy hat. She seemed cheerful but looked poor enough to have slept in her clothes. All bar two of her front teeth were missing. Her limited Spanish included much repetition of *regalame*, which I took to mean *give me a present*. We gave her a cheese sandwich which she ate straight away and enthusiastically. Our impression of Peru was that people weren't too badly off except at the margins, which in this case meant at high altitude.

Another day walk took us up to 15,000 ft and the much visited Laguna 69 where a sliver of a waterfall fell over rocks into a pale blue glacial meltwater lake. The young couple walking up the path behind us were speaking Hebrew but it included words that I recognised. I stopped and turned to the guy. *Did you just say 'Walton on Thames'*, I asked – not the question you would expect to ask of a young Israeli walking high in the Andes. But yes, some of his family lived in suburban Surrey where I was brought up.

The centrepiece of our stay in Huaraz was the Santa Cruz trek, a four day walk in the mountains that involved camping and a lot of preparation. Jo's Place, as you might imagine, was set up for backpacking, mountain-walking visitors and he introduced us to a young woman who could help us prepare for the trek. Lena was around twenty years old, outgoing, knowledgeable and a great help to us. She didn't speak Quechua and wasn't so squat and solid looking as the locals but was of some native South American background. I thought she looked Nepalese and was also, I've got to say it, moderately gorgeous. She arranged for an *arriero*, a donkey driver, to come with us and carry our equipment. On the day before we set off she spent a lot of time helping Flic to prepare:

Had an amazing morning shopping at the mercado, 60 bread rolls. The market half indoors and half outdoors. Villagers come to town to sell: bags of live guinea pigs, sacks of hens and ducks all alive, eggs cheese parsley potatoes corn, avocados, strawberries, roast pigs and calves and fruit. It was good fun going with Lena and coming back in a motocarro with all our supplies. I bought some roast piglet and small potatoes and salad to have for lunch.

After lunch Lena and I put the tent up and got things ready – pans, sleeping bags, mats, mugs, plates *etc*. Richard couldn't help with anything, he is feeling so ill today. He keeps going to sleep and hoping to feel better then he wakes up but not improving. He's worrying but he does feel OK sometimes so let's hope it's the next four days.

The next morning we set off at six to travel by taxi to

Cashapampa where Lena would introduce us to our *arriero* and we would begin the trek. On the way she pointed out a place called Yungay, where, in the 1970 earthquake, 20,000 people were killed when a landslide of rock, snow and ice destroyed the town. Only ninety-two people escaped death – they were at the cemetery on a hill above the town when it happened.

The taxi ride took three hours, much of it on very rough dirt tracks, and we stopped halfway to get some breakfast. It was our first of many morning drinks of a sort of liquid porridge called quinoa, properly pronounced *kinwa*. After driving up and up on rougher and rougher tracks we stopped at the house of the man who was to be our *arriero*, Pedro. He was, as Flic said, an amazingly nice man. Smiley red brown face, big hat, lovely dog. He spoke no English so we had to use our feeble Spanish. Fortunately Flic was talking to his wife, not to him, when she said *estoy caliente*, which means *I feel horny*, not *I am hot*, as she intended.

Pedro was sixty-one years old and had nine children. He lived in a handsome adobe house on a small-holding surrounded by pastures and trees with a mountain stream flowing by. It looked like a healthy lifestyle in beautiful surroundings. And Pedro had about him a calm wisdom you would expect from someone in such a place. I wrote in my blog that he was one of the nicest men I have ever met – very kind, gentle and helpful. He was aware of my difficulties and quite simply took it upon himself to do everything he could to help. He would be ahead of us on the trail with his two donkeys and companionable dog and would set up camp and prepare food in advance of our arrival. He did much more than we asked of him and did it as if it was a noble calling; with not a hint of subservience but with a lot of kindness.

From my blog: *I can't begin to describe the strange vegetation, the lakes and glaciers, the waterfalls, the high peaks, snowfields, and the very special people we met along the way.*

I think the truth is that I couldn't describe much of the landscape because we couldn't see it very well for the mist and low clouds and rain that got in our way. But I can describe two of the people. We met Pascal and Christa in a valley bottom campsite in the rain. Our cooker wasn't working and Pedro had to borrow the use of theirs. Besides that he was a friend of their *arriero*, Amador.

Pascal and Christa were from Switzerland. He was a slim, dark man with a modest manner. Christa was blonde, less slim, ebullient, and friendly. They were in the middle of a sailing trip back and forth and around the world. I think they had been away six years when we met them. Pascal had been a mountain guide but was unable to work at his profession because of injuries sustained in a parachuting accident. He had jumped off a mountain and his parachute hadn't opened properly. He'd fallen a long way and was buried in the snow for five hours before being found. He never much liked the cold after that and with his new partner, Christa, took to sailing around the tropical seas, as you do under such circumstances. They had left their boat in the Caribbean somewhere and travelled up the Amazon into Peru and the Andes while waiting out the hurricane season.

I check out their website now (three years later) and find that they have quit sailing, sold their boat, and settled in Andalucía. Christa describes their meeting with us: *Il a bien du mérite Richard (55 ans) qui depuis 6 ans souffre de la maladie du Parkinson. Avant que sa maladie ne dégénère complètement, il profite, en compagnie de sa femme Phill, de faire un maximum de trekking. Quel courage et quel lucidité !* I don't know much about *courage* and *lucidité* but then again I don't remember a wife called Phill.

In Flic's diary I find that she had been subject to a moment's sexual harassment when she was walking alone on the trail; a man called out to her, *oyé bonita*, hello gorgeous. It made her day.

When we had completed the trek and I had given a tip to Pedro, *el mejor arriero del mundo*, the best *arriero* in the world, as I described him, we were left at the side of a road in a remote village waiting for the doubtful possibility of a bus. There were four of us, with Pascal and Christa, and we had an amazing amount of camping equipment. No bus came but Pascal negotiated a ride for us on a passing lorry. It was a big vehicle, which was a very good thing as there were already six people riding in the cab. Pascal rode on top and I wanted to but thought better of it.

The road out of the mountains was the most dangerous we had experienced; and remember that comes after many a bus journey in the Nepal Himalayas. There was a section of lorry-wide dirt track that hairpinned its way down an unrelentingly sheer slope for, I don't know, several thousand feet. There may have been thirty or forty hairpin bends and viewed from the cab the lorry appeared to put one wheel out over the edge of the road on each bend. It was too crazily, ridiculously dangerous to take in and beyond scary. It made us laugh. A couple of hours later we had descended far enough for it to get very warm. All the Peruvians in the cab had fallen asleep except the driver, who I thought gave every appearance of being about to drop off. I suggested to Christa, who spoke good Spanish, that she talked to him to keep him awake. She thought that seemed like a good idea. Eventually we arrived in a small town from where we caught a minibus back to Huaraz.

We stayed about two and half weeks in Huaraz and the mountains and despite the very great difficulties with my health we had some extraordinary adventures. There are more stories I could tell of our time there but I want to move on. We travelled from Huaraz to Trujillo and then to Lima by bus. Then we flew down to Arequipa and stayed around there for a while. On the way we had one difficult moment which I described enthusiastically in my blog:

Yesterday we got robbed. We were in the bus station at Trujillo and I was trying to keep an eye on our four bags. But a man kept tapping me on the shoulder saying 'taxi, taxi', and eventually I turned to him and simultaneously another man dropped a bunch of keys on the floor in front of Flic to distract her. I looked back to the bags and, sure enough, one had gone. Another man had taken my small bag while our backs were turned – the bag with most of my medication and other valuable things in it. This is a very short story. The whole incident took place in a few seconds. But wait – there's a tiny bit more. Yes, I ran out of the bus station onto the street, caught a glimpse of my bag in the hands of a guy walking briskly away, and grabbed it back off him. He let go straight away and all three guys melted away into the morning crowds. Hooray! It was so exciting.

I knew that bus station, with three different entrances onto the street, was dodgy and I was on the ball and quick and also lucky. The man chose to let go of my bag rather than risk further trouble; perhaps there were police around. I might have got a punch in the face or worse doing what I did. I know that I was tremendously happy to have rescued my bag and I walked back into the bus station with a big smile on my face. I felt like the conquering hero.

T is for Tel Aviv (Israel)

Tel-Aviv is wonderful city. The old port of Jaffa, where we stayed, is both decrepit and revamped, historical and modern, laid back and vibrant, artsy, earthy, picturesque and zany.

The people are friendly and helpful and there's a little buzz in the air, something that reminds you of New York. The place is multi-ethnic and multi-cultural. Road signs are in Hebrew, Arabic and English. In Jaffa you can hear the Muslim call to prayer five times a day and church bells ringing on a Sunday.

I felt at home in Tel Aviv. But an hour or so away is the border with the Palestinian Occupied Territories and down the coast is the Gaza Strip. The list of injustices against the Palestinian people since 1948 is too long to recount here.

We cycled along the seafront into Tel Aviv and saw the burnt out shell of the Dolphinarium nightclub where twenty-one teenagers on a night out were killed by a suicide bomber in 2001. There have been eight such attacks since the year 2000. That's the other side of a complicated story.

People all over the Middle East are warm hearted and fun to be with. They greet each other with a *salaam* or a *shalom* – words meaning *peace*.

21

At the End of the Road to Nowhere

I read Flic's journals for our South America trip and find three noticeable preoccupations. First there are the daily descriptions of the food we ate; that runs through all her diaries. And then there are her regular descriptions of my state of health. It makes me feel sad to think that her happiness was so much determined by my ups and downs. Did I say *ups and downs?* Think of a yo-yo on a roller coaster ride and you will get the idea. And think of a drizzly winter's day when it's getting dark at four o'clock and how hard it is to imagine at such a time that summer ever existed or will exist again. You try to imagine the sun still hot enough to lie on the grass in just a pair of shorts but outside it's cold and wet; you know summer will come back again, of course it will, but it's hard to really believe it. And so it is with my health; when I'm seriously disabled and in great discomfort (which happens for part of every day) I can't always imagine that in an hour or maybe in a day's time I will be fine. It seems so unlikely. So my emotional state is, to put it mildly, somewhat variable. Poor Flic has to cope with this when we travel. At home she can go out and forget about me for a while.

The third of her preoccupations in the journal is the frequent comparison of South America to India. In India there is endless hassle and often enough it's useful. Look lost and someone will help you find your way. Get tired and a tuk tuk or a taxi will magically pull up beside you. People are interested in foreigners and it's not just a question of separating you from your money. But in South America there is so much reserve. It's OK but sometimes you miss the interaction. And India is so profoundly foreign and colourful. Anywhere else in the world will be disappointing after India. We both felt that when we first arrived in Peru.

It was in Arequipa that Flic made a note of a young teenager (she didn't specify gender), wearing a t-shirt bearing the words, *Vida con no sexo es no vida (vida sin sexo* sounds better Spanish to me but that's what she wrote in her diary). *Life without sex is no life.* Yes, in South America sex officially exists. Maybe in some mountain communities it's a little hidden away but in most places you will see couples on the streets walking arm in arm or hand in hand or more. You will see a young woman wearing moderately sexy clothes and catching the eye of men in the street. It looks so normal and healthy and joyful and it contrasts with those buttoned-up parts of the world we have visited like India or Nepal or the Muslim countries.

Unfortunately the greatest difference between South America and Asia is the amount of crime in the former. We met a number of people who had been victims of crime and there were so many places where we were less relaxed than we might have been because of this. It's a shame.

Peru is big and empty and we travelled big distances by bus but also took an aeroplane a couple of times. After staying a night at Casa Ana in Lima we flew down to Arequipa in the south of Peru where we stayed off and on for between two and three weeks. It's a handsome town with many fine old buildings from the colonial period; one church, for instance, has the date 1698 carved into the stone-work. And the view from the rooftops takes in a vast open landscape dotted with snow-capped volcanoes. But our reason for being in that part of Peru was to go hiking in the famous Colca Canyon. The landscape around there has a very special arid, high altitude beauty that left a great impression on me.

In Arequipa you can see notices in travel agent's windows

advertising whole day tours to the Colca Canyon. We spent ten days in and around the canyon. That's the way we travel. Our first stop was Chivay, a small, high town three hours away from Arequipa. We got off the bus in a dusty square and followed a helpful man to his hotel. We had a little walk around the streets and then we got up on the roof to watch the light fade. We looked over the low roofs of the scruffy town and out at the bare hills. The light, at that altitude and in that dry atmosphere, was clearer than we ever experience at home. The mountains were lit sharply against a cold sky. As the sun descended the colours changed and shadows filled the hollows. Flic drew and painted, I took photos, and we both wished we hadn't left some of our warm clothes behind in Arequipa. Flic wrote: I feel very happy here, it's so beautiful and peaceful.

I found an internet place down the street and blogged: *High in the mountains again. Vast wild landscape, populated by scattered flocks of alpacas, llamas, sometimes a shepherd, sometimes delicate wild deer. Snow on the tops. Big yellow flowers like chrysanthemums on the cactus trees. In the small town of Chivay. Half the population, the female half, are in fancy dress, as they are every day – very, very colourful clothes and improbable hats. The men more ordinary but with cowboy hats. Amazing market, whole skinned alpacas hanging up. Everything more amazing and beautiful than words can tell. Happy us.*

And the next evening I recorded: *A walk in the countryside this morning. We saw a sort of giant humming bird, about the size of a starling, hovering with its beak in a flower. Later we found out it's called Picaflores gigante. We passed a woman with a baby on her back, knitting as she walked along the road. A boy herding a few donkeys and sheep on a bicycle (he was on the bicycle). A man ploughing a field with two little oxen – he wanted to talk to us in Quechua but got a better response when he changed to Spanish. We crossed a deep gorge on a suspension bridge and looked down on 'hanging tombs' constructed in the cliff-face. We saw Inca terraces and irrigation systems. Fields planted with broad beans. It was really hot but we saw fresh snow on the mountain tops. And more besides. And then we hitched a lift back to our hotel.*

The next day we caught the bus to Cabanaconde, about thirty-five miles away. In the morning I woke Flic at half past five and we walked through the town to the bus station arriving an hour early in the true Collins manner. So we wandered around and came across two bullfighting arenas, the new one inaccessible as it was surrounded by a corrugated iron fence, and the old one, built of stone and with a painting of a bull with a condor strapped to its back on one door. The heavily symbolic and ritualistic nature of the bullfight is sometimes taken a step further by the addition of condors, a practice that continues to this day in one or two remote parts of the Andes, but probably not here, in Chivay.

The bus was a local one with no tourists on board but just village people; the men wearing big brown cowboy hats and the women in very colourful skirts and aprons and embroidered hats. The time has come for me to say more about hats. The fact is that women in Peru and other Andean countries wear extraordinary hats. Here's a short list of some we came across (from my blog):

- *Huaraz*: the stove-pipe trilby, taller in the crown that is practicable on a crowded bus, worn at a jaunty angle
- *Chavin*: felt hats with plastic flowers affixed
- *Chavay*: sequined boaters
- *Puno*: bell-shaped bowlers with two tassels hanging over the left ear
- *Llachon*: four-cornered felt hats with bobbles
- *Cusco*: cream-coloured tapering top hats.

As you can tell, traditional (i.e. everyday) dress is subject to quite distinct local variation. Every woman among the *campesinos* will wear the local hat and the local style of clothes. It's a huge cultural difference from our society where people dress more or less individually. An anthropologist might explain it but I can't. Obviously the main factor is that people don't travel around much and distinct local cultures develop and carry on. And they are carrying on: young people as well as old wear traditional clothes. Did I say *people*? I should say *women*, because men dress in more modern, what we would call if we weren't so far west, *Western* clothes. It was the same in parts of India. You might guess from this that men in these societies are able to move around more and are less parochial in outlook. That might explain it.

Back on the bus now: we found seats but the aisle was full of people standing and what with dirt on the windows and the hats on the heads we could only get glimpses of a beautiful landscape. The road to Cabanaconde runs along the rim of the canyon, three or four thousand feet above the valley floor and with the mountains around several thousand feet higher again. The land has been formed by recent volcanic activity and the hills look burnt, as if made of cinders, which they more or less are. And the higher of these grey-brown-yellow-black mountains are topped by snow. Add some llamas and alpacas on the high slopes and Inca terraces lower down and condors flying overhead and you might imagine that quite a few tourists come here. They do. Halfway to Cabanaconde is a viewpoint called Cruz de la Condor, where it is possible to see condors drifting by on outstretched wings. It is a tourist honey pot visited by coach loads of day-trippers from Arequipa. The canyon itself is popular with trekkers and has simple backpacker accommodation in several of its villages. But somehow the vast landscapes and the rural way of life remains if not untouched then certainly unspoilt by tourism. And if you want to get away from your fellow tourists or fellow travellers you just have to take a little more time and step off the well worn path.

When we arrived in Cabanaconde we found a very cheap hotel and got ourselves up on the roof from where we could look down on the square, the sprawling little town, the dry fields around and the mountaintops beyond. Cabanaconde was a quiet, one horse, one llama, kind of place at the end of a road to nowhere. The buildings, for the most part, were scruffy, dirty, shapeless things built of adobe and rough stone with flat cement or gently sloping tin roofs. Think of a Mexican town in a low budget Hollywood western and you're halfway there. The *Plaza de Armas* (as the town square is called in Peru) had been tastelessly revamped in recent years and featured a water-less fountain and weird geometric-shaped patches of almost-grass behind little hedges. There was a huge, squat, white-washed church and a lorry parked across the street with the words *Christo es el Camino* written above the cab. There were window-less shops and cafés with hand-painted signs on the doors. There were torn posters over peeling paint over crumbling plaster and an air of in-built decrepitude. We liked the place very much indeed.

Cabanaconde really is at the end of the road. The tarmac stops here and beyond the town are only rough dirt tracks. In the afternoon we wandered out of town towards a viewpoint overlooking the canyon. At that altitude (over 10,000 feet) and in that dry climate there was an exceptional quality of light and clarity to the air that added some drama and beauty to an astounding landscape. Around us were pastures and dried out arable fields on gently sloping land leading up to small hills and mountains beyond. There were rock outcrops and boulders lying on the stony ground and stone walls, some topped off with a row of cactus pnts in lieu of barbed wire and others in varying states of disrepair.

We walked past an old bullfighting ring occupied by a single donkey and a football field more dusty than grassy. In shallow places between the hills the ground was washed out by the rains of a different season. There were cacti large and small, the biggest like fifteen foot high candelabras. We walked to a little flat-topped hill where there stood an adobe barn with a tin roof and next to it a timber cross decorated by bits of coloured material and carpet and a garish plastic head of Jesus. Then we went across to the edge of the gorge.

The land dropped away in front of us with cliffs and steep slopes leading down several thousand feet to the valley floor where the Colca River was just visible as a winding strip of blue among the rocks and trees. The slopes opposite us were not so very steep and we could see distant villages halfway up the canyon side. And higher above them were the mountains, cinder grey and yellow and sometimes white with patches of snow. We wandered about for a while until we were too hot and tired and thirsty and needed to go back to our hotel.

In the morning we were out in the square by five for a walk before breakfast. I guess there was little to do in the evenings here and we had got more into the habit of going to bed early and rising early to make the most of the twelve hours of sunlight. Flic seemed to get used to her day starting with the sound of my voice saying, excitedly, *Flic, Flic wake up, it's nearly light*. We weren't the only people about. A woman crossed the square carrying a mattock on her shoulder, another came by with a bundle of green animal fodder of some sort, and a man came the other way with a huge bag of corn stalks. Two shops were open and then we saw a woman putting out a table with two chairs and a stall with some breakfast food. We sat and had hot sweet quinoa drink and cheese and avocado rolls.

A little later a queue formed for the six-thirty bus out of town. Most of the women here wore traditional clothes as everyday attire but the women in the queue outshone everyone else in their finery. Flic noted velvet sleeves, embroidered waistcoats and hats, and full bright coloured skirts with embroidered hems. They all carried huge bundles and were headed for Cruz del Condor where they would make some money selling gaudy craftwork to the tourists. And we were headed that way too.

Cruz del Condor is a viewpoint with parking for cars and coaches and plenty of walled terraces from which you can look out across the canyon and are very likely to see condors drifting past on the updraft. It was cold there sitting around in the early morning even wearing the extra jumpers we had bought in Chivay. Buses pulled in and the crowds grew and the sun warmed us a little. We talked to a German couple who were travelling in a camper van and therefore, I thought, missing the joys of public transport and contact with the local population. And then the condors came quite suddenly and quite close, not beautiful birds but impressively large. We saw maybe eight or nine, rising up on the breeze and cruising past on outstretched wings. Then we set off to walk back to Cabanaconde.

When we were coming along this stretch of road the day before I so wanted to be out on foot or on a bicycle and not looking at the world through the window of a crowded bus. The walk back to town took us three hours and was as dramatic as I had thought. When we got close to town we passed a man leading a bull by a rope and I found myself thinking about the male animal in South America.

At home it is the female domestic animal that earns a farmer a living. Ewes give us lambs to rear for meat and cows yield milk and hens lay eggs; the rams and bulls and cockerels are relatively superfluous or at least limited in their usefulness. So in Peru I was struck by how many cockerels you would hear in the early mornings and how often you came across bulls in the countryside. Of course they are important for cock fighting and bull fighting. Both sports seem to us unpleasantly aggressive and very different from the way animals are cared for at home or revered in India. You might think that South America had a more macho society. But in Peru men tend to have a modest and gentle demeanour, not at as aggressive as you might anticipate.

And while we're on the subject of preconceptions overturned I had better tell you that the buses run on time in Peru and if they are a minute or two late in leaving there will generally be one or two old ladies calling impatiently from the back of the bus, *vamos, vamos*. Let's go. People aren't so laid back as you would expect.

The next morning we set off to spend a few days in the canyon. At first we met giggling school children coming up the track and then as we got further down there were backpackers looking very exhausted and hot. We made it to the bottom of the canyon quite early in the day and decided to stay in a little wooden hut at a place called the Oasis. It was the greenest place for miles around with little grassy fields and eucalyptus and palm trees growing among the rocks. Spring water had been diverted into swimming pools for the delight of foot-tourists like us. The river ran fast around boulders. There was a patch of handsome large cacti with yellow flowers. It was beautiful but somehow phoney; a far too small area of fertile land to support a village. My health continued to be a problem as Flic recorded in the evening: Richard loved the walk down, he kept saying how he loves travelling but now he doesn't know if he'll be able to walk across to the bar and get dinner. I told him he had to and he did but went back to lie down straight away afterwards.

The next day we had a challenging walk that took us to the village of Tocay situated on some less steeply sloping ground halfway up the other side of the canyon. It was a beautiful place that could be reached only on foot and was totally unspoilt. Fortunately there was one simple guesthouse. Flic noted: the streets are mud and stone. There are blossoms outside our window and tiny apples on the tree. There's a beautiful church here and we were welcomed into the village by a lamb and a sheep and an alpaca. We liked that place very much and stayed a couple of nights, pottering about above the village among fields with huge rocks and cacti and eucalyptus trees. From there we could see the path leading back to Cabanaconde. It went up three thousand feet or so of the almost vertical canyon wall. Flic followed the path with her eyes, counting forty-five bends in the bottom two-thirds of its zigzag route to the top. It looked daunting.

We stayed the next night at a hostel in the bottom of the canyon. Flic recorded: the path of tomorrow rises above us like a terrible snake. It's like going into labour or diving off a high cliff into the sea. Horrible fear. We have been watching people coming down, they took three hours so that means at least six hours up. Richard is terrified, he has gone to sleep which is his way of coping with unthinkable situations.

Part of the challenge of that path would be coping with the heat as the sun rose higher towards the middle of the day. And so we went to bed at eight that evening and got up at four, setting off in the dark at four thirty. There are, as a taxi driver told us on one of our first days in Huaraz, *bastante perros en Peru*. Plenty of dogs. They run wild much of the time and there are so many because Peruvians think it cruel to castrate the males. I have always been nervous around dogs and it was a problem for me at times. At five o'clock in the morning in the dark at the bottom of the canyon we were subject to a dog attack. They came at us suddenly, barking, wagging their tails and jumping up to be stroked. This, I have to say, is unusual behaviour for a Peruvian dog. Normally they ignore you altogether.

We came to the bottom of the path up the canyon side at five fifteen and set off carrying a few biscuits and some bananas and three bottles of water each. It wasn't as steep as it looked from the other side and the path was wide and safe. What's more we felt good. We were fit and, as I liked to say afterwards, we *stormed* it, arriving at Cabanaconde at ten in the morning. On the way up we had seen two more giant hummingbirds (*Picaflores gigantes*) and a condor, and witnessed the wonderful confusion that occurs when two groups of donkeys coming from different directions meet up on a narrow mountain trail.

In the afternoon we went for a walk out to the top of the canyon where we could look down on the route we had taken and the tiny villages we had passed through. As we were very short of cash we stayed in a more comfortable hotel (the only halfway posh one in Cabanaconde) where we could pay with our cards. Then in the morning we took the bus back to Arequipa.

We felt good. We had stormed up the side of the Colca Canyon and now, after nearly five weeks at or above ten thousand feet, we were more acclimatised to high altitude than ever in our travels. That's why we couldn't resist the challenge of *El Misti*, the snow-topped volcano that rises above Arequipa. At 5,822 metres the summit would be the highest we had been in the world.

On the second morning back in Arequipa we set off with a guide and another man to help carry camping stuff and drove and then walked up and up the slope of the volcano. We camped about two thirds of the way to the summit. I later wrote in my blog: *When it got darker the city looked fabulous from so high above. Like looking down from an aeroplane but without the aeroplane and therefore very cold. For some reason we had to set out at two a.m. for the summit. It was steep in places, dark because the moon had gone down, cold, and I really couldn't do it. We went quite a way but my legs wouldn't work. Scary for a moment but we got back to 'basecamp' and rested and then the sun came up and it was rather beautiful and strange and I felt OK again. It was trying to exercise at two in the morning that was a mistake. It was an amazing place and it wasn't too big a disappointment not making it to the top. We bit off more than we could chew.*

But looking back it seems that El Misti was significant. It was the first time in our travels that I had been unable to meet a challenge. I'm not a competitive person but overcoming difficulties and getting to a big summit had been one way of denying our friend Mr Parkinson. This time he won. I wasn't entirely happy about that.

U is for Urubamba (Peru)

We walked out of Urubamba one morning along a randomly chosen country road that led through beautiful countryside up into the mountains. As we climbed higher the land became poorer and signs of human activity became scarcer. We came to a road sign that read something like this: **Corralbamba 1,562 km**. Imagine that, a land so vast and empty that a country road leads hundreds of miles through the mountains before it arrives at the next settlement. What an extraordinary continent. And we had seen it from the aeroplane; huge areas of uninhabited and uninhabitable wilderness.

A little further down the road, not much more than a kilometre away, we came to the village of Corralbamba. We now know that in Spanish speaking countries the decimal point is replaced with a comma. And in some places they measure road distances with great accuracy, down to three decimal places. Well, I never...

Another peculiarity of Urubamba was the frequent occurrence of a type of sign that we couldn't understand. Outside some houses there would be a big bamboo stick, maybe eight or ten foot long, with a piece of red plastic bag tied to the end. We tried to guess what it meant: *vote Gonzales* maybe; or *no rubbish to collect this week*. Eventually we asked someone who spoke enough English for us to understand. It signified a place where *chicha*, maize beer, had recently been brewed and was available. A couple of times we were passing by people sitting outside in their gardens and invited in to drink some. It tasted OK.

22

The Sky Was Working Overtime

After Arequipa we went to stay for a while around Lake Titicaca. It's so big that in some places you can't see across to the opposite shore and we found ourselves referring to it as the sea though it lies 12,500 feet above sea level. There are some very touristy spots around the lake but it's easy to avoid them and spend time in less visited areas. It's one of the most beautiful places that I have ever been to.

This is how I prepare myself to write this chapter about Lake Titicaca:

≈ I read Flic's diary. At this time she was writing in a little exercise book that she could pull out of her bag at any idle moment and so some of it is in the present tense — we're on a boat heading for Llachon. We're the only foreigners and everyone else is Peruvian and women are dressed in thick felt skirts, patterned blouses and cardigans and shawls. We bought some lunch, a small plastic bag with two boiled eggs and two small baked potatoes, warm. All the adults are chewing coca leafs and the men wear brightly coloured hats — we could make a map of the world in breakfasts.

≈ I do some remembering, about the hats for instance — I remember them changing their broad-brimmed felt hats for *gorros* (Peruvian wool hats) when we got out on the water. I remember cold two-hat mornings around Titicaca when the men would wear a gorro under their big hat.

≈ Then I look in Flic's sketchbook. There's a pen and ink

drawing of El Capitan (Angelino, he was called) and his mate in the back of the boat. El Capitan has his head down and his hand in a bag of coca leaves while the mate looks ahead with a hand on the tiller. There's another drawing looking into the small cabin where the locals are all hunched down on the floor looking unhappy; they really don't like being out on the water. The colours are written in and were painted later on.

≈ Then there are my photos. I see that I took one of an old steamer with a red funnel that was out of commission and permanently moored at the dockside. Another photo shows just the glossy calm water of the lake reflecting a blue and white striped sky and a distant shore just a dark smudge on the horizon.

≈ There are Flic's photos and she's not as shy as I am of photographing people when they will allow it. There's a photo of the captain and mate showing their handsome broad faces and thick lips – quite different from the people in other parts of Peru. There's a picture of me with a woman in the background covering her face as though in superstitious fear of the camera.

≈ I do some more remembering. I remember cruising out along a sort of canal between very tall reeds before we reached open water. And the husband and wife teams out fishing in small boats, the men handling the nets, the women... at the helm as I remember, but was there an outboard motor or just oars?

≈ I use the internet to look at other people's photos but I can't see outboard motors. I do see the decorative reed boats made just for tourists and the tourists themselves and then more tourists and I'm aware that we did well to miss some of that.

≈ And then there's YouTube, perhaps I can see people's holiday videos. But first I come across a documentary in Spanish. There's a young man on the back of a boat talking to camera and the water behind him is an implausible blue, just as I remember it. Now a cut to him getting off the boat at a rough stone jetty that looks like... and yes, it is the exact place we went ashore on the Llachon Peninsula. He stumbles a bit over the boulders and then strides up the stone jetty, not carrying backpacks as we were. He looks around and the camera pans and it's just how it was then, the water, the clear light, the eucalyptus trees and the cultivated fields on the slopes by the shore. And I'm pretty much there for a moment myself and I feel strange, I'm smiling but my eyes are watering too. To find myself back in such a place again...

≋ I read my blog, a piece dated Thursday, 13 October 2011: *We keep calling it the sea. It is 100 miles long, 60(?) wide, profoundly beautiful, and it has a silly name – Lake Titicaca. We avoided the most touristy bits by going straight to a quiet, roadless (at the end) peninsula. We stayed three days. In the mornings and evenings it reminded us of the west of Scotland; in the middle of the day when the sun was hot and the sea (lake) was blue it looked like the Mediterranean in spring. As beautiful as either place but different – different from anywhere we've ever been. The sky was working overtime.*

The sky was working overtime because the light was startlingly clear and there were banks of cloud and storms chasing across the water and impressive sunrises and sunsets and the vast open space over the lake and between far distant Andean mountain tops in Peru on one side and Bolivia on the other.

Perhaps we took an hour to cross the water from Puno to the end of the peninsula that was marked Llachon on my little map.

The water was calm but the dozen or so local people on the boat crouched down on the floor of the cabin, some with heads covered, others obviously asleep, one or two reaching into small bags and taking out coca leaves to chew. For island people they were surprisingly scared of seafaring. When we pulled up by the jetty at the end of a peninsula they all stayed on the boat and it chugged away leaving us completely alone. We walked up a grassy path to a grassy track running between low stone walls. There was no-one around at all and there was absolute quiet. No machines or cars or planes overhead. We understood that we would find some simple accommodation in a small farmhouse or suchlike but we didn't know where. I felt dysfunctional and rough so I had a little sleep on a stone slab in the shade of a tree. Flic wrote in her diary for a while and made a sketch of the clouds over the lake. When I woke up we pottered about and found a young German woman sitting behind a rock reading a novel. She had caught the ferry from the nearby island of Amantani where she was staying but didn't know anything about places to stay here.

We set off along the track. We were passing through farmland of tilled fields and pastures sloping down to the... to the sea I want to say, because at this time of day in the heat and bright sunshine it felt like we were on a Greek island. We met no-one. The silence and emptiness felt strange enough to remind us of John Fowles' *The Magus*. We walked along and things very gradually picked up. The path was less grass and more dried up mud as if people had actually walked there. We came across simple rough-built houses. Flic walked down into the yard of one house and found a young woman to speak to but just got a blank look in return. We walked on getting hotter and mildly concerned.

Then two women came towards us dressed as if for a wedding or for a tourist's photo. They understood Flic's request for somewhere to stay and took us back to a simple and charming house we had passed. There was an outhouse built of stone, mud, reeds and timber that had been converted into a simple bedroom and we waited while they made up two beds. Then the more communicative and younger of the women slipped away and we didn't know if we should ask for food or if it would be provided. Everything around us was rustic and beautiful to the point of idyllic but I felt uneasy. I was hungry and I didn't know where my next meal was coming from.

Reader, don't worry; lunch did come, and in the evening supper came too. Both were cooked not on a stove but for some reason over an open fire in the barn attached to the house. The young man who brought us our food smelt strongly of woodsmoke and we could see the shadows and the light of leaping flames in the evening. The place was, as Flic put it, *rustico*, with rain dripping on my bed in the night.

The next day we breakfasted on egg, potato and an orange root, lumpy and veined and tasting like salsify and hot water with coco leaves and sugar, Flic wrote. The family didn't interact with us much and didn't expect us to stay a second night. I did manage to find out from the man of the house that we had just spent the night in Santa Maria and hadn't arrived yet in Llachon, as we thought – that was further down the track.

The morning was cold and cloudy, much better for walking with our rucksacks and so we set off. The hour's walk was quiet and Flic recorded only: I saw a dog chasing a hare across a field below us by the lake. He ran so fast he did a somersault. Then later a hare ran past us on the track. We've been watching a yellow-bellied snake-necked woodpecker. Watched a humming bird – dull and brown with long thin beak, as it flew towards us it had an emerald breast. We didn't see any vehicles but the track widened out and we did see tyre marks.

At Llachon we came across a guesthouse with simple accommodation and a restaurant. There was a crowd of German tourists outside being subjected to a tourist experience;

locals in hi-vis traditional clothes were dressing them up for a photo session and trying to sell them souvenirs. I was mildly horrified but Flic didn't seem to mind. Of course it brought to an end my sense of being in a remote place of unspoilt beauty but the Germans, it must be said, were having a lot of fun and the locals were making some much needed cash. After an hour or so they had all gone; the tourists walked down to the lake shore and left on a small boat and the locals packed up their gear and walked off. We checked in at the guesthouse (for want of a better word, it was too primitive to call a hotel) and were the only foreigners around once again.

The land all around sloped down to the lake but just here there was a step in the hillside so that the guesthouse sat on a little flat area above a small cliff. Below us was a sandy beach and a small harbour with a stone jetty. By now the day had brightened, the sun was out and the water was as blue as could possibly be. We asked the proprietor, Valentino, about the canoes that we had heard were available here. He took us down to a shed by the water and there, inside, were a number of shiny new yellow kayaks complete with paddles, spraydecks and lifejackets. They seemed to belong to some foreign adventure sport outfit with which he had connections.

I am, at heart, a paddle-my-own-canoe kind of guy (and Flic is a paddle-her-own-canoe kind of woman) but these were two person boats. We took a chance and set off together along the coast, headed towards the place where we had been dropped off the day before. It was a fine thing to be out on the water and but it was very slow going. In that huge landscape we didn't seem to make much progress and it was very tiring. I had never found canoeing that hard before and I couldn't think of why it should be so. Only now do I realise that we were at 12,500 feet where all exercise is hard. We were rather used to the idea that water accumulates at low levels and it didn't occur to us that we were doing was, in fact, high-altitude kayaking.

We stayed at Valentino's for couple of nights and did some walking around the area. We were on a peninsula long enough and narrow enough to give us the sense of being on an island. When we walked to the tops of the low hills we could see across the lake to the mountains above the wild Bolivian shore fifty miles away to the east, across a shorter stretch of water to the Peruvian city of Puno with its buildings climbing up the hills to the west, and to the nearby pyramidal shaped island of Amantani to the south. The land around us dropped down with slightly terraced irregular shaped fields, mostly in that fallow condition between one harvest and the next rainy season's new crops, until it met the lakeshore with its beaches and rocky outcrops. We saw strange succulent wild plants with flame coloured flowers and blue-green iridescent bodied flies on the drystone walls. We passed an old woman driving a mixed herd/flock of cows, calves and sheep out to graze.

At one point an old couple coming towards us on the path nudged each other and smiled at the sight of the strangely-dressed gringos. The woman couldn't contain herself and laughed out loud. Later a younger man looked at me and commented in Spanish as we passed: *pantalones cortos*, he said. It was hot enough here for me to wear shorts for the first time since we had arrived in Peru and they were the cause of the hilarity. I didn't wear them again.

One afternoon we walked northwards along the track that soon turned into a red dirt road and we saw no less than three motorised vehicles: a lorry, a minibus and a motorbike. The fields were flatter, larger and on richer soil and one or two farmers were wealthy enough to be driving tractors. It gave us a sense of how simple and poor the lives of those at the far end of the peninsula were, their prospects limited by the steepness of the land and its inaccessibility.

It's over to Flic for the next part of our time on Titicaca: had doughnuts and jam for breakfast and asked the señora about a boat to Amantani. She made a phone call on her mobile and at 7.15 a small wooden boat with a motor turned up at the quayside. The lake was very calm but later it got choppy and the boat slapped down on the waves. It was fun sat at the front watching the shoreline. It only took an hour.

At Amantani local women came to greet us and we followed one up a steep slope to her house where she settled us in a room. Her husband, Victoriano, took us along a path behind their house past his land some of which was furrowed diagonally. He pointed the way to the plaza. We stopped there for a tea, taking two chairs out to sit in the sun rather than indoors which is the norm here. After tea the señora from the café pointed the path out up the hill leading to archaeological sites, Pachamama and Pachapata. The island is cone shaped. A man called Gabriel walked up with us and we found out about his life. He is forty and has two girls and a boy but his wife died last year. He carried a pickaxe on his shoulder and was going up to break up the soil on his land. We left him to work while we walked to the top. It's so stony here and between each patch of land there are high stone walls, often just one layer thick so you can see the sky through them. Beyond Pachamama were big cliffs and rocks descending to the lake.

Next day it was beautiful and bright. I went out for a walk, Richard said he'd catch me up but he didn't. I walked along the stony beach and up a track to the plaza. Everybody says *buenos dias* or *hola* and although it's before six a.m. there are a lot of people around. The lake looks good.

When I got back to the room Rich was really fed up as he hadn't been able to walk and he couldn't eat breakfast alone as he can't pour out the hot water from the flask or butter bread. We have decided to go back to Puno by boat.

And that is how it was. I had good days and rough ones. My health was deteriorating and because it was unpredictable Flic wasn't always there when I needed her. I hadn't learned to be patient, to sit out the bad moments and quietly wait for things to get better. I allowed myself to get miserable at times. Amantani wasn't great for me but there were good times to follow.

We went to Chucuito in a mini-bus full of women, some very wide. They piled blankets full of onions on the roof. Thus begins Flic's journal entry describing a day trip we made from Puno. It continues: there were supposed to be stone phalluses here but they look more like mushrooms. Yes, the archaeological remains were very boring and it was no wonder that we were the only gringos in town. But there was something about the place that made us hang around for a while and we were glad that we did.

Chucuito is a small town situated a little above the main road that runs along the coastal plain by Lake Titicaca on the way to the nearby Bolivian border. We arrived there around mid-morning on a clear sunny day. After we had checked out the phalluses we wandered around the quiet streets. It was an ordinary town but there were some handsome older buildings of adobe and stone with red sandstone lintels across the doors. We soon found ourselves hanging out in the Plaza de Armas, the town square.

The square was on sloping ground with the usual formal park area in middle: little stretches of concrete path around patches of grass and trees and benches to sit on all geometrically arranged. On two sides of the square were low buildings, some of them housing modest little shops and cafés. On another side was a large modern concrete building with *Municipalidad Distrital de Chucuito* written across the front in big letters – the town hall. On the fourth side overlooking it all was big old church, a fine building up on a bank behind a colonnade of red and white painted arches. On the road running around the square stalls had been set up, most them bearing adverts for *Cusqueña*, the Peruvian beer, complete with government health warnings, *Tomar Bebidas Alcohólicas es Dañino*.

There was nothing going on at all but we sat in shade for a while watching the street. Flic asked a woman passing by if there was to be a *fiesta* and was told *mañana*, tomorrow. It was getting hotter and we thought of getting the next bus back to Puno but we liked this town. We wandered again, had some lunch in a big empty café, and came back to the square. There were a few more people around, the women in fairly smart traditional dress. We sat down and Flic got her journal out. She wrote: **a man has just crossed the square in a silver and purple costume, maybe a dancer.** We sat some more and then she wrote: also men on horseback. Now the locals began to gather by the town hall and we went over and joined them.

We sat on a low wall and watched. Half a dozen women with their hair worn in plaits that went down to their waists and an array of different hats (straw boaters and bowlers and one *gorro* – I have a photo here now) sat down on the kerb in front of us. More and more people turned up including some men leading horses and plenty of wide (as Flic might say) women in bright colours. Things began to happen. A brass band consisting of trumpets and tubas and a big bass drum played a couple of numbers. The mayor gave a speech. The slim young man who was sitting next to us said something about a *corrida*. We struggled to understand so by way of explanation he got out his wallet and showed us his union card. He pointed out the name of his profession: *matador*. He was a stranger in town himself, come to take part in this afternoon's bullfight – not in the ring but to officiate in some way.

The doors of the town hall were thrown open and everybody went in leaving the square empty except for a few tethered horses. We wandered yet again and found a viewpoint on the edge of the village from which we could see the land drop away to the plain and then the lake beyond. There below us, on the opposite side of the main road, was a football field in which stood the temporary bullring, a simple affair of wooden fences with a small grandstand on one side. Perhaps the event was sponsored by Cusqueña, the beer company, for they had a big banner sign here too. The health warning seemed a little out of place in the context of what was to happen this afternoon.

Back at the square we took a look at the squat colonial church, the biggest and oldest building in the town as it is in some small towns in Peru. It was a grand affair painted pale yellow and dark red with a massive green wooden door and a corrugated iron roof. Then people came out of the town hall where, we guessed, they had eaten some lunch. The band, a couple of dignitaries on horseback and the matadors paraded around the square and set off towards the bullring. We found a place to watch from the hill as did half the townsfolk, while the other half gathered around the ring. The people around us stood quietly, not smiling much and saying little. They didn't interact with us at all, as if we were invisible. A couple of women came along handing out homemade icecreams from insulated boxes but they didn't look that nice and we didn't try them for fear of upsetting our stomachs. Down below people were parking *camionetas*, pickup trucks, close to the ring and standing on them for a good view of the action to come.

Flic recorded: it took a couple of hours before the first bull, a brown one, was let into the ring. It tried to toss the matador but got confused as it got tangled up in his red cloak. After not long they let it go and another one was brought in, a lively black one but still small. This charged around a bit with someone on a loud speaker shouting *olé*. Then this one was released and a bigger brown bull came in and this one did stir up dust pawing the ground and looked a bit angry. I suggested that we leave now as I didn't want to see anyone, bull or man, hurt so we walked back to the plaza. She went on to say that the people watching were as interesting as the bullfight itself, which was a bit of an act.

I remember that the first bull seemed to tire easily and lose interest in the matador. The second one was a little timid. They weren't injured in any way and I imagined that later in the day they were grazing quietly in a field somewhere wondering what that had been all about. Did the bullfight get more serious after we left? I don't know.

We caught the minibus back to Puno glad to have witnessed, by accident, an extraordinary part of life in Peru. It was a memorable day, something that happens when you have the time to travel independently far from home.

After our day at the bullfight at Chucuito we went on around the lake and across the border into Bolivia. We stayed a few days in a town called Copacabana. You've already heard a little about this place and I'm not going to say much more here. It was seedier, scruffier and smellier than any place we had visited in Peru but we liked it. The landscape around was rocky and steep and the town felt safe and friendly. Our idea was to travel on to La Paz, the capital city of Bolivia but the roads were closed because of some political action. We got impatient waiting and decided to see more of Peru. We took a bus back across the border to Puno and then headed for Cusco, the Sacred Valley, and Machu Pichu.

V is for Varanasi (India)

We were in a rooftop café in Varanasi. We looked out across the water to the sandbanks on the opposite shore and at the rowing boats overloaded with pilgrims in brightly coloured clothes and at the broad sweep of the river stretching into the distance upstream and downstream. We looked down at the smoke rising from cremations on the burning ghats and at people ducking their heads in the water at the bathing ghats. We watched the monkeys gathering on the next door rooftop.

Then our food arrived. I can't remember what we ate, only what I didn't eat. It was a chapatti whipped off my plate by a monkey that leapt off the parapet and bounded past, snatching and grabbing as it went.

Monkeys are a sacred animal in India as well as a nuisance. A few years ago a government minister fell to his death from a balcony during an altercation with a monkey. There was talk of controlling the increasing numbers of these large holy vermin in New Delhi, where it happened, but I don't think anything was ever done.

It was in Varanasi that we found a monkey skull on the ground where we walked along the river bank. Its mouth grinned at us and its empty eye sockets stared up at us. It was sinister, being almost human. Perhaps the skull had fallen from a nearby rooftop where the animal had died and decomposed. There is so much life and so much death in India. It's not hidden away. Particularly in Varanasi.

23

The Sacred Valley

We stayed in Cusco at the *Hospedaje Inka*, a sort of backpackers' hostel or guesthouse that consisted of an ancient farmhouse and outbuildings that sat on the ridge overlooking the old part of the city. *Qué rústico, bonito y simpatico* are some words that come to mind; yes, that's right, it was rustic and charming and friendly. You might also use the same words to describe the proprietor, Americo, whose family had owned the property for five generations. He ran the Hospedaje with the help of two enthusiastic young men, Harry, who took time off only to look after his 300 guinea pigs, and Cipriano, whose special project was himself, if the amount of time he spent looking in the mirror was anything to go by. There was also Julio, a tiny eccentric old man dressed like one of the Blues Brothers complete with shades worn indoors and out. He said nothing and did nothing but added something to the place anyway. I think he might be described as having learning difficulties.

The hospedaje was a great place. The buildings were constructed out of the usual mixture of rough stone and adobe bricks covered over with crumbling plaster which had once been whitewashed. To get to the bedrooms you went up outdoor staircases and across wonky wooden balconies under pantiled roofs. The kitchen was across a cobblestone yard. Indoors the furniture was ancient and characterful and outdoors there were stone and wooden benches and cactus plants and flowers. Best of all was the view. The land dropped away in front of the house and all the old city lay spread out below, church towers and tiled roofs in abundance. Around the city was a ring of bare-topped hills except to the west where the valley opened out and the newer parts of town spread onto the plains. And, when the light was clear, you could see one distant snow-capped mountain making friends with the clouds.

The lovely strange thing about this place was that there had developed a kind of communal eating arraignment. When we arrived we were invited to eat by a Dutchman called Peter who had been staying there some time and during our stay we cooked (hmm... I think I mean Flic cooked) and other people cooked and people came and went and sometimes shared food in the big kitchen. It was sociable and we got to meet some interesting people.

Americo was a distinguished middle-aged man who spoke no English. The place was rustic but he had a good internet connection and liked to give little concerts of his favourite classical music on YouTube in the evenings. Peter, the Dutchman, was a nice old hippy, a true eccentric, full of bizarre theories and crazy talk and kindness and frantic inaction. We met an Icelander who knitted and a Swede who talked at length about milk and a German woman who had been to the rainforest to see a shaman and had come back to Cusco very ill. There was Claus, part Swedish, part Peruvian, completely bonkers and who believed that he had supernatural powers and was engaged in some struggle to save the world. And there were more because we stayed there for a few days either side of visiting the Sacred Valley and Machu Pichu.

I liked Hospedaje Inka and it has good memories for me so I'm surprised to read this passage in Flic's journal: Richard is feeling hopeless sometimes about his inability to do anything, dressing, packing, washing, shaving are all getting very difficult and it's hard to know what he will do when we get home. Walking he can do. Usually. For now we are in Peru and it's all new and I am here and we are having a good time but the future I don't know.

This trip was turning out differently from our trips to India and Nepal; much harder, and with bad times almost as often as good. I have got into the habit of discounting the horrible stuff. It's the good experiences that matter, isn't it? I have to think of it this way and I would like to keep Mr Parkinson out of this story for a while but I can't. We had fantastic, really fantastic, adventures despite his presence. It makes me sad to think how preoccupied Flic had become with my illness. I'm sorry to have caused her so much worry. But despite the problems the good times continue. My state of health is increasingly up and down. But I have, as my son Kit recently observed, a miraculous recovery several times a day. Not many people can say that.

From Cusco we went to *El Valle Sagrado de los Incas*, the Sacred Valley of the *Incas*, a few words about which might be a good idea. We shouldn't really call them the Incas as that is the name of their kings; the people we might describe as *Quechua*, which is also the name of their language, still widely spoken today. They had a short-lived empire centred around what we now call Peru, Ecuador and Bolivia for the hundred years before the Spanish turned up in the 1530s (i.e. not that long ago). Their architecture was amazing; sometimes massive blocks were fitted together with great (but not inexplicable) accuracy. They built Machu Pichu and other monuments and the foundations of Inca buildings are clearly visible in places like Ollantaytambo and Cusco, where the present day buildings, which date from colonial times, sit on top of them. The Sacred Valley is also referred to by the name of its river and central town, *Urubamba*.

First we travelled by bus, a real bus with real people, as Flic described it, from Cusco to Chinchero, high above the Sacred Valley at 12,500 feet. The town, she wrote, is set in marvellous scenery, huge rocks, valleys with winding streams, and Inca terraces, stretches of flat lawns, small curved terraced fields. Some of the great rocks have steps carved in them. We looked to see some sheep wandering into a field of barley and children running after them and chasing them back, hitting them with their jumpers. We had lunch at a stall in the market place: roast pork, potatoes and sweet-corn, all fished out of a vat of bubbling oil in which floated the pig's tail. We sat on a tiny bench and ate, like everyone else, with our fingers, cleaning up afterwards with toilet paper, a roll of which is found on the tables of cheap cafés in Peru in lieu of napkins. Here we encountered a new hat, a maroon flying saucer, which was quite common here alongside the aforemen-tioned hybrid somewhere between a trilby and a top hat in white or cream colour.

In Chinchero we stayed the night in a small tacky cold hotel and ate fish and chips off cold plates in a cold dining room. In the morning we walked down and down a steep path along the side of a little valley that led eventually into the Sacred Valley. We found a moderately unpleasant place to stay in the town of Urubamba and went back by bus to Chinchero to pick up our things.

This was one of the fullest buses we have ever been on and we foolishly had seats at the back. When we got near to Chinchero we had the laughably impossible task of pushing our way through the people standing in the aisle to get to the door. I really hadn't thought about it but had assumed that the impressive girth of Peruvian *campesinas* was one part woman and an equal part layers of petticoat and skirt. Not so. How can I put this delicately? Let's just say that the idea of obesity as a feature of decadent lazy *Western* society is myth. There are fat people and thin people scattered about all over the world. But on the bus to Chinchero that afternoon the thin people were noticeably absent.

Flic says that I use the word *beautiful* too often. What can I do? The walk down the valley and the bus ride back took us through an impressive and wonderful landscape. There was snow on the peaks and extraordinary flowers and insects on the ground (including stick insects that we had never seen in the wild before). There was red earth, purple dust and green rocks; agave plants and huge cacti and, lower down, acres of maize, fields of flowers, avocado, papaya and peach trees. It was pretty damn good. And at the bottom, after seeing no-one for most of the day, we came to a house where the people were taking a rest from the making of adobe bricks. They invited us in to drink chicha, maize beer, and eat some salad. Both these items could possibly give us stomach troubles but we accepted their hospitality and survived. It was a very good day.

On the following morning we found a great place to stay on the edge of Urubamba. Flic thought it was delightful,

we have a balcony overlooking a garden full of blossom and fruit, hens, guinea pigs, bees, humming birds, passion fruit vine, peach, pear, tree tomatoes, a brown bird on a nest at eye level, a ping pong room, shame Richard doesn't play. Humming birds seem to purr more than hum and they cheep too. They are tiny and iridescent green and blue and brown and grey. Our hotel is on a dirt road on the edge of Urubamba. Beyond it are fields of maize and potatoes and cabbages. Mud walls. Beyond the fields are mountains.

Large bundles of barley are sold and you see people lugging it home on their backs. Sheep are herded along. There's a town square with beautiful trees in blossom, blue, pink and red. Red petals fall to the ground and look like parrots beaks. Hibiscus trees line the road. It feels like summer.

Urubamba was at a much lower elevation than Chinchero and it was much warmer and it was a lovely ordinary town with markets and town squares and no tourists apart from ourselves. It was a good base for little trips along the valley. There are famous much-visited Inca ruins close by but first we wanted to go to Salineros, where a salt rich stream flows out of the hillside into a number of pools from which the salt is harvested.

We took a bus up the hill towards Chinchero and got off at a junction. Then a shared taxi took us a short distance to a little village with a big church clinging to the hillside. We were high above the Urubamba Valley in a vast open landscape with mountains all around. The slopes here were convex, that is to say the ground fell away in front of us more and more steeply, so we couldn't see the salt pans of Salineros but knew they were below us somewhere. Our plan was to walk down to them and then carry on to the valley floor where we could catch a bus back to Urubamba. We set off down a dusty track through pasturelands and cultivated fields that were maybe quite green at other times of year but now looked dry and barren. Far away on the opposite side of the valley we could see quite large areas of land blackened by recent fires.

We met a man leading a donkey and asked the way. He muttered one or two words in Quechua or Spanish and waved his arm vaguely downwards. We carried on for a while. Then the track divided to form two paths on each side of a widening gulley; if we went wrong we would go very wrong but we had to choose. We took the left hand path and continued. An hour passed and we still saw no sign of Salinas. The sun was very high now, we were very hot and we had finished most of our water. The path subdivided and we chose to follow some tyre tracks but they led us into a field. We turned back, took the second path and carried on descending. I was limping a little and doubted that we would make it back up to the village; we had to carry on down.

After a while a little smoke and the not unpleasant smell of burning herbs drifted up to us on the breeze. Then we turned a corner in the path and there was a fire, the crackling sound of burning vegetation, the smoke and flames apparently coming towards us. We turned and ran.

Of course we couldn't run far uphill. We stopped and waited but the fire didn't seem to be getting closer. We walked down again for a better look and found that the fire was small and was only on one side of the track. We made a decision and ran down, feeling rather warm for a few paces before coming through and away. We were genuinely scared for a few minutes and now were relieved. And we felt better again when we got our first view of Salinas.

We saw the steep slope below us terraced and divided up into a patchwork of little areas separated from each other by banks in exactly the same way that rice fields are in the Himalayas. These weren't fields but pools of water evaporating to leave a deposit of salt. The pools were in different stages of use, some newly filled with water from the stream, others half dried out and turning brown and grey, others glistening white with salt where the water had all gone. As we got closer we saw a few men at work, shovelling the salt into sacks and carrying it up the bank to a track. It looked like a tough way to earn a living.

The place was visited by a few people who came up by car from the road in the bottom of the valley below. This meant that there was a café and we found ourselves suddenly transformed from intrepid adventurers crossing a barren land under a burning sun into tourists sitting in the shade and eating icecreams. We didn't mind at all.

We made other day trips and took walks from Urubamba and then went to Ollantaytambu and Machu Pichu further down the Sacred Valley. There's a problem with these places: they are touristy to the point of feeling unreal, they are like theme parks where tourism is the only visible activity and the ordinary life of the country is submerged beneath it. What was very real was the rain, which we had experienced very little of for a month but which fell heavily on our arrival at Ollantaytambu. The other uncomfortably real thing was: a political rally with amplified speeches in a town square. It seems a lot of nonsense, hundreds of people are listening, most in their costumes, men in orange boiler

suits and yellow hard hats, school uniforms on girls, women in traditional gear. Policemen and firemen and magistrates and town chiefs.
Loud interminable speeches. We climbed high up above town to
get away from the noise but we didn't succeed.

From Ollantaytambo we travelled down to Aguas Calientes,
below Machu Pichu, on a special tourist train. I found myself
sitting next to a young Englishman. He really didn't want to
talk much but somehow I managed to draw him out and learnt
a bit about his circumstances. I never found out his name. He
was a graphic artist by profession and had been living in
California, making a lot of money and saving up to buy a house
and settle down with his girlfriend, with whom he was very
much in love. She left him and he was shattered. He gave up
his job, took his surf board (a seven foot *longboard*) and
headed south. He travelled to Mexico and various other Latin
American countries, spending most of his time by the ocean
but also travelling far inland and into the hills, taking his board
with him on public transport. It must have been an incongruous
sight. I'm reminded of Odysseus who was told by the blind
soothsayer, Teiresias, that he must

> *go overland on foot, and take an oar,*
> *until you come one day where men have lived*
> *with meat unsalted, never known the sea*

in order to placate Poseidon, the sea god, who he had upset
badly. The Odysseus sitting next to me had by now left his
board behind somewhere along the way. I don't know if he still
had it with him in Quito, where, he told me, he had been beaten
up a little and robbed. It wasn't a traumatic experience for him
because he had done some boxing in his time and was used to
being hit. In fact when the two guys had cornered him that
night he had thought about throwing some punches but decided
against it; he was a small man and it was two to one. We never

bumped into him again but I expect he has had some more adventures since then. He seemed a little accident prone.

The Urubamba River flows steeply down from Ollantaytambu to Aguas Calientes which is less than 7,000 feet above sea level, much lower than the places we had been staying most of the time in Peru and therefore in a completely different natural environment, something like tropical rain-forest. In fact the river is a tributary of the Amazon and its waters carry on out to the Atlantic Ocean nearly 4,000 miles away. So while Aguas Calientes is a tourist town serving visitors to Machu Pichu it was for us something else too: a chance to experience tropical jungle.

We walked downstream from the town along a track beside the railway line that took us to a sort of private piece of half jungle and half botanic garden. Here we followed a path to a waterfall. There were orchids and bromeliads, tree ferns and giant ferns, a type of courgette or squash plant thirty metres long, a parrot with a red and orange head (called the Cock of the Rock), big colourful butterflies, and the almost continuous noise of an insect that sounded like a dentist's drill. For us, who never made it to the rain forest in all our time in South America, it was a special experience.

Then we went to Machu Pichu, the *Lost City of the Incas*, which must be one of the most tourist infested places in the world. We had bought our ticket in Cusco two weeks in advance as visitor numbers are limited to a mere 2,500 per day. To beat the crowds we got up at 4.30 in the morning and got one of the first buses up the hill. The extraordinary nature of Machu Pichu is partly its setting, on a very high, very steep hilltop in the jungle. We couldn't see this because of the rain and mist. It seemed like we had chosen the wrong day. But we continued with our plan to go up Wayna Pichu, which is a thousand foot high, jungle-clad pillar of rock overlooking the main part of the site. For me, with a moderate fear of heights and with Parkinson's disease affecting my movement, it was a challenge. But we were fit and very acclimatised to altitude and managed to be among the first people on the top. The clouds opened a little and through the gaps we could see the ruins of Machu Pichu right below us and the Urubamba River snaking through the forest further down again. You can choose your own clichéd superlatives; I'm just going to say that it looked pretty good. And, despite the tourist overload, we were glad we went there.

W is for Westport (Ireland)

Eric Clapton's *Layla* was in the charts so that must make it 1971 or 1972. I was camping near Westport, County Mayo, with the school scouts. Oh, really? Yes, the scouts. I was fifteen or sixteen years old.

Sometimes I see a human being as a building that survives over the years, still recognisable from the outside despite increasing decrepitude and botched renovations. But inside there are many changes. Occupants come and go as time passes; some of them barely memorable in future years. And so it is that I would recognise myself in a photo taken in 1971 or 72, the outside of the building, as it were. But I'm not sure that I would be able to recognise much of the inside, the person that I was then. I'm not convinced that I even want to try.

Westport is situated at the end of Clew Bay, where, legend has it, there are 365 islands. There are, in truth, only 117, including sandbars and rocks (but not submerged drumlins). They have names like Carrigeennaronty and Freaghillanluggagh, and John Lennon once owned one of them.

I can remember that we were taken out in boats to fish for mackerel in the bay and that we would reel in several at a time on the multi-hooked fishing lines. I remember that they tasted good cooked over an open fire.

So, there it is. A one-time occupant of this building, long since fled, has left a little something behind.

24

The Earth Moved

Huaraz and the Cordillera Blanca; Arequipa and the Colca Canyon; Lake Titicaca; and then Cusco and the Sacred Valley. We had adventured for between two and three weeks in each of these four areas and although it had been difficult at times it had often enough been a more than moderately wonderful experience. Now we went back to Lima and set off by bus on a leisurely overland journey from that capital city to Quito, the capital of Ecuador. It took about three weeks during which we had some memorable times, including one of the most exciting moments of all our travels.

In the bus station at Lima we had a new insight into Peruvian culture. We had to wait a while for our bus and watched television on a large overhead screen. Most people in Peru are of mixed race, that of the native Americans (for South Americans the word *America* describes their continent and they deplore the use of it to mean the United States) mixed with some blood of the Spanish invaders, or they are pure blooded native people. They all look Peruvian; that was our experience in the two months we had been there. But there are a few people of more or less pure Spanish blood who, of course, look rather European, and who form much of the wealthy and powerful ruling elite. We never met them. In the bus station we sat among ordinary Peruvians and watched Peruvian television, soap operas and news programmes and adverts, in which *all* the participants were of European blood. People from another world. What does that tell you about that society? I'm not sure, but it isn't good.

Then we saw a cow fall from the sky, but that was after we had got on the bus and that was on television too. (I mentioned it in chapter five.) We travelled northwards to Pacosmayo on the Pacific coast. It turned out to be a strange town with weird birds over the sea including pelicans, turkey vultures, which are as ugly as those two words added together might incline you to imagine, and a bird we didn't know the name of but if I call it the greater cormorant kite you'll get an idea of how it looks. There were a few fishing boats, the world's most dangerously decrepit pier, and some big waves which lured the occasional surfer including an American, oops, North American who we met over breakfast.

Next stop was Cajamarca when we got stuck in our hotel and later trapped in a shop by a massive demonstration against an American, oops, North American, mining company. The streets echoed to the cry *El Pueblo, unido, jamas sera vencido (the people, united, will never be defeated)*. The speeches in the town square got more and more heated but then the thing fizzled out. Being rich foreigners we kept a low profile throughout.

On the bus to Celandin there was an Englishman, let's call him Kevin, with his recently acquired Taiwanese girlfriend. They weren't getting on well to the point that when he got off, she stayed on. He was another accident prone guy. It turned out that they had been robbed at gunpoint on a night bus a few days previously. He had his thousand pound laptop stolen and went to the police station to report its loss to be able to claim on the insurance. They asked to see his passport and it was then that his girlfriend discovered that he had pointlessly lied about his age to her, taking ten off his forty something years. While he phoned the insurance company to find that his computer wasn't covered she was able to think about his lie. She thought some more during the course of the day with predictable consequences. All this he told us with great frankness and honesty; after all we were his friends, with whom he had a different standard of truthfulness to that which he practised with a lover.

It was in Celandin that we saw a man walking a dog on a lead, a strange occurrence that we hadn't witnessed for a long time. Dogs are allowed to run wild in Peru. In the mornings and evenings they are very active, meeting and greeting friends in the usual unmentionable doggy ways, sometimes hanging out in amiable packs of half a dozen or more. In the heat of the day they are asleep and you might have to step over one in a doorway or on the street. They are never taken for walks on leads. When we got closer to this particular dog we saw that it was, in fact, a pig. This was quite normal; animals of all sorts are taken out in the morning and tethered to graze or root on some local patch of dirt.

Animals are much more a part of daily life in South America in the same way that we saw in India and Nepal. In a later blog post I mention: *cows, sheep, goats, hens, pigs, llamas, alpacas, donkeys, horses, guinea pigs and dogs* seen on a single walk in the countryside. And we saw a man trying to get on the bus with a cockerel under his arm. But these are modern times; the bird was required to travel in with the luggage at the back. We heard it crowing from time to time along the way.

We were in this relatively little visited area of Peru because we wanted to visit a place called Kuélap, a mighty hilltop fortress of the pre-Inca people known as the Chachapoyas, the people of the clouds. We met the Chachapoyas in the form of 200 or so mummified corpses in the museum at Leymebamba. They were mostly skin and bone, tiny figures bound up tightly, their knees pulled up against their chests and arms tucked in close so that their hands covered their faces, mouths open, as if in pain or fear. The museum was funded from abroad and we met a Swedish dentist working there, taking the mummies out of their temperature and humidity controlled room one at a time and determining the age, at death, of each one by examining their teeth. And so we got to see a five hundred year old teenager as close up as you could wish. He had skin but no flesh, teeth but no eyes, and colourless rags that had once been clothes. He didn't look happy.

Kevin, on the other hand, who we bumped into again at Leymebamba and who came to the museum with us, did seem happier than before. But I noticed that his misfortunes extended to a resemblance to David Cameron. These things can't be helped.

We found Kuélap difficult to get to, which made it seem a little bit of an adventure. We left Leymabamba early one Sunday morning in a *colectivo*, a cheap shared taxi which would take us to a place where there was a market that attracted village people from all around. The market was a very busy affair with an earthy character and it sold basic foods and necessities to ordinary people. Then we found a *combi*, as we had learnt to call the privately run mini-buses, to a road junction at a place called Tingo. It was a low lying place with semi-tropical vegetation and it was very hot. A small road from there wound up and up into the hills for several thousand feet to tiny misty villages and eventually to Kuélap. We hung about awkwardly hoping to maybe hitch a lift. Eventually a rough-looking old taxi with a rough-looking young driver stopped for us. The guy had a mean look, spoke little, and wanted to charge a lot of money. I felt uncomfortable but we took a chance. We had been robbed once before and had met quite a few others that had had the same experience so this was not exactly paranoia on my part, just caution.

We hadn't gone far before I noticed the guy had a photo of a baby stuck to the dashboard. Straight away my perceptions were completely changed; this was a young newly married man trying hard to make enough money to feed the beginnings of a family. A nice guy. And when we came to realise how far and how high and what a rough road we were to travel with him that afternoon it didn't seem so very expensive after all.

Maria, where we stayed for the next two nights, was a pretty village in a stupendous setting. It rested near the top of a ridge thousands of feet above the valley floor in the greenest landscape we had seen in Peru. There were lush fields of grass with cows grazing, ploughed fields of rich dark soil, and plenty of woodlands on the steepest slopes. A patchwork of different colours and textures all appearing and disappearing as clouds and shafts of sunlight drifted over the land. It reminded us of Wales but with a many times greater range of altitude and with every tree and shrub and flower and bird and insect different from those we would see at home. There were, for example, a number of hummingbird species, some with gorgeous colours, some with long tails. We came across their thumb-sized nests in the vegetation alongside the road. And in the evening we saw fireflies looking like hundreds of tiny florescent lights switching on and off as they drifted about among the trees. There were towering clouds and rainbows and, of course, wonderful sunrises and sunsets. And rain, plenty of rain.

We found a small guesthouse in Maria with a concrete patio at the back from which we had a view across the valley. It was mid-afternoon and we had time to visit Kuélap, two hours walk up a small country road. Kuélap is just a massive stone wall with few ruined circular buildings inside but it's on top of a very high hill in a dramatically beautiful landscape. There were very few people there and we enjoyed clambering about enough to go back the next day. Flic described it thus:

After breakfast today we set out to walk or cadge a lift to Kuélap again. We walked a little then a lorry came and gave us a lift. The cab was full so we were told to climb up a ladder on the side. Richard went first and jumped down inside the lorry and stood up so he could see. I went up and sat on some planks of wood above the driver's cab. It was a brilliant way to travel, head out in the air, landscape falling away below. I had to duck for branches occasionally. Got to Kuélap rather elated.

At first we were the only people there. It's quite overgrown and mysterious with so much hanging grey lichen and big red bromeliads. We watched lizards and sky and landscape. Then a bunch of Peruvians came and made a lot of noise and took photos of each other and then took photos of us.

And I photographed them high on the edge of the fortress, the modern day People of the Clouds, silhouetted against a stormy sky. They were having more fun than their ancestors in Leylebamba, wore brightly coloured clothes, and weren't fleshless at all. Far from it.

Just as we were leaving the site we came across a tourist group who had just arrived in a minibus. I recognised one of them and called out his name, Kevin. He didn't want to talk to us much. He had clearly got over the loss of one girlfriend and was in animated conversation with a new potential conquest. I wished him luck.

Kuélap is sometimes talked of as the Machu Pichu of the north. Although it's not so impressive it is in a similarly astounding hilltop setting. But walking and hitching along a quiet country lane and being alone there in the quiet of the morning is a much happier and rewarding experience than being part of the tourist mass at Machu Pichu. And Maria is an unspoilt village with a meaning in the landscape and a community connected to the land itself. It was a good place to be at the end of our visit to Peru.

A few days later we were on the border of Ecuador at a remote place called La Bolsa. We reached it in a beaten-up shared taxi driving down a dirt road through lush steamy tropical forest and farmland. Across the river, on the Ecuadorian side, the track was rougher and wound up a very steep slope through the trees. La Bolsa wasn't even a village, just a few buildings and a couple of cafés. There was no traffic unless you counted the two cows wandering back and forth. We crossed a smart new concrete bridge and got our passports stamped in a little office. They didn't have a computer on which to log our arrival so a couple of weeks later we had difficulty leaving the country on account of not having officially arrived. We sat in the shade outside a café for three hours waiting for transport to the nearest town. It wasn't completely uneventful; every now and then a flying ant would fall to the dusty ground and get pecked up by a chicken.

Transport, when it arrived, turned out to be a *ranchero*, a truck with seats fitted onto the back, open sided but with a canvas awning to keep off the sun. It was a fine way to travel. Our first few hours in Ecuador were spent driving along an exceedingly poor dirt road cut into steep slopes of something that looked more like mud than rock. We could see that it must be very prone to landslides and that choosing that route at that time of year, the beginning of the rainy season, was taking a chance. It really was a road less travelled.

When we arrived at the bus station outside Zumba, our first Ecuadorian town, a man offered me something to eat out of a plastic container. I had a few of what looked like currants but which were crunchy and salty. They seemed nice until I looked more closely at them. They were flying ants, without their wings and fried but ants all the same. I didn't feel like eating any more.

Ecuador didn't make such a great impression on me after Peru. The landscapes are less dramatic, the people less colourful. I'm not going to say much about Vilcabamba, the weird place where people enjoy great longevity. I blogged: *weird because there are a lot of middle-aged Americans who have moved into the area and weirder because of the sacred healing mystic nonsense people who are here in great numbers. The locals seem disgruntled but some of them are friendly. We walked along a dried up river bed looking at birds and fantastic butterflies and were interrupted in our nature studies by a young man called Charles Darwin; he showed us his I.D. to prove it. We have already met a Victor Hugo here so we weren't too surprised. He asked us for twenty dollars but was very polite when we refused.*

I'm not going to say much about Riobamba, where we stayed in: *a small hostal with rooms set around a courtyard garden. Last night, as the light faded, we became less aware of the dozen or so gold painted concrete statues and other paraphernalia as our attention focused on the illuminated father Christmases and snowmen, the lights suspended in the trees, the hundreds of little red and green moving lights, like glow-worms, projected somehow onto the vegetation, and the elevator music coming from speakers hidden in the trees. Someone came in and I found myself saying 'buenos noches, feliz navidad'. Good evening, Happy Christmas.*

I'm really not going to say much about the day trip we made from Riobamba with an adventure tour company. We were taken up the side of the volcano called Chimborazo in a van with bikes on the back. After a short walk to a refuge at high altitude we were kitted up with waterproof jackets and trousers, balaclavas, cycle helmets, knee pads and elbow pads. Then we set off for what should have been a rather wonderful ride down something between six and seven thousand feet on dirt tracks and then metalled roads. The bikes had the brakes set up differently from at home with the back brake (essential for going downhill on a loose surface) on the right, which was almost impossible for me to use. I had to be picked up by the van and driven back. The weather was rough too with rain, hail, sleet and snow. We picked Flic up further down the hill.

And I'm not going to say much about travelling in a *lechero*, a milk truck: *just a truck with three large plastic barrels in the back and all the other available space filled with standing passengers. Every now and then we stopped and someone would pass up a plastic bottle or bucket of fresh milk and it would be poured through a strainer into one of the barrels.*

I will say a few words about our stay in Baños. First I'll quote Flic:

Baños is a small holiday kind of town. It's cheerful and has two plazas and a church with big paintings of disasters like an eruption of the volcano above the town and people fleeing, a flood and fire. A small picture of the virgin is in every picture. Some tradition. Around the church are stalls selling religious souvenirs and plastic inflatable ducks and rubber rings as there are many pools here filled with hot water from the volcano. We walked with our backpacks looking for somewhere nice to stay in. We found a hotel with my name on, *El Eden*.

Baños is surrounded by high hills and a volcano so as you walk around your eyes are drawn to the tops of the hills and you walk very upright, head held high.

We walked to a bridge over a canyon that led to a road winding up away from the town, trying to get a good view of the volcano. It had been active last April but is quiet now. The last time it erupted was in 2006 and the town had to be evacuated.

Flic and I followed a signpost to a *mirador*, or viewpoint, and walked along a track until we came to a large house with a sign outside reading *soda bar*. The building was fairly new, four storeys high, and had a concrete ramp zigzagging up the outside to the top floor. We made our way up the ramp past pots of geraniums and were met on the third storey by a friendly black labrador and on the fourth storey by a man in a wheelchair. He introduced himself as Alfonso and invited us in. The top floor of the house was one big open plan space with a kitchen hidden in the corner, a bar in front, one or two chairs and tables and the rest of the area filled by the curious junk that you might find in an attic. There were windows and sliding doors onto the balcony which ran the width of the building.

Alfonso was a genial smartly dressed man in early middle age. He wheeled himself across the room and opened the door for us all to go onto the balcony. We looked out across the slopes of the valley covered in verdant farmland and orchards and dotted with eucalyptus trees. Below us we could see the gorge that held a broad fast-flowing river, the bridge that crossed it, the small town beyond, and above the town the volcano, Tungurahua, the upper slopes of which were covered in snow. Alfonzo got us some fizzy drinks and told us a little about himself. He had been in an accident twenty years ago at work and since then had played a part in the town council, promoting disabled access among other things. He showed us framed certificates and newspaper cuttings that congratulated him on his achievements. From time to time his dog bumped against us affectionately. Then Alfonso took us down the ramps and showed us the accommodation available, for the place was a guesthouse too. We decided to move up here from the town the next day. It turned out to be a good decision.

We hung out in Baños for a few days. Downstream of the town the gorge deepened and there were a number of impressive waterfalls. We rented bikes and cycled down the busy main road, the famous *Route de la Cascades*. The bikes were terrible and we ended up stopping a *camioneta*, a pick-up taxi, to transport us back to town where we managed to get our money back. We decided to tour the waterfalls in true tourist style in something called a *chiva*, an open-sided truck like a ranchero but with flashing lights and disco music to help us enjoy the natural beauty of our surroundings. We were the only gringos on board as Baños is a big-time resort for Ecuadorans. It was our first experience of South American style tourism, Peru being a less affluent country where people are too busy earning a living to indulge in such things. Everyone on board the *chiva* had a great time except us. The music was really loud, really awful and it was to me a torture. We did stop and cross the gorge on a little cable car and then later walk down for a close look at a waterfall. But then it was on the truck again in the now fading light and all the way back to town in our very own version of disco hell.

Flic tried out the thermal baths in the town and found herself to be the only pale person in an early morning crowd of brown people. The waters are supposed to be curative and there were a number of sick and disabled people among the bathers. She also shopped for presents as this was one of our final stops before Quito and the flights home. But the real high point of our stay was not a tourist experience but a natural phenomenon that we really hadn't anticipated.

While we were in Ecuador we experienced proper mountain weather, none of that wall-to-wall sunshine stuff but big towering clouds and heavy showers and rainbows and intermittent bright sun lighting up the hillsides. And so when we heard a rumbling sound one evening we imagined it to be thunder. Its real cause was outside of our experience and beyond our imagination. But I did make a little joke when we turned off the light go to sleep that evening in our room-with-a-view at Alfonso's. I said *wake me up if the volcano starts erupting*.

At four in the morning on November the twenty-eighth, 2011, I woke Flic up. I was as excited and happy as I had ever been. Reader, the Earth moved. I was woken by a tremendous roaring sound and the windows were shaking. I leapt out of bed and rushed across the room to look out. It was very dark outside, being well before dawn and a moonless night. Across the valley, above the town, Tungurahua was erupting. Red hot lava was flowing down the slopes of the volcano and huge red hot rocks were flying through the air. We watched individual boulders and counted the seconds before they hit the ground. Some were airborne nine or ten seconds. Is that possible? It's what I remember. These rocks were travelling up hundreds of feet and we could see them from... I don't know, five miles away? They were the size of houses? No, maybe not but possibly the size of a car or lorry and each weighing several tons. Those are the sort of forces we're talking about.

We dressed and went outside to watch, sitting against the wall for about an hour before it began to get light. All the time we waited to hear the sound of sirens and fully expected to see the flow of traffic as the town was evacuated. The mountain would go quiet and then we would hear another great rumble, more lava would flow, more rocks would fly. It was, as they say, compulsive viewing. A marvellous experience.

It was less dramatic in the light of the day. We couldn't see the red glow of the molten rock but we could see smoke and steam coming off it, a plume of smoke coming out of the mouth of the volcano, and the black marks where the lava had crossed and swept away the snow. The town was quiet. This was, apparently, a minor eruption and no threat to life or livelihood. It was exciting enough for us. In the afternoon we got a lift up the hill behind Alfonso's and had a great view of the volcano. In the evening we sat outside and watched the show again.

A day later we left Baños and went by bus to Quito, the handsome crime-ridden city that I described earlier. We were there a few days before saying good bye to South America and setting off for home.

Flying across the Atlantic in the night was a strange thing. We were suspended in a thin tube of warm air in a cold empty sky above a cold empty sea, between continents, between time zones, out of this world. I had the opportunity to think of this as I was unable to sleep. Everybody else had their eyes shut and were deep in their dreams. I decided to set my watch to UK time; after all we were going east, rushing to meet the dawn. And so it was that I found myself a day ahead of my companions. They were sound asleep on Friday and I was wide awake on Saturday. South America had been difficult for me. I was pleased to be going home.

X is for Xania (Greece)

Xania, or *Chania*, as it is more often spelled, is a pretty harbour town on the north coast of Crete. I was there in 1976 having set out for Lapland and taken a wrong turning. I remember sitting in a bar with a Canadian friend, a young woman called Carla, on a stormy summer day, listening to old Beatles songs and watching the waves come into the harbour, break against the wall and flow across the street towards us. Sometimes the foamy water would come right up into the bar and we would lift our feet to let it pass under our chairs.

I was there again with Flic in 1990. She was seven months pregnant and we toured the island on bicycles that we had brought with us on the plane. Coming down a long steep hill into Chania, or it might have been Rethymnon, we hit a patch of mud brought onto the road by builder's trucks. Flic braked and skidded and ended up on her back on the tarmac. She and the lump that was to become Kit, our first born, weren't injured.

In 1997 the now four of us, Flic, Kit, Peter and myself, had a very short holiday in Crete and stayed in Chania. It may have been there that I started to go the wrong way around a round-about and stopped the car (which we had hired), got out and walked off a little way to de-stress before carrying on.

These are unreliable memories of unreliable memories and are totally untrustworthy. My guess is that memories are turned into stories and are drafted, edited and fictionalised within moments of an event happening. When they are re-remembered they are changed again. There must be so many things that shape our personal fictions: a particular understanding of human nature; a world view complete with religious belief or its absence; a narative of a relationship; wishful thinking; a tendency towards denial. Most of all there is the need to tell a good story.

25

The World Turned Upside Down

This is the chapter I have been looking forward to, the one I so much want to write. It's about our visit to the Middle East; to Jordan, Israel, Palestine and a tiny bit of Egypt. Nowhere in these countries did we see anything like the beauty of the Himalayas or the Andes or the Mediterranean or, for that matter, Wales. But we were engaged and stimulated in a different way. There are big issues here; things to weigh up and think about before you even set foot in the area. It was in Israel in particular that we had our preconceptions – prejudices I should say – challenged and somewhat overturned. We came away with more questions rather than with answers. Questions like this: why do good people do bad things?

Towards the end of 2012 Hamas were firing rockets from Gaza into suburban Jerusalem and Tel Aviv with the possibility of killing civilian Israelis. Israel was likely to respond with brutal punishment attacks and the violence would probably escalate. Meanwhile in Syria, to the north, a bloody civil war was carrying on with tens of thousands of people killed and tens of thousands fleeing to neighbouring countries. In Egypt the so called Arab Spring had led to the overthrow of a despotic regime and its replacement with one less popular; lawlessness and chaos continued. In Jordan there were street protests which had included an attack on a police station. We had already bought air tickets and planned a rough itinerary for a trip around this part of the world. We could have changed our minds but we decided to go. We started off with the least troubled country, the one officially known as the Hashemite Kingdom of Jordan.

We flew to Aman airport on November 19th, 2012, and went by taxi not to the capital city itself, which I didn't fancy, but to nearby Madaba, a smallish town, ordinary enough for me to think of it as the Walton-on-Thames of the Middle East. We arrived at a tacky cheap hotel in the early evening and went up onto the roof. From there we could see the big church opposite the hotel with the cross on its roof outlined in electric lights and down the street a little way the floodlit domes and minarets of a mosque. Madaba has a mix of Orthodox Christians and Muslims living side by side very comfortably and the town is proud of its reputation for tolerance.

In the morning we were on the roof again watching the town come to life. Madaba did look ordinary but there is always something special about waking in a new place and not knowing what to expect. We noted that many women here wore headscarves but other than that were in *Western* clothes and I remember thinking that they were more outgoing than I expected. I think that says something about my preconceptions. And when we walked around the town we came across a shoe shop with red leather thigh-high boots in the window and another shop selling Christmas dresses with extraordinary short skirts. So much for the sexual repression that we imagined dominated Muslim countries. We also saw two armed policemen greet each other with a handshake followed by kisses on both cheeks. I'm not sure what that tells you but they don't do it at home.

We made an afternoon trip out by bus from Madaba to Mount Nebo: *the place where Moses saw the Promised Land. It didn't look very promising to us – just desert and scrub and a few places fertile enough to grow olives. And plastic bags blowing on the wind.* Or, as Flic wrote: nothing much to see, stones, lizards, thorny bushes, ants. The sound of hundreds of goat bells tinkling.

Jordan is not densely populated and there is not necessarily public transport to the places you want to go; after all most of it is desert or scrubby semi-desert. And so we travelled by taxi to our next destination, the Dead Sea, and it wasn't that cheap. I reminded Flic that we shouldn't worry about the expense too much because with my illness getting worse this would be our last special adventure together. I had used this argument from time to time in many different countries on several continents during the previous half-a-dozen years. It always seemed to work.

At the Dead Sea we stayed in one of a number of stone chalets by the entrance to Wadi Mujib nature reserve. The Wadi was a gorge, very narrow in some places and therefore danger-ous in the season in which there was a chance of heavy rain. We stood in the intense heat under a desert sun and read a sign telling us that the reserve was closed due to the possibility of flooding. This, you might say, was a low point, for we were 1,200 and something feet below sea level and at the lowest place on earth. And it was not particularly beautiful.

Of course we bathed in the sticky water of the so-called sea. I say bathed because our bodies tended to float so high that our arms and legs couldn't make enough contact with the water for us to swim. We laughed and paddled ourselves about with our hands like awkward boats. When we got out we found ourselves set upon by flies, the only thing that lives around there. Yes, the sea really is dead: no fish and no fishing boats and no villages lining its shores. No waves either, just the glossy viscous blue water stretching into the hazy distance. Desert all around. And Israel just visible on the far shore.

We stayed only one night at Wadi Mujib but we spent the evening in good company. We met a couple of about our age who were travelling around having visited their daughter who worked in Hebron, in the Occupied Territories. Let's call them Elena and Stan. And they picked up a big genial man with a distinguished accent who might have been called Tom. Elena loved travelling and Stan was amiable enough to tag along. She was English in every discernible way apart from that of her nationality, which she informed us was Dutch. Stan was laid back with something of the old hippy about him; a nice guy. We spent the evening with them and talked about all sorts of things, including, of course, Israel. Elena summed up the situation thus: *Israelis are evil and Palestinians are stupid.* She was a kind hearted woman but not frightened of forming an opinion. We later found out that she was Jewish herself, and had lost family members of the older generation in the Nazi death camps. I remember Elena was keen to make a list, some sort of A to Z of foreign places which they had visited. I think it may have stuck in my mind.

Our plan was that after leaving Wadi Mujib we should travel to the north of Jordan and then into Israel to spend a few days in Jerusalem. Then we would go south and visit the Red Sea coast of Egypt, cross the water by ferry to Aqaba and travel up through Jordan again. An anti-clockwise loop. And so it was that we accepted a lift from Elena and Stan and went with them and Tom by car the next day to Jerash, in the north of Jordan.

Jerash was another Walton on Thames or, as it was larger than Madaba, let's say a Swindon of the Middle East. A commonplace town in a landscape of rolling hills covered by fig trees, like a humdrum version of Tuscany. Oh dear, not the beauty or fascination of the other places we had visited in recent years. Why were we here? Well, Jerash had some Roman ruins and we wanted to see them.

At first we were underwhelmed, you might say. A few old columns amid the dust and scrub, a hippodrome, where terraced seating surrounded an arena where horse racing once took place. We walked on. A ruined temple, more columns, taller this time, lining a paved street. Flic noticed the ruts made in the limestone paving slabs by the passage of chariots. And so the place came a little alive for us and as we went further the size of the site gradually became apparent. We found a beautifully preserved Roman theatre. Then two temples with massive columns. And more. This wasn't a few ruins but a whole town, and a magnificent one, a place you could wander around in for some hours. As such it gave us a taste of the grandeur of past civilisations. Something we were to experience a few times in this part of the world.

At home in between our big journeys I tended to do some research on the internet after waking at five in the morning and not feeling comfortable enough to get back to sleep. The issue of Israel's occupation of the West Bank and their treatment of the Palestinians couldn't be avoided. I tried to see both sides of the situation but found myself increasingly sympathising with the Palestinians. We wouldn't visit much of Israel, I thought, only the contested city of Jerusalem, where we would stay in a Palestinian owned hotel.

And I worried about border crossings. I read stories of people being detained by Israeli security personnel for many hours, even overnight. Airport security had always been a problem for me as it was very difficult for me to get things in and out of bags or take my belt or shoes off without help. I tended to get panicky and seize up and then get waved through sympathetically. Sympathy, however, was apparently not a strong point at Israeli border checks. And politeness could often be in very short supply. I was particularly worried about being separated from my medication. I couldn't face going over the border at the Sheikh Hussein crossing, as it is known to Jordanians. And so we put off visiting Israel for a while, abandoned our anti-clockwise route and headed south to the much visited historical site of Petra.

I said a few words about our bus ride to Petra in chapter five. Here's Flic's version: *on the bus to Petra the Koran is playing on the speakers. It's interminable but not everyone is listening. The man* in front of me has the red and white Jordanian head-dress and black rope. A woman all in black has gold embroidered wrist cuffs and gold sequins by her eyes. The Koran wails on. It's Friday. In the desert are flocks of sheep and Bedouins walking slowly in front. At 12.45 the bus stops by a mosque and most of the men get off. A woman turns to us and says *they are praying, it is good.*

In Wadi Musa, the town that serves the needs of visitors to the archaeological site, we found a hotel shabby enough for our taste, or I might say for our pocket as everything was more expensive here than in other places we had visited over the years. We looked through the door and could see a young man praying. It felt wrong to disturb him and we started to walk away but he came out and welcomed us into the hotel. We were soon on the roof looking out over the town.

Wadi Musa is a likeable new town. Why *likeable*? I don't know, maybe because of its setting, in a basin shaped piece of land on the side of a hill overlooking the steep rocky outcrops around Petra. There is some beauty in that red-stone, red-dirt, high landscape. And the town itself has a nice ordinary bustle to it. Right below our hotel was a big mosque with the call to prayer (seriously cacophonous in this town) sounding out and people coming and going, and meeting and greeting, on the steps outside.

We got up at 5.45 the next morning to be the first visitors to the ruins. We were badly scammed by taking the *free* donkey rides down to the site and having an expensive tip extracted from us on arrival. Never mind. Then we walked down the *siq*, a narrow gorge that opened out after a few hundred yards and gave us the view of the treasury, a 150 foot tall facade of pillars and doorways carved out of the soft sandstone cliff. It was the first of a number of handsome buildings, or at least fronts of buildings, that were spread about over hundreds of acres of rock desert. The biggest of them, the so called monastery, had a doorway the height of an ordinary house. It was a spectacular place with, as the day went on, a spectacular number of tourist visitors.

We went back the next day and spent nine hours exploring. We started by trying an alternative route into the site down a different *siq*. We were alone there and it became impassable and dangerous enough for us to turn back. So we entered Petra the usual way and went through the shanty town of cafés and trinket shops in the busiest area. I was appalled that such a place should be spoilt in such a way. The Jordanian government promote Petra as an archaeological wonder, which it is, charge a fortune for entry, fair enough, but then allow the local Bedouin to turn it into scruffy shopping mall. I thought some more and changed my mind. The Bedouin have lived here for generations, making use of the tombs carved into the rocks to shelter their families and their livestock. And then in more recent times they have benefitted from tourism, earning some cash and improving their standard of living in an environment largely devoid of opportunities. The Bedouin are not, by the way, proud and noble tribes-people ranging over a harsh desert landscape on camel back but, from our experience, ordinary enough folk trying get by. And in Petra they deal out a great deal of humour along with the hassle.

We wandered off away from our fellow tourists fairly quickly and were in a less visited part of the site when a couple of Bedouin children ran down to invite us to visit their family for tea. This happened to us later in other places and seems to be one part genuine hospitality and one part enterprise. We accepted and went up to their home. They lived in a big square cave-like tomb carved into the cliff decorated inside with plastic flowers and rugs and outside with more rugs, cushions and plastic water butts. We met the children's father, Aaron, a short handsome man with a cheeky smile and enough vanity to enjoy posing with his children for a photo. He wore ordinary clothes but with a cloth around his head. He told us that he spoke Arabic and a language called *tourist* which seemed to be mainly English.

Aaron made us some mint tea and told us a little more about himself. He had two wives, twelve children, and a pick-up truck as well as a Nabataean tomb with a view dating back perhaps 2,000 years for his accommodation. He looked older than his thirty-three years but I put that down to the hot sun and the dry desert air. He and his family (that is to say the two girls, a lad wearing an Arsenal FC baseball cap, and one wife that were present) were friendly, relaxed and cheerful.

We asked Aaron to show us to the path that led up the hill behind us and ended up engaging him as a guide for the afternoon. We walked for a couple of hours up to a wild flat hilltop with a stupendous view. The land was rock desert: sandstone carved by wind and occasional rain into ridges and plateaus deeply cut with steep-sided and sheer-sided gorges. The rock was striped with red, yellow, ochre and black. There were a few spiny shrubs dotted about and narrow ribbons of green in the wadi bottoms. We could see the broad valley with the ruins of Petra and beyond it the dirty whites and greys of the town. Above us the sky was patched with clouds that gave intermittent relief from the sun. We sat and Aaron talked a little of the kindness of the late King Hussein towards the Bedouin people and the mixed feelings about the new village that had been built for them.

Our long day got longer as Aaron took us down and some distance along a wadi. He wanted to show us something very special and very important to him. We saw oleanders and tamarisks and even a few olive and lemon trees growing. We passed by a herd of black goats wearing bells on collars around their necks. We got more and more tired but he wanted us to go on. Eventually, after an hour's hike, we had reached our destination. Aaron asked us to stop at a point on the path a little above the valley floor. He indicated that we should listen carefully. From below us came the sound of trickling water. He pointed to a gap in the scrubby bushes and there it was, a tiny stream flowing between the rocks. I don't know, perhaps we tried to give the impression that it was worth walking all that way. We didn't explain that we came from a country where the sight of water was not a miraculous thing. I'm not sure that he would have understood.

From Petra we went on southwards to the Dana Nature Reserve. We stayed in the old Ottoman village above the reserve and hiked down the valley. The village was being reconstructed as a small tourist destination and lacked heart and soul. The valley was surprisingly free of wildlife experience. But we did visit a Bedouin family at the bottom of the valley. They seemed as poor as any people we had met in the poorest parts of India or Tanzania with very few possessions and a very rough physical environment. Their tents were patched together from goat hair blankets and fertiliser sacks but were very big inside with much more space for children to run around than you would get in a council house or a Welsh cottage. Snotty nosed children did come and go along with various animals including some goats, a hen with her chicks and a rabbit. Some days I can walk and I can lie down with my eyes closed but other things, sitting on the floor of a Bedouin tent waiting for tea to be made over a fire of sticks for example, I find very difficult. So we didn't stay long. We saw more than one old person around the encampment who looked very poor, just skin and bones and rags, as Flic described them.

From Dana we went on to Aqaba. On the way there we had to change buses in an ordinary desert town called Ma-an where we seemed to be the only foreigners. I was sitting on an old sofa outside a café in the bus station when Flic decided to take a photo of me. There were three local men in various combinations of Western and traditional clothing seated at tables in front of the café who would inevitably be in the picture too. It seemed polite to ask if they minded and Flic gesticulated and pointed at me and at them. They misunderstood and without hesitation jumped up and joined me on the sofa. One put his arm around my shoulders and they all beamed smiles at the camera. And that's the way people are in Jordan. For a brief moment they might look unapproachable but they are actually very friendly and full of good humour. They pride themselves on their hospitality.

We stayed in the Bedouin Moon Hostel on South Beach outside Aqaba and snorkelled a little over some dead coral and looked at the tropical fish. We looked out across the Red Sea to Egypt and to the tiny stretch of coast belonging to Israel at Eilat. We noticed that Jordan is so crime-free that locals left two laptops lying around in the bar all night while the doors weren't locked. And then we moved on. We wanted to go to Jerusalem.

I had been to Israel something like thirty years before and worked as a volunteer on a kibbutz. When I told people about this I always explained, *but I didn't know anything of the politics then*. Now I did know. I understood how the state of Israel came into being in 1948 after one third of the world's Jewish population had been quietly murdered by the Nazis. I also understood that in 1948 700,000 Palestinians fled for their lives and lost their homes and land to remain refugees ever since. I had read of the brutalities of the IDF, the Israeli Defence Force, in the West Bank and Gaza and of the ongoing injustice suffered by the Palestinian people. We wanted to go to Jerusalem and that city, for the time being, was entirely in Israeli hands. We would cross the border at Eilat and travel the six hours or so to Jerusalem by bus. I remember thinking *but the bus will be full of Israelis*. I wasn't looking forward to it.

The first words I heard in Israel were *don't worry, bout a thing, cause every little thing, gonna be alright*. They were playing Bob Marley in the customs building. And the young guy on security had long hair and wore trainers on his feet as well as a machine gun hanging casually from his shoulder. It felt like a young country. We showed our passports and were asked to wait. Then I was called into an office to be questioned. The woman behind the desk looked me in the eye all the time as she spoke. I explained why we were travelling and waited for her to ask if we would go into the Palestinian Territories. I knew that I must answer *no*, when, in truth, the answer was *maybe*. She didn't ask. She was amazed and a little thrown by our very small rucksacks. She asked if I had been to Israel before. *Yes, in 1978, I think*. For how long? *Four months*. Four months? What were you doing all that time? *I worked on a kibbutz*. I was relaxed and vague. She held eye contact. And then she smiled and handed me my passport. Easy.

We caught a taxi into Eilat and went into the bus station. There was a wait of five hours for the first bus to Jerusalem but only one hour for the bus to Tel Aviv. We bought tickets to Tel Aviv. To pass the time we walked down to the posh hotels and restaurants at the water's edge and then came back to the bus station. It was there, in the waiting room, in the sensitive border town of a country on constant alert to the terrorist threat, that I reached into my bag and took out a bottle of fizzy drink. Flic describes what happened next: we have put fanta in a water bottle and as Richard opens it, it explodes with a loud bang and the top flies off. A few people laugh. No-one arrests him. I remember a nice older couple sitting opposite us smiling sympathetically.

The bus to Tel Aviv was full of Israelis and many of them were soldiers. Of course they were just young guys doing what they had to do. They didn't look so very different from our sons, Kit and Peter. We travelled up the Jordan Valley and could see, through the haze, the great escarpment in Jordan where we had looked westward at sunset from the village of Dana. We were passing through the same barren desert of the rift valley that we had seen around the Dead Sea and on our way down to Aqaba. We had really seen more than enough of it by now. But there was a difference on this side of the valley. From time to time we would pass large areas of intensive agriculture: acres of greenhouses, date palm plantations, and sometimes groves of lemon trees. And, as we drove towards the Mediterranean coast and got closer to Tel Aviv, the sky became cloudy and the land beneath it became much greener. It felt like a relief.

I had made a mental note of a place to stay in Tel Aviv, or at least in the old port of Jaffa, now a suburb of the city. So when we arrived at the bus station we asked how to get to Jaffa and got on a local bus that would pass close enough. Someone told us where to get off and we walked down some ordinarily unpleasant city streets towards the sea. After half a mile or so the buildings began to look older and more characterful and the sky looked different, as it often does as you get close to the sea. This felt right but it was disturbing that we were walking up hill. And then we came out on a promenade on top of a low cliff.

In front of us was the Mediterranean, not as stunningly beautiful as it is in somewhere like Greece but nice enough. On our left the ground sloped up and there were handsome old limestone buildings and trees. To our right we looked out at the curving line of the coast backed by a cityscape of tall buildings. We walked along a little. There were people jogging and cycling and hanging out in cafés. There was a bizarre old junkshop. There was some very classy graffiti. And wherever there was a patch of open ground there was the colour green. We were in a sophisticated cultured city and we weren't in the desert anymore. It looked good.

Jaffa had plenty of old buildings from the Ottoman period (the Turks ruled this part of the world for three hundred years until the First World War) some beautifully restored, some pleasantly decrepit, and many in a state somewhere in between.

We saw a fine church by the side of a park and a fine mosque by a busy street. And on the opposite side of the road from a busy market stood the Old Jaffa Hostel. We checked in and the young man at the desk told us we would like it there. He was right.

In the hallway was a plaque engraved in Hebrew and English with the words: *This house is dedicated to my parents, Mali and Itzhak Salman, who had love, compassion and respect for every living soul*. Upstairs in the kitchen on the roof we met an older Israeli woman who said: *It's our land – the Palestinians are trying to take our land away from us*. Confused? Welcome to Israel.

The hostel housed an eccentric collection of old furniture and photographs and our room had a balcony overlooking the street. We looked down on market stalls selling carpets and antiques and fruit and children's toys looked after by middle-aged Jews in skull caps. They spent the day arguing good-naturedly, playing backgammon, arguing again, serving the occasional customer and arguing some more. A large man of diminished mental capacity walked up and down looking self-important and sometimes organising people who didn't need organising. He was a fixture and tolerated by all. While we were there we saw the market vendors set up in the morning and take down in the evening and found something likeable in their good-humoured disputatious manner.

On the rooftop were banana trees, cacti, bougainvillea, and views over the patched up roofs of the market stalls, the old buildings and new buildings and a mosque at the end of the street that broadcast the call to prayer five times a day.

In the morning we walked around the hill to the old harbour which housed a fleet of smallish fishing boats and a large number of gulls, cormorants and white egrets. There were warehouses with imaginative graffiti on the walls and an exhibition of big photographs on controversial themes and posters advertising art exhibitions and joggers and dog walkers. We passed *The Arab Hebrew Theatre* and *A Stage for the Deaf-Blind* and saw signs written in Hebrew, Arabic, English and sometimes Russian. We visited the park where we saw hoopoes feeding on the grass, looked past a modern sculpture to the big city buildings beyond and listened to church bells ringing. Across a little gulley near the top of the hill a footbridge had been built. A sign in English among other languages read *Hope Bridge*. Another sign read *Closed – Do Not Approach*. It was badly in need of repair.

Back in the harbour we saw a bird that we had seen once in India: the pied kingfisher that hovered like a kestrel and dived like a gannet. From the sea wall I pointed out the rock where Jonah was said to have been eaten by a whale. Flic wrote: this country is full of places where things were supposed to have happened. In a café we saw a woman well into her sixties who wore her hair cropped and dyed blond with one very long thin plait. Flic said, *I like your hair*, to which the woman replied, *my mother doesn't like it*.

There was an energy and creativity about Jaffa that reminded us of New York. Flic commented in her journal: clever people have worked hard to make this country something. We didn't buy an *I Love Tel Aviv* t-shirt; I don't think it would have gone down well at home. But in the course of a morning there we found ourselves immensely stimulated. We felt at home and happy. It was not what we had anticipated.

In the afternoon we went to a cycle hire shop and rented bikes. Then I felt ill and dysfunctional. Flic took the bikes back and returned to the hostel to find me feeling better. We went back to the bike shop. The woman there was kind and understanding and we set off again cycling along the seaside. We stopped at one of the many beaches and Flic swam. I commented that she had bathed in three seas on our trip: the Dead, the Red and the Med. We spent a long afternoon cycling the length of the city's sea front and returning to Jaffa.

In the evening we had to come to terms with some new perceptions: we loved Tel Aviv; we liked Israel; we found Israelis to be, in our very limited experience, rather nice people: warm hearted, kind and fun. Yes, I know, there is the issue of Palestine and the appalling treatment of the Palestinians, how does that fit in? We had yet to decide. The next morning we walked all around Old Jaffa and the harbour again. In the afternoon we went to a very good modern art gallery. And the next day we set off for Jerusalem and the Palestinian West Bank. We had more to see and more to learn.

In Jerusalem we stayed in the old city, in a Palestinian-owned hotel by the Jaffa Gate. The place was run by unhelpful teenage boys who offered us an appalling tiny room downstairs. We settled in but then asked for another room. And then changed again to be higher up. Now we had a cold room with brown nylon curtains, a fluorescent light, and sheets of wrapping paper glued to the windows in lieu of net curtains. It was raining outside and on the metal balcony we had our own private puddle. We weren't happy.

But, in truth, the place had the seedy charm of faded grandeur. On our floor was a large space that may have once been a ballroom, at one end of which was a view of the city through cracked and dirty windows. And when we went upstairs onto the flat roof we found that the Citadel Hotel, as it was called, had the best possible view of the old city of Jerusalem. The land sloped gently away from us and we could see flat roofs and domed roofs and church towers and minarets and television aerials and water tanks in abundance. Most eye-catching was a large mosque some distance away, its roof covered in gold. Beyond that were hilltops outside of the city with posh new apartment blocks and more church towers.

I read somewhere that *Tel Aviv plays and Jerusalem prays*. It's true. We preferred Tel Aviv but Jerusalem was a fascinating city. We visited religious sites and saw pilgrims aplenty. It reinforced my atheism. First we went to the Western or Wailing Wall. This is the part of the wall surrounding the Dome on the Rock (the gold roofed mosque that we could see from our hotel) the site of which is immensely significant to Jews, Christians and Muslims. They have been arguing about the rocks and stones in this little corner of the world for centuries. Religiously inclined Jews pray there in large numbers and carry out strange bobbing motions as they do so. Flic commented: we began to walk down to the face of the wall but I was asked to go to a different end of it for women. I couldn't be bothered. How will the world ever be peaceful while people hold such ridiculous rituals so seriously?

We visited the church of the Holy Sepulchre, the place where Jesus was supposedly buried. It is very important to the various Orthodox Christian churches who have argued about access for, you guessed it, centuries, to the extent that the key to the door is traditionally kept by two local Muslim families. Greek Orthodox and Armenian monks have come to blows quite recently and had to be separated by Israeli police. Inside we saw nuns and headscarfed orthodox Russian women pilgrims crossing themselves and kissing a stone. It all seems mad, Flic wrote.

We couldn't enter the area around the Dome on the Rock; it always seemed to be the wrong time or the wrong day. We didn't go into, or even notice, any synagogues because they are such modest buildings as to be invisible. We did see and visit some more churches. And Jerusalem was full of pilgrims and other pious folk. We noticed that Muslim men often carried prayer mats on their shoulders. We saw Orthodox priests with their long black robes and dark beards. There were very many Hasidic Jews, always hurrying, nearly always bespectacled, and looking particularly strange, with homburgs on top of skull caps and occasionally a hat like a cake tin covered in fur. We saw joyous colourfully-dressed pilgrims from African countries. And one morning we stepped out of our room to find the hotel full of devout headscarf-wearing Russian women and their Orthodox priests.

We took a walk along the city walls and came down by the Damascus Gate where we dropped into a café owned by a Palestinian who spoke good English. His sense of humour failed to hide his sadness and cynicism. *Jerusalem, Jerusalem, Jerusalem,* he said, *the centre of all the misery in the world. I don't give a fuck* [he really did speak good English] *if you're Jewish, Christian, or Muslim...* and he went on to say that what he really objected to was Zionism – the belief that Jews have a God-given right to take other people's land. He showed us copies of old photographs of the Damascus gate under Turkish, British and Jordanian rule. *All gone,* he said. *And one day the Israelis will be gone too.*

I have two very positive memories of Jerusalem. First there's the icecream in the Italian icecream shop in New Jerusalem. The best I've ever tasted. And then there's the Israel Museum. I don't like museums that much; I like to be outdoors and I like to see the world as it is, not dusty relics of the world as it was. But the new museum in Jerusalem is wonderful. It is situated on a hilltop and has a good sculpture garden including a work by the British artist Anish Kapoor. This is a highly polished stainless steel tube, shaped like an hour glass. It gives marvellous distorted reflections, changing as you move around it. The concave surface gives an inverted image, hence the name of the piece: *Turning the World Upside Down.*

Inside the museum two things struck me. The architecture is beyond brilliant. There is a sloping entrance corridor 50 feet wide and maybe 200 yards long lit by translucent glass on one side, all muted silvery grey but leading up to a great spectrum of colour on the top wall. It houses only three sculptures but also a host of shadows and reflections and silhouettes of people passing along. The other thing is the archaeological section. I'm not much interested in archaeology and I'm not much interested in history but I was enthralled. What can I say? *The Land of Israel has been home to peoples of different cultures and faiths for more than one and a half million years*, as it says when you come in. That's a long time, a lot of culture and many faiths. I would be daft to even begin to describe it here. I can say that like most people I was struck by the human-shaped clay coffins (anthropoid sarcophagi, if you need more syllables), dated 1,400 years BCE, and a stone mask, 9,000 years old.

We spent just one day in the Palestinian Occupied Territories, in the area known as the West Bank. We had been recommended a particular Palestinian taxi driver called Khaled who would give us a tour. We caught a bus at the Palestinian terminal outside the Damascus Gate of Jerusalem and met Khaled outside of Bethlehem where the bus route terminated. The political geography around Jerusalem is complicated but all the same you would expect there to be a clearly marked border between Israel and the West Bank with passport controls and security procedures. There wasn't. We showed our passports to Israeli soldiers on the bus coming back but not on the way out. We didn't have them stamped. The other passengers on the buses were Palestinians who had their papers checked in the same way as we did.

Khaled was an ordinary family man who we got to know a little during the day. At one point he made a phone call on his mobile and then a short detour and picked up two of his children so they could come out with us. The son was a shy twelve-year-old and the daughter was a quiet twenty year old with a baby. She was dressed very modestly in a long coat and headscarf. Flic managed to find out that she didn't have a husband but it didn't seem to be an issue. Khaled told us more than once that he loved his grandchild more than he loved his children and carried the baby about proudly whenever we were out of the car.

Khaled spoke with some sadness and anger about the Separation Wall. It had been built by Israelis to improve their security, in particular to keep out terrorist suicide bombers. Unfortunately it didn't keep to the border but wandered into Palestinian territory causing all sorts of problems. But Khaled was an ordinary working man who wasn't too bothered by politics. He believed that some sort of just peace settlement would come in time; it was a matter of waiting. He was genuinely optimistic. He had struggled and succeeded in learning Hebrew because he thought it would be useful for him. At some point in the day he spoke of jobs he'd had working for Israeli families. He spoke warmly about them and said that they had been very good employers. *It is governments that are the problem*, he said. *Not the people.*

We went first to see part of the separation wall that was covered with lots of graffiti. There were big murals including one of a female Palestinian terrorist/freedom fighter carrying a machine gun. Nearby someone had stencilled very neatly the words *Until justice rolls like water and righteousness like a mighty stream*. Further along were the words *They will force us, they will degrade us, they will not control us. We will be...* and the words ended there. I don't know why. We read *don't forget the struggle* and *LOVE* and *Make hummus not walls*. There was very little written in Arabic.

Khaled then took us to an awful souvenir shop packed with useless items carved out of olive wood. We were determined to buy something as a gesture of support but it was hard. I bought a tiny box. When we asked if they had any Banksy postcards the shop man showed us some unenthusiastically. They found it hard to understand why we didn't want their beautiful trinkets and instead bought postcards of graffiti.

We went on to see some Banksy murals including the one of a protester flinging a bunch of flowers which is on the wall of a petrol station. Khaled had met Banksy and like the other locals didn't get along with him. It sounded like the artist worked in a vacuum and didn't connect with people very much.

We also visited the church built on the place where Jesus was born. On three different dates, as Flic noted. And outside, in Manger Square, we saw a very large, very fake Christmas tree being erected.

I noticed a pointy shaped hill nearby that I thought would have a good view and asked Khaled to take us there. He parked at the bottom and we walked up. It had some religious significance unknown to us and was under control of the Israelis and we would have to pay to get to the top. I don't know why but I got a little hot under the collar about paying Israelis to go up a hill that wasn't in their country and we decided to go to Jericho where there was a cable car owned by Palestinians. We would pay Palestinians to go up a hill in Palestine.

Khaled and his children enjoyed Jericho very much and so did we. The cable car took us to a monastery on the side of a hill where something was supposed to once have happened. I think Jesus might have been involved. We treated the family to a meal in a café in the seedy desert town of Jericho and then we went back to Jerusalem.

We spent only a day in the West Bank and I don't want to say much about it beyond describing our limited experience. We saw very grand Israeli settlements on the hilltops. We drove along a smart new road that had been paid for by the EU because the old transport hub was Jerusalem to which Palestinians were not allowed to travel. We went to ordinary Middle Eastern towns where people didn't seem particularly poor or well off. And we went on the lowest cable car on Earth, at the top of which, we were told, we were still below sea level.

I have read much and thought a lot about Israel and Palestine – more than many people I meet who are fiercely opinionated on the subject. I know a little about why the Israelis treat the Palestinians so badly. But most of all I am aware of how much more there is to understand. I realise now that as well as disapproving of Israel's treatment of the Palestinians I was prejudiced against the Israeli people themselves. But I had the experience of meeting many kind and friendly Israelis and getting to know them to be just ordinary people, with all the good and bad characteristics of people anywhere in the world. I remember that before travelling to Jerusalem I was feeling very negative about being on a bus full of Israelis. I never had that thought about a bus full of Peruvians or Turks or Indians or Tanzanians or any other people. I was wrong to be prejudiced. On the last of our big adventures I learnt something that I need to remember. Perhaps Khaled was right and it is governments, not ordinary people, that create problems. Is it as simple as that? I really don't know.

We got up early on our last morning in Jerusalem, walked out of the Jaffa Gate, took a tram to the multi-storey bus station, a bus to Eilat, and crossed the border into Egypt. There were no signs or help or explanation at the border crossing. We bought a visa which we didn't need, asked for a refund, and, because there was a shortage of change, were given more money back than we paid. We took a taxi along the coast, overtook a Toyota pick-up truck with a camel in the back, and arrived at a small resort called Dahab. We checked into a cheap hotel and went up onto the roof to watch the sunset.

Dahab was a tourist resort, nothing more. In front of our hotel was a promenade, a few metres of beach and then the Red Sea. Behind was a dusty road, some suburban streets, then the large steep hills of the Sinai Desert. But it was warm enough to wander around in shorts and swim in the sea and we liked it there. One thing that struck us about the Middle East was the lack of wildlife. But here we could swim ten metres out to where the reef dropped away and snorkel among any number of colourful fish and extraordinary coral formations.

After a few days in Dahab we took the ferry from Nuweiba across the sea to Aqaba. We went to see the stupendous desert scenery at Wadi Rum. And then we went home. Here is part of the last blog post I wrote before we flew back to the UK. It's dated December 17th, 2012:

We are in Aqaba, it's a lovely warm evening and we don't want to come home. We fly back tomorrow afternoon. It's been good. I think this trip has challenged our preconceptions of the Middle East. We have felt more comfortable and safer here than on our other trips; very little crime, no bad tummy issues, friendly helpful people. I think that at home there is a kind of background noise of prejudice against both Muslims and Jews. I wasn't aware of it until we came here and kept being surprised at how approachable and friendly people are – why so surprised? Hmmmm.... I spoke of this to an American volunteering for the National Park at Wadi Rum (a retired man, very nice). 'That's the value of travelling,' he said. 'It breaks down barriers between people, challenges prejudice. Don't forget to tell people when you get home'. OK, point taken. I won't forget.

It was in Wadi Rum that we also met a nice Israeli peace activist called Elon, an intelligent well-informed man. Flic said to him something like, *so you're on the Palestinian's side?* He replied, *no, I am on everybody's side*. Of course that is the right answer. I am on everybody's side too. I like to think of the people of the Middle East as a whole and say that they are good people with a great deal of warmth, humour, kindness and friendliness. I'm not being soppy or unduly idealistic; that was our experience there. I talked to Elon for a while and ended up asking him the question: *is there a chance for peace in the area?* He didn't pause for a moment before answering: *No*, he said, *there is no chance.*

We have to hope that time will prove him wrong.

Y is for York (England)

One time I was in York with my old school friend, Phil (you may remember him from Fort William; he's the one who may or may not be building compost toilets in Tahiti). We crossed the river by climbing on the metal girders under one of the bridges. We arrived at the other side and let ourselves down into a sort of builder's yard. Someone shouted from the bridge that there was a fierce dog there and we had to climb up and back across the river. I don't know why we did it. Perhaps we were drunk.

Phil and I were at school together. Tiffin Boys School was modelled on the old public schools and had an ex-army head master, Brigadier JJ Harper. He was a monocle-wearing authoritarian who addressed his pupils with the words *you boy* and was answered in fearful sentences ending in *sir*. I remember some sixth formers starting an independent school magazine and being called to his office and threatened with expulsion. We were under a totalitarian regime.

Pupils wore stripy blue and maroon blazers, ties and caps in the earlier years and black blazers in the sixth form. In very hot summer weather we might be given permission to take them off. Even the pupils in their final year who might be old enough to vote or get married were not allowed out at lunchtime without a note from their parents. But the greatest injustice we experienced was not being allowed to grow our hair long. This was the early nineteen seventies and we were listening to Pink Floyd, Jethro Tull and Hawkwind. Long hair, and facial hair if you could manage it, was important. It was a statement of anti-establishment idealism. It could change the world.

I remember wearing shorts on bitterly cold afternoons on the rugby field and long trousers on glorious summer days on the cricket field. I remember the extensive school grounds: tarmac and grass and trees surrounding fine buildings. I remember the school bell that signalled the end of a lesson and the end of the school day. The words *five past four* have a special, liberating sound for me to this day. And so it was on the final five past four, on my last day at school, that I stepped out of the school gates and found myself breaking into a run. I felt that my life was just beginning.

26

The Road to Zagora

A great deal of discomfort, some pain, a feeling of humiliation, loss of self-esteem, frustration, anger, sadness. Then, several times a day, miraculous recovery. That's my life with Parkinson's disease. They say that depression is a very common symptom but I don't experience that. I'm down and I'm up. Sometimes it seems as grim as can be. Sometimes, quite often as it happens, I'm in a mental state of mild euphoria; I call it *happy moron syndrome*. And I should also mention sleeplessness; I'm writing this at four o'clock in the morning.

I have found that denial and not looking into the future are important ways of coping with the illness to some extent but they have their limitations. And so, a few years ago, I read up about the possible later stages of the disease. It can be very bad indeed with very severe disablement, incontinence and depression among the symptoms. I have heard of hospitalised Parkinson's patients who are unable to swallow being fed by means of a tube. I decided that a long term plan might include suicide and I came to think of myself as having a terminal illness. I must say that the thought of suicide generally cheers me up considerably. There is a way out. And being alive suddenly seems a very wonderful thing. The world looks especially beautiful. I am struck by the need to live for now; to try to live more intensely. To travel.

I have been lucky enough to have a great travelling companion in the shape of Flic and my illness has brought us closer together. She recently said that Parkinson's has changed me and that when I feel rough I can be disagreeable. *Disafuckingreeable*, I snarled, *in what way?* Which made us laugh. Yes, humour is another strategy for coping, and one that we use on a daily basis.

Now I had better mention two things that I have become aware of this year. I've noticed that the illness is progressing more slowly than I anticipated and I also have heard a lot about new treatments and possible cures. So, as I write this, suicide is not on the agenda; you'll be pleased to hear that.

At the beginning of this book I said that travelling changes a person. It does. We now have lasting connections to the places we have visited and the people that live there. We follow the news from the Indian subcontinent. I have tried to learn more about the politics of Latin American countries. And, of course, there is the Middle East, especially the Israel/Palestine situation. I find my opinion of the issues there shifting with every new piece of information. I have to say that I found Israel to be, in many ways, a fine country and Israelis, in many ways, good people. But that fine country and those good people are responsible for a great deal of suffering and injustice experienced by their neighbours, the Palestinians. Why is that? I'm afraid you'll have to find out for yourself; I am not the person and this is not the time to go into all the complexities of those issues.

Our connection with the Middle East did lead us to read a wonderful book by an Israeli writer called Amos Oz – *A Tale of Love and Darkness*. It is a very personal memoir of his childhood in Jerusalem in the 1940s and beyond. Sari Nusseibeh, a Palestinian who grew up a few streets away has also written a fine book about his life – *Once Upon a Country*. The books tell of very different experiences of the same place. The two men have both known unhappiness and injustice and have the right to be bitter and angry. They have reason be enemies. They are, in fact, great friends, visiting each other's houses and both playing a part in the peace movement. They have both made the effort to learn from each other and understand the other one's viewpoint. I admire these guys. I find myself wanting to emulate their open-mindedness, their willingness to learn from each other. And that is something that travel has done for me. It has brushed away some preconceptions, misconceptions and prejudices. And it has allowed me to see into other peoples' worlds. To be lastingly connected to them.

Our last big trip abroad consisted of four weeks in Morocco in February and March 2013. It seems like a long time ago now and we are sure, really this time we're sure, that we won't go travelling again. There are times of day and night when I'm very seriously disabled by this illness (I'm not going to give you all the details) and to be so ill far away from home is out of the question. Now it feels like we made a very good decision several times over in the last few years: to make a very special journey, a trip of a lifetime. And to be more intensely alive for a while.

I don't want to say much about Morocco. Don't get me wrong, it's a fine country and we had a good time there. I would recommend it. It's just that we had made five big trips to extraordinary parts of the world before we went there and we had begun to lose our capacity for wonder and our excitement at being somewhere new. So I only want to give some snapshots of some of the places we visited, a little taste of what made that country different and special.

First there was Marrakesh. It's a short flight from the UK but you get off the plane, take a bus ride into town and arrive at the square called Djemaa El-Fna, and are deep in the heart of an exotic culture, very different from our own. There are story tellers and acrobats, and live music and dancers and snake charmers. Some of it is put on for the tourists but much of it is for locals. We also loved the parks and gardens in Marrakech; sunshine and the smell of orange blossom are not things you find much of at home in February. And we came across a sort of *hiring fair*, I think it might have been called years ago in Britain; guys sitting in a row by their mopeds or bikes advertising their trade by displaying, for instance, some copper piping or electrical wires or carpentry tools, and waiting for someone to offer them work. Flic asked if she could take a photograph of them and they were fine about it.

We went to Essaouira, an important fishing port on the Atlantic coast; touristy but with a huge fleet of boats big and small, and fish being bartered for on the quayside and a sky full of seagulls. We stayed in ordinary towns like Tiznit and watched the street life: the handcart men, the beggars, the brightly dressed women and the guys with pointy hoods like something out of Lord of the Rings.

We stayed in Tafraout and did some cycling and walking among the curious rock formations of the Anti-Atlas. We came across a wild boar and tried to follow it which gave me the opportunity of writing the blog post title: *Sometimes seeing more boar spoor – sometimes not so sure.*

One of my favourite places was Agdz where we stayed in a guesthouse on the edge of a *palmerie*, a sort of oasis with date palms, pomegranates, almonds, barley, and beans growing in the valley bottom surrounded by arid stark hills. The land was divided up by mud walls and people came and went on little donkey carts. It was especially beautiful at dawn and dusk.

We had our usual bad moments with my health. Times when I would feel scared of being so helplessly disabled so far from home. Flic would patiently wait for me to feel better and braver and we would go on. We had gone through this often enough in South America and the Middle East for her to be an expert at not panicking and at being patient with me.

I never wrote of these moments in my blogs. Denial, as they say, is not a river in Egypt. It's a useful strategy for dealing with a long term serious illness. And so my blog posts would be all sunshine and light, like this one:

Yesterday we tried to get a bus up into the mountains but the road was blocked by snow. That surprised us as it was hot in the day and warm at night in Taroudant where we were staying. So this morning we set off for Ouarzazate. But the bus stopped in this little town (can't remember what it's called) and we got off because it looked nice. The light is very clear here and the barren hills stand out against a blue sky. There are kasbahs, mudwalled castles, in various states of decay dotted about the landscape. The valley floor is very green with palm trees, alfalfa, barley etc. We walked through the farmland and along a river bank – yes, that's right, a river with water in it. People wave to us and call out bonjour. Storks, six of them, drift about above the town in the wind.

Travelling is a different state of being. You see new things every day: strange birds, flowers, trees; a thousand ways of meeting and greeting with combinations of handshakes, hands to heart, hugs, air kisses, kisses on top of the head and so on; a profusion of head coverings with hoods and turbans and baseball caps and more worn in combinations (yes, two hats per head sometimes – why not); unusual architecture, different ways of behaving...

To while away the time on long bus journeys in Morocco we made an A to Z of place names, each one the name of a town we had been to and each one in a different country. It wasn't easy and we got stuck on the letter Z. Then it looked like we might go to an end-of-the-road, edge-of-the-desert town called Zagora. Some of the places we visited along the way were moderately wonderful and we didn't hurry. We dawdled in the *palmeries* of Agdz for far too long, ran out of time, and headed for home. There was a plane we had to catch and there were other places we wanted to visit on the way. We wanted to walk in the High Atlas Mountains and we had to go to back to Marrakesh. We never made it to Zagora.

It was in Marrakesh nearly a month earlier that I had what felt like a significant moment on a rooftop. It was before sunrise but I was awake early, as usual, and up on the roof watching the day begin. I could see palm trees and minarets and countless other rooftops with their water tanks and TV aerials. In the south the snow-capped Atlas Mountains were catching the morning light.

Then the call to prayer sounded out some distance away across the city and came in a wave towards me, getting louder as it got close and more voices joined in. It can be a beautiful sound in the Middle East or other places but somehow they do it differently in Morocco; it's more like the braying of a thousand donkeys than anything else. I think the job of *muezzin*, the man in the minaret, is passed down from father to son and not awarded on talent. That's my guess because there's some rough and tuneless calling to prayer going on there. Or at least that's how it sounded to me.

Eventually the local *muezzin* in the local mosque, quite close by, started his call. He really did have a rough voice and, to my ears, it was not a good sound. But he was loud and he was enthusiastic, you had to say that. The call to prayer is amplified over loudspeakers these days but it's live, not pre-recorded. And so it was that I heard one man's heartfelt song above the general cacophony and got a sense of what it meant to him. His voice rose and his passion grew and I was unexpectedly moved. It was a lump-in-throat, teary-eyed moment. Belief in a bigger, more profound purpose and meaning to our existence, and a joy in that purpose and meaning, echoed across the city. And one man's voice sung out above the rest.

Most of all I was moved by a sense of something special about humanity, about the strength of the human spirit maybe. But I also couldn't help but think, just for a moment, that there might be inside each of us something much bigger than us. This felt like a revelation, an almost spiritual experience. I had a strong sense of something much larger of which we are all a part. That's as far as I'm willing to go. I have been an atheist all my life but in recent years I have sometimes wanted to be an agnostic, someone who admits to the possibility of a deeper meaning. And for a moment, between first light and sunrise, on a rooftop in Marrakesh, I moved a step closer to the possibility of belief. It felt good at the time.

In Morocco signs are often written in our script as well as in Arabic. I noticed that shops are often named *Al Quds*, after the Holy City. *Jerusalem, Jerusalem, Jerusalem, the centre of all the misery in the world*, as we heard it described when we were there. I remember our experience in that city now and I think of it as the antidote to belief. And I remember Lumbini, in Nepal, and the temples that made up what I thought of as the *Birthplace of the Buddha Theme Park*. I think of the improbable multilimbed Hindu gods in India and the libations to Pachamama in Bolivia. It all looks, from the outside, like superstition. So much for deeper meanings. Never mind.

I think the meaning of life is in the living of it, nothing more. It feels pretty good to me. Perhaps this is a sort of existentialism but not of the angst-ridden miserable variety, more of a happy existentialism. Zagora may or may not be a worthwhile destination but it's the journey that matters. Like everybody else I've experienced sadness and pain. But I've been lucky; much of the time my journey has been a happy experience. Not deeply meaningful but profoundly worthwhile.

Afterword

I am the princess and the pea. My glass is less than half-full. Sometimes I sing *Nelly the elephant packs her trunk* while walking through deep snow. And I am on the railway station at the end of the universe again.

It is August, 2014, and I am with Bill, who has come to help me while Flic is away for the third year in a row. We are on the platform of Dyfi Junction station looking out across the marshes and the estuary towards the sea. Sand dunes form the horizon in that direction and around and behind us are green-grey hills with rough pastures, forestry plantations and patches of oak woodlands. Shafts of sunlight come through broken clouds and illuminate random farmhouses and meadows and trees. The wind is blowing from the north-west and the air is cool.

I notice that Bill has a wonderful way of looking out at the landscape and taking it all in, enjoying the distances, the space and the sense of wildness. Now he walks to the end of the platform and watches an osprey circling above its nest. I am happy to see how much he likes it here. But before our train arrives I interrupt his reverie and tell him about an experience I had on a boat earlier this year. I don't know what makes me think of it.

Flic and I were coming back from a brief holiday in the Canary Islands with friends, a trip that may very possibly be my last venture abroad, given the difficulties I now have at some times of the day. We were on the ferry from La Gomera to Tenerife and I was walking a deserted upper deck, swaying from side to side like a drunken man, partly because of the movement of the boat but also because of the effects of Parkinson's disease. I felt weak, unsteady on my feet, and I needed to use the toilet. I came across a door with a symbol of a man on it. So far so good. The door was held shut by what seemed to me, in my weakened state, to be a very strong spring. I guess it had to be able to take the force of wind and waves in the event of a big storm. I pushed and pushed, leaned my weight against it and finally it gave way. I fell forward and staggered in, the door slammed shut behind me and I found myself in total darkness.

I blundered around for a while, bumping into urinals and wash basins, hoping to find a light switch or the way out. At this point in the story I would like to say that I was in a state of complete sensory deprivation. This, unfortunately, was not the case. All around the ship music was being played over speakers. You could barely hear it on deck above the noises of the ship's engines and the wind blowing but here, in the darkness and with the door shut firmly, it sounded very loud. It was disco music, maybe from the eighties, something like *that's the way, uh-huh uh-huh, I like it, uh-uh uh-huh*. It made my need of escape from that place feel more urgent.

I began to imagine the ship reaching port and Flic and our friends deciding that I must have got off before them. They would leave the boat and it would set sail again, back to La Gomera, with me crashing around in the darkness, madness setting in, my cries for help drowned out by the awful sound of *that's the way, uh-huh uh-huh, I like it, uh-uh uh-huh*. Perhaps some days would pass before I was discovered, stretched out on the floor, semi-conscious, my body still twitching in time to the music…

The train pulls in and we wheel our bikes on board. We are off for another day's adventuring. Half an hour later we get off the train at Tywyn and cycle towards the Dysynni Valley. But before we are out of town my body seizes up and we have to stop. I lie down on a bench in front of the cinema until I am able to move again. Then we cycle over the hill on little used tracks and roads to Dolgellau and back along the estuary to Morfa Mawddach from where we get the train home. It's wonderful but it's tough. For long sections of the ride I struggle to keep my feet on the pedals, my bottom on the saddle, and the bike on the road. I tumble off a couple of times when we are going up very steep hills. And when we get home I don't get the usual feeling of triumph, of *yes, I did it*. Instead I find myself questioning if it was worth the effort. I wonder how many more times I will find the energy and enthusiasm for such adventures.

I remember that a few years ago, after our second trip to the Himalayas, I was possibly fitter than I had ever been in my life. Fitter than I had been before suffering from Parkinson's. I dreamed up the idea of what I called a triathlon, a canoeing and cycling and mountain walking day trip from the mouth of the Dyfi Estuary to the top of Cadair Idris and down to Dolgellau, making the journey home by bus. Flic and I did it together one day when the wind and tides were right, going back to collect one abandoned car, two bicycles and two kayaks later in the week. If it sounds crazy to you I have to say that such things are not an unheard of response to the disease. At any one time there are a few Parkinson's sufferers in the UK running marathons.

Bill stays for a week and we find ourselves talking about Parkinson's often enough for he is also a friend of Glynis, whose emails, you might remember, I ignored in chapter six. Bill says that Glynis sometimes worries that people think she's faking it. She will be in a wheelchair one minute and walking fairly normally the next – that must make people suspicious she thinks. Oh, yes, I know about this. I often run to the post box in the village because I have such difficulty walking. I imagine people looking out of their windows and tut-tutting, *isn't he supposed to be ill?* And I have discovered this year that I can play tennis. That's right. The little messages from the brain to the body like *walk across the kitchen without falling over* often fail to get through. But the big messages like *run around this tennis court and hit the ball as if you're a young man again* do make it, intermittently, but often enough. And so there are days when I am helped into and out of the car and I limp awkwardly onto the tennis court and confidently play three sets.

Back at home I wear a buzzer alarm when I'm on my own because sometimes I sink to the floor and am unable to get up. I press the red button and a neighbour comes to help. I've had to use it three or four times this year. The people who see me run to the post box or hit the ball around the tennis court don't see this. Not being able to do the washing up and finding it difficult to get my wallet out of my pocket are two other things that could arouse people's suspicions. *How very convenient for him*, they might think, *he can do the things he wants to do*. If only that was true. Music was always important to me but I can rarely play the guitar or piano now. I joke that I suffer from diminishing repertoire syndrome. It's not that funny.

And while we are close to the subject I had better explain *Nelly the elephant*. It's what I do sometimes when my feet won't move – I sing *Nelly the elephant packed her trunk* and pretend that I'm walking through deep snow. It works for me. *And the princess and the pea?* I hear you ask. Perhaps you don't know the story of the young woman who was proved to be a princess by her delicate sensitivity. She was kept awake at night by the presence a single pea that she could feel through countless mattresses and eiderdowns. And that's the way in which, when my illness is at its worse, I find small discomforts exaggerated, particularly in the evenings and at night when I struggle to get comfortable enough to sleep. Did I say struggle? Not me. That's another aspect of dealing with the illness, coping with the psychological aspects. So it's not a *struggle* it's a *challenge*. My glass is nearly half-full if I can make myself think of it that way.

Here is another strange thing. The illness makes it difficult for me to concentrate enough to read but I am still able to write. As I write this Bill sits in the kitchen and reads the beginning of this book. I hope he will find it enjoyable and will correct some of my grammatical errors. The time has come for me to say a big thank you to Bill for his help. I would also like to thank Nigel Judge and Geri Skeens for the careful reading of an early draft and for their thoughtful comments.

I have to end the book as I began it, with a massive thank you to Flic, who seems to be stuck with me now for better and worse. I like to think that the journeys we made together have been as worthwhile to her as they have been to me. Quite recently at the end of a busy day together we were drifting off to sleep and I found myself saying to her the words *I'm glad I met you*. There was only a tiny moment's silence before she replied *I bet you are*. Then, as sleep overcame me, I thought I heard her say something more. I couldn't quite make out the words.